MASTER GUIDE
TO FIELD SALES MANAGEMENT
TACTICS AND TECHNIQUES

Howard S. Bishop

PRENTICE HALL
Englewood Cliffs, New Jersey 07632

Prentice-Hall International, Inc., *London*
Prentice-Hall of Australia, Pty. Ltd., *Sydney*
Prentice-Hall Canada, Inc., *Toronto*
Prentice-Hall of India Private Ltd., *New Delhi*
Prentice-Hall of Japan, Inc., *Tokyo*
Prentice-Hall of Southeast Asia Pte. Ltd., *Singapore*
Editora Prentice-Hall do Brasil Ltda., *Rio de Janeiro*
Prentice-Hall Hispanoamericana, S.A., *Mexico*

© 1987 *by*

PRENTICE-HALL, INC.
Englewood Cliffs, N.J.

10 9 8 7 6 5 4 3 2 1

Library of Congress Cataloging-in-Publication Data

Bishop, Howard
  Master guide to field sales management tactics and
techniques.

  Includes index.
  1. Sales management.   2. Traveling sales personnel.
I. Title.
HF5438.4.B57   1987   658.8′1   87-17425

ISBN 0-13-559840-0

PRENTICE HALL
BUSINESS & PROFESSIONAL DIVISION
A division of Simon & Schuster
Englewood Cliffs, New Jersey 07632

Printed in the United States of America

Acknowledgments

I'm told that acknowledgments should be brief. This means that many of the sales professionals who contributed to this book will not be mentioned. Some special mentions:

Sherie and Rob, Wendy, Kristen, and David, my beautiful adults (no longer children) were very helpful in their "go ahead, Dad—you can do it" support, prayers, and love.

Dottie Balceniuk was with me during previous book efforts and at the beginning of this one.

Very helpful in reviewing sections of the book were Ron Gilrain, Vice President, Public Affairs for Stanley Works; John Hall, Vice President, Sales, North Penn Machine; Bob Fritsch, President, Hunt Manufacturing Co.; Jim Nichols, President, Nichols Advertising and a former Director of Communications for Sperry (Unisys), Al Magid, President, Joshua Meir Corp., and many others.

Bette Schwartzberg, my editor, always had confidence in this book and, with Cindy Micucci's help, backed up her convictions with action and help.

Sidney Mehlman, production editor, provided very helpful suggestions with a sense of balance and a sense of humor.

Many thanks and much love to you all.

About the Author

HOWARD BISHOP is President of BOPCO, a company he founded in 1978 that offers marketing, distribution, sales management, and sales training services. The firm has solved marketing problems for several hundred clients including Meilink Safe Company where Bishop acted as National Director of Special Projects (sales and marketing) and Multimate International where he acted as Vice President, Sales. BOPCO is also associated with the consulting firm Bove/Feinberg Associates.

His sales and marketing responsibilities have included the titles of Advertising Manager, Sales Service Manager, Product Manager, Sales Manager, General Sales Manager, Director of Marketing, Vice President of Sales, and President with Berol Corporation, Stanley Works, Magic Marker, Victor Systems, Sperry Remington Machines, and Sperry Corp.

Bishop, who is also a Certified Public Accountant, authored a series of marketing articles for *Keynotes*, the national magazine of the Associated Locksmiths of America and, as President of MGB Business Services, edited and co-authored *Framework Made Easier* published by Prentice-Hall.

He has faced marketplace realities by starting from scratch his own national fulfillment center, national wholesale distributorship, regional office services company, and commercial stationery operation.

Why You Should Read This Book

Whatever your title, your situation as a salesperson-turned-manager is probably a common one. You may have been promoted either from the ranks of your sales peers or from a lesser managerial position. Either way, your background and skills are for the most part related to sales. Prior to being a manager, you were a skilled sales professional whose personal success and contribution to the company were gauged easily in terms of dollars and cents.

As a manager, your responsiblities are different, and your effectiveness is measured with a different yardstick. Your achievements result from how well you manage other people, directly or indirectly. You still have to meet group sales quotas, and you are undoubtedly responsible for a profit and loss budget, as well as, perhaps, for certain prescribed managerial objectives. To be successful, you have to train, direct, and motivate salespersons, who might be former peers but who are certainly very much like your co-salespersons of the past. In either case, they probably perceive you as someone who did the same things that they are doing now. Consequently, they might expect more sympathy from you than you can give them. You also have to cope with the paperwork, problem-solving, and administrative duties that are part and parcel of any managerial function. This *Master Guide to Field Sales Management Tactics and Techniques* will show you how to effectively manage these responsibilities.

Your perspective must be altered. As a salesperson, company directives might have seemed restrictive or at least irrelevant to your efforts. Issuers of memos may have seemed out of touch with your needs and with the demands placed on you by customers. When you become a manager, you are a member of the corporate leadership. You can now appreciate the basis for some of those directives. Even when you are obliged to implement an instruction with which you disagree, your responsibility is to do so without the subliminal grousing permitted among the sales staff. You are part of the company's leadership. By applying and implementing the techniques in *Master Guide to Field Sales Management Tactics and Techniques*, you can become a more effective leader and demonstrate improved performance and profits through the use of smart management strategies.

In short, you find yourself, by reason of your sales effectiveness, in a position that requires new skills, new thought patterns, new behaviors—all of which will be illustrated, step-by-step, in this book. Your primary responsibility is to grow as a person and as a professional. You recognize that, to avoid professional stagnation, you must never stop learning. Providing you with these management tools to meet that challenge is the purpose of the *Master Guide to Field Sales Management Tactics and Techniques.*

My career path demonstrates that challenge. At first, as a CPA, I looked at sales from a nonsalesperson's point of view. Later, as an internal audit manager, I reviewed expense accounts and recommended sales quotas—again, without any experience in selling.

Then I got into sales and sales management—and realized the kind of professionalism needed to perform this difficult job effectively. Fortunately, the accounting background helped me deal with the numbers and paperwork. In dealing with the home office, my facts and figures were straight enough—and my language skills polished enough—to make an effective, believable presentation.

By getting into sales and sales management in this way, there was a lot to learn. And, by using a disciplined approach—that is, examining all the strategies and approaches instead of merely accepting them—I learned quickly. More important, I listened to the successful professionals in the field, summarized their sometimes intuitive methods, and distilled from them valuable elements. Even more important, like an accountant, I documented them.

As a result, I've had most of the standard sales and marketing titles and responsibilities—from cold-call salesperson to sales vice president to president—for small firms and multibillion-dollar conglomerates. In the last ten years, my consulting practice has enabled me to deal with more sales management situations than most people see in an entire career. This book is a distillation of those 20-plus years of learning from management professionals and from clients. And in the *Master Guide to Field Sales Management Tactics and Techniques*, I show you how to make these proven successful techniques work for you.

HOW THIS BOOK IS ORGANIZED

The first chapters are most helpful to the manager who needs to organize or reorganize a sales territory, whether it is local or national. There are also time-proven techniques for you to use to increase your effectiveness in generating profits.

Later chapters deal largely with the day-to-day and ongoing aspects of managing the territory, as well as the planning and other long-range functions of your position. You'll see how to control your budget, manage your time, hire the right people to get the results you want.

One of the most important features of this book is that it enables you to customize your managerial and organizational approach. Read the Table of Contents and pick out your most pressing problem and start reading there. As you read, keep a notepad at your side. Many significant benefits of this book come from your own thoughts and implementation. The *Master Sales Guide to Field Sales Management Tactics and Techniques* is intended as a guide, catalyst, and stimulant. Only you can develop the actual plan that makes you successful.

Ten Mistakes You Don't Get to Make Twice

Here are some of the reasons that field sales managers don't make it:

1. Trying to be either a "boss" or a "democratic manager" instead of a leader—and not knowing the difference.

2. Assuming that the abilities and performance they exhibited as field salespersons or as regional managers will work as effectively in their new position.

3. Appointing or promoting the wrong people.

4. Not recognizing that the regional or national job is *qualitatively*, not just quantitatively, different from the field sales position and not making the necessary adjustments.

5. Not setting quotas fairly or equitably, thereby undercutting the credibility of the whole management process.

6. Not thinking through and assigning territories based on *today's* marketplace realities—accepting what always worked in the past without question.

7. Falling behind on paperwork; making only inadequate or arbitrary reviews of expense accounts and performance.

8. Not using statistical and other information tools to develop a *conceptual* understanding of the task and how to manage it.

9. Not developing the right kind of relationship with the home office (in a regional sales manager assignment) or colleagues in the home office (in a national sales manager assignment).

10. Spending too much time on many trivial tasks and too little on the critical few.

I'll show you how to avoid all of these mistakes in the pages that follow.

Contents

CHAPTER 3

PROVEN TECHNIQUES FOR INCREASING AND ACCELERATING SALES REVENUES AND PROFITS   19

CHAPTER 4

SPENDING TIME WHERE IT COUNTS— ACCOUNT STRATIFICATION   30

CHAPTER 5

SUCCESS-PROVEN CALL FREQUENCY PLANNING THAT BRINGS IN INCREASED SALES REVENUES   42

CHAPTER 6

HOW TO MAXIMIZE PROFITABILITY USING ACCOUNTING TECHNIQUES TO SET YOUR SALES BUDGET   57

CHAPTER 7

ALLOCATING YOUR TOTAL BUDGET TO SPEND DOLLARS WHERE THEY COUNT   73

CHAPTER 8

HOW TO MANAGE YOUR SALES MANAGEMENT TIME EFFECTIVELY   83

CHAPTER 9

HIRING SALESPEOPLE WHO WILL PRODUCE THE RESULTS YOU WANT   100

CHAPTER 10

USING THE PAINLESS THREE-MONTH PLAN ON THOSE WHO AREN'T CUTTING IT—AND HOW TO TELL THEM   116

CHAPTER 11

HOLDING EFFECTIVE SALES MEETINGS 124

CHAPTER 12

AVOIDING THE TEN BIGGEST MONEY-LOSING MISTAKES MADE AT INDUSTRY SHOWS AND CONVENTIONS   151

CHAPTER 13

HOW TO GET YOUR MAJOR ACCOUNT—AND MAKE YOUR CAREER   167

CHAPTER 17

USING TELEMARKETING AND DIRECT MAIL TO INCREASE SALES WHILE CUTTING COSTS   233

1

How to Determine Your Real Responsibilities

Field sales management can be among the most exciting, interesting, and challenging jobs in the business world. Your success in the position, however, depends on your ability to get things done through other people—a much different situation from being an effective salesperson. Being effective in management therefore means making the transition from sales to leadership, and separating false perceptions (or myths) from the realities.

ARE YOU THE "BOSS"?

Are you the "boss"? Can you see yourself in any of the following answers to this question?

1. You're darn right I am. I *run* this organization and nobody makes any mistake about that. Just ask anybody.
2. Well, we kind of all work as a team. Yes, I have the title of sales manager, but everyone is important. I deal with the home office and handle their requests, but everyone knows what our assignment is.
3. If you mean "manager," then, yes, I am. However, I would prefer the term "leader." Bosses belong on chain gangs. Managers belong in home offices, administrating. I'm a *leader*!

Which of these would be your answer?

Underlying each of these responses are myths about field sales management. To learn something about the mindsets of the people who responded in these ways, let's examine a couple of myths.

Myth: The Field Sales Manager Must Be a "Boss"

"Bosses" went out in the thirties. There have been too many years of participative management, rights of the individual, "Japanese" style of management and its variation, Theory Z. (The so-called Japanese management style, by the way, originated in the United States in the fifties and should really be called the Deming style of management.) The people who expect to be "bosses" are kidding themselves if they think that managerial techniques have not changed in half a century. They may have gotten their management experience from the military (but even the military isn't the military a lot of us knew). Their people may swear undying allegiance to their "boss," but they're on their own as soon as the door to the office closes.

Ironically, this kind of manager gets the job done with an effective and loyal sales force. In most cases, there are two reasons for such effectiveness:

1. They are really benevolent despots. They are quick to be hurt when a salesperson has a problem. They are the first to jump in and help, no matter how misguided and late the help is.
2. The consistency in their efforts and relationships is what people need most. Better an absolute tyrant that you can count on than someone who is a tyrant one day and a nice guy the next.

The reasons for being effective, however, are not all good ones. The disguised benevolent has to be wasting some energy that could be put to more productive purposes.

Steps To Take If You're the "Boss"

Obviously, if the approach is clearly effective, it should not be changed. If, however, it is proving to be ineffective, your responsibility is to seek other managerial styles. Even after many years of "bossing" an operation, you would probably not find it difficult to deal with employees differently. Here are some points to think about:

1. If you are really a tyrant and everything seems to be going well, you are not going to change overnight, no matter how convincing the arguments may be. You might, however, consider making some changes in your behavior and relationship patterns to become even more effective.

2. Think about whether the "leader" mantle might fit better than the title of "boss." You can still "run things." The only difference is that while being more objective about goals and tasks, you support your people and look on them as a "team" that works *with* you instead of *for* you.

3. Remember that your people need stroking or positive feedback, even from a "boss." Make this part of your style. You can continue to tell them in a quiet and

tactful way when they do something that you feel is wrong. Yet also remember to tell them when they do something right. Make it a point to catch your people in the "act" of doing something right. By following this tack, you create the kind of environment in which your people will tell their friends, "He's tough, but he's fair and always tells you when you do something right." If you remember that consistency is the most important attribute and provide the occasional thank-you for something well-handled, you can create this kind of environment—without changing your basic style.

HOW TO TELL IF YOU'RE A DEMOCRATIC MANAGER

The democratic manager learned to get ahead by getting along. The company may want a democratic manager, but, with such a manager, *no one* is in charge. Such a company is no place for the manager whose goal is effectiveness. If the democratic approach works for you, be certain that the home office doesn't want a boss who seeks results.

More importantly, salespeople *don't* want a manager who lets them do what they want. Selling is a lonely enough job as it is. Salespeople *want and need* direction, motivation, and supervision. The democratic manager doesn't meet these needs and is therefore often less effective.

What to Do If You Are a "Democratic Leader"

1. Set specific goals, either of your own choosing or in collaboration with the sales force.
2. Communicate these goals to your people in a clear and specific way, complete with numbers and dates.
3. Hold your people to these goals. Keep a tickler file of due dates for assigned projects and follow up on any overdue projects right away.
4. Keep the "team" idea but make it clear—by setting and enforcing standards—that the team has a leader.

HOW TO EVALUATE YOUR LEADERSHIP ABILITY

Managing is different from leadership. Some businesses are undermanaged, but many are overmanaged—and underled. Particularly in the field, leadership counts for a lot more than management.

The leader is a special kind of person; disciplined but charismatic, result-oriented but supportive, organized but flexible. The leader's job is to motivate salespeople to do their best to achieve their goals and those of the company—to the point of making sacrifices in time, but never in purpose or principle.

That is the ideal manager! Perhaps the best definition of a manager is "a person whose job it is to *assist* those others to do the best job they can." The word "assist" is key. Go to a well-run manufacturing assembly plant, such as that of a computer company, and you'll find the floor supervisors carrying tote boxes to their workers to keep things going. You can picture your role as manager in this way.

Much of the information in this book is aimed at helping this kind of sales manager and persuading others to adopt the style. The main principle, however, is that the effective field sales manager's job is to *assist* the sales staff to do the best job they are capable of doing. The myth is that the effective field sales manager is a star. The reality is that the manager is a helper. Good salespeople usually do not make good sales managers unless they learn—or someone teaches them—how to be effective field sales managers!

What to Do If You Are the "Leader"

1. Use your charisma to motivate people to live up to and to exceed the required achievement levels.
2. Set specific goals, with numbers and dates. Don't rely on your leadership abilities to get the job done if you haven't spelled out to your people the details of the job and your requirements.
3. Use sales meetings with your people to motivate *them* to set specific goals and monitor their own progress.
4. Remember that you are a leader, not a star. In your present position, you get things done through other people even if it means submerging your ego and giving other people full credit for successes you have achieved jointly.

HOW TO PROMOTE THE "RIGHT" PEOPLE

The candidate, of course, has the same options that you faced as a would-be salesperson-turned-manager. Presenting these options to the candidate and discussing them thoroughly is one way to avoid setting up a candidate for "a fall." Yet this takes you only halfway to making sure you avoid that all-too-typical situation. Let's look at the other half and set up a checklist:

1. Spell out in *complete written detail*, the functions, responsibilities, duties, and expectations of the job. Make sure you really know what you want the person to do. See Figure 1.1, "Functional Responsibility Outline (FRO)," for an example of how to do this formally. (Format and related questions are discussed later.)

2. Make sure that the FRO is in line with what the company expects of you and the position. Of course, you will have cleared the FRO with your boss and perhaps the Personnel Department.

3. Ask "Why do I really want this person in this job?" Is it because the individual is the best salesperson? Is it because this person sees most things my way? (Remember that when two people agree on everything, one of them is unnecessary.) Or is this person the best equipped to *lead*?

PURPOSE: The purpose of this FRO is to define the duties and responsibilities of the Regional Managers of the company who report to the Field Sales Manager.

RESPONSIBILITIES:

1. Manage, train, direct, develop, and motivate all District Managers in the region assigned.

2. Recommend to the Field Sales Manager all hirings, dismissals, salary adjustments, promotions, changes in job assignments, and incentive compensation changes. (While the FSM has the final approval, such recommendations by the RM's will carry a great deal of weight.)

3. Approve all regional and district customer service, administrative, and other support personnel.

4. Implement all company sales, marketing, and promotional programs to ensure the attainment or exceeding of assigned quotas by district and for the region.

5. Recommend to the FSM regional promotional programs and suggest national marketing programs. Develop and implement region-wide programs. Develop and implement region-wide programs consistent with overall company marketing plan and objectives and ensure follow-through by the District Managers.

6. Monitor regional and district expenses to ensure that expenditures stay within assigned budgets.

7. Organize, manage, and participate in all regional trade shows and exhibits approved in the annual marketing plan.

8. Participate as an active member of the company Sales Planning Committee chaired by the Field Sales Manager.

9. Maintain active relationships with key regional accounts, coordinating efforts with the activities of the District Managers.

10. Any other duties and responsibilities which might be assigned by the Field Sales Manager.

Figure 1.1
Functional Responsibility Outline

4. Consider other ways of filling the position. Have you considered looking outside the company? In the staff organization? In other territories? And so on.

5. If you decide to promote the salesperson, make sure that you have adequately communicated the requirements of the position—from your viewpoint and the company's. Does the candidate realize the position's requirements? Or is he or she just enamored of the title of "Regional Manager"?

Sit down with one or more candidates and explain the position as it really is. Make sure that they understand that while the job has its prestigious aspects, it comes with responsibilities and pressures, too. The best way to put this point across is to put it in writing. When your words are committed to paper, the things you have talked about seem more "real."

Again, Figure 1.1 shows a way to put your points in writing. The phrase "Functional Responsibility Outline" isn't just a euphemism for "job description." *Functional* means describing the function. *Responsibility* means that it is not just a description: It defines responsibilities. *Outline* means keep it simple—one page if possible.

6. Make sure you have a specific plan, along with a set of goals and objectives, against which to measure your regional manager. Also be certain that the plan is in an easily communicated form. (Later chapters show you how to develop your specific plan and provide guidelines on implementing it.)

7. Arrange for a training program to help the new manager to acquire the needed skills. Determine how you will fit into the training and how much time you have to devote to it.

8. Finally, think about how you will handle the situation if the candidate does not make the grade. After, say, three months, are you prepared to fire or reassign the individual? Is she or he willing to take a reassignment? How will you deal with your boss, who may have graduated from training school with the promotee?

Again, there are no definite answers in such matters. A popular notion is that there is a "cure" or "quick fix" for managerial problems. The reality is that, in this area, the best anyone can do is to raise the right questions and suggest that you come up with *your* answers. Nevertheless, "a problem well defined is half solved," said William James. When you are dealing with so many intangibles, a precise statement of the problem should answer at least 75 percent of the existing or potential questions.

IN CLOSING...

Determining your "real" job as a field sales manager entails, for starters, ascertaining your managerial style—boss, democratic manager, or leader. This first step calls for a great deal of reflection and honesty on your part. What *is* your present style? Is is effective? Could you be more effective if you were to change your style?

When you have given these questions thought and answered them to your satisfaction, proceed to Chapter 2, which deals with specific techniques for enhancing your effectiveness.

2

How to Outperform
Your Peers
Every Quarter, Every Year

HANDLING THE DAY-TO-DAY
DEMANDS SYSTEMATICALLY

As a salesperson, you had demands placed on you—by customers, by your manager, and perhaps by others. Yet meeting those demands was almost exclusively up to you and you alone. By reason of the fact that you have reached a managerial level, you must have been very effective in handling such things as customer complaints, difficult presentations, or sales-related paperwork. Occasional inquiries from the manager might have been a nuisance, but they were certainly manageable.

Now in management, you face not only different but probably escalated demands. Many more people need your time, and you seem to have much less of it to give. In all, you might be wondering what, specifically, is your job? Are you a manager, trainer, or salesperson? If you have entertained such thoughts, be gratified that *professionals* raise such issues with themselves. Others don't ask the right questions until they are demoted.

Most demands on the time of a field sales manager can be categorized as follows:

1. Managing the paperwork.
2. Learning how to get things done through the efforts of others.
3. Meeting the needs of the home office.

Let's look at each of these areas.

HOW TO EFFECTIVELY MANAGE THE PAPERWORK

Not having all your paperwork completed on time is probably a new experience for you. Now your in-box seems to overflow with demands for reports, market information, and other paper—all arriving daily. Handling a lot of paperwork can present a psychological barrier to many people, but it can be a particular problem to sales managers, who are generally oriented to taking action and to getting things done. The longer you put off doing this work, the harder it is to get started on it.

Once again, if you regard the paperwork as a necessary part of the job, you can approach it more systematically and effectively. Although you undoubtedly receive much unnecessary mail, a certain percentage of it *is* necessary, useful, or even valuable as a source of new ideas.

TIMESAVING CHECKLIST FOR HANDLING THE PAPER

1. As much as possible, regulate the amount of paperwork coming in to you. You cannot control what you get from your superiors or peers, but you can stem the flow from those who report to you. For example:

- Tell your people what you want to see copies of and what you don't need to see. Perhaps you want to see major proposals to important customers; "major" might be defined as over a certain dollar amount.
- You should be alerted to problem areas not mentioned in the normal activity report.
- New product opportunities, market segments, or promotional ideas should be brought to your attention.
- You *don't* want copies of routine appointment or follow-up letters.
- Standardize the call reports. Some salespeople have to be compelled to hand in these reports while others tell you what they had for lunch every day. Figures 2.1, 2.2, and 2.3 are examples of simple but effective ways to make these reports more consistent—and easier for you to review. You can create your own standardized report forms for other areas as well.

Figure 2.1, by the way, shows a formal "Administrative Procedure" with a masthead, subject, number, and date. Such formality provides more credibility and permanence than a memo that gets forgotten one to thirty days after it is written and distributed.

2. Sort your incoming mail, or have your administrative assistant sort it, according to its urgency. Create three piles, such as "Important," "Later," and "Read." If the day gets hectic, you can focus on the "Important" items and deal with the other stacks toward the end of the day or perhaps after business hours.

EFSM CO.	Date:
ADMINISTRATIVE PROCEDURE	
Subject	**No:**

PURPOSE: The purpose of this procedure is to define the steps to be followed to provide necessary customer information for salespeople and sales management.

PROCEDURE:

1. An account profile sheet will be prepared for each account. (See Figure 2.2.)

2. Two copies of this account profile and call sheet will be maintained—one for the salesperson and one for the sales manager.

3. The salesperson will complete an account profile and call sheet for every account and maintain them in alphabetical order within the designations A accounts, B accounts, and C accounts.

4. All activity (mailings, telephone calls and personal visits) will be briefly entered on the sheet with the date and a brief description of what happens. (Figure 2.3 attached provides a continuation sheet.)

5. Each Friday copies of the sheets with entries for that week will be given (sent) to the sales manager.

6. The sales manager will review the activity and discuss with the salesperson any questions or suggestions.

7. The updated sheets will then be placed in the sales manager's master binder and the old sheets and the old sheets will be removed.

8. Copies of newly filled-out sheets for new accounts will, of course, also be given to the sales manager.

In this way, all salespeople will have a good working tool to govern and organize their activities and the sales manager will have an up to date (no more than one week behind) record of everything done with the account with a minimum of paper work and call report hassle.

Figure 2.1

ACCOUNT PROFILE AND CALL SHEET

Company
Name_____ Contact_____

Address _____ Alternate _____

City_____ State_____ Zip_____ Phone_____

Hot Buttons _____

Comments _____

_____

_____

Date   *Activity*

_____

_____

_____

_____

_____

_____

_____

_____

_____

_____

_____

_____

_____

_____

_____

_____

_____

_____

Figure 2.2

ACCOUNT CALL SHEET

Date   *Activity*

_____

_____

_____

_____

_____

_____

_____

_____

_____

_____

_____

_____

_____

_____

_____

_____

_____

_____

_____

_____

_____

_____

_____

_____

_____

Figure 2.3

3. Handle each memo or other piece of paperwork *once*:

- If you really don't feel comfortable making a decision right now, mark it for "follow-up" with a date.

- If the response should be made by one of your people, reroute it right away. Provide instructions in the form of a short handwritten note on the document itself.

- Throw it away. Paperwork surveys have shown that less than 10 percent of filed material is ever referred to again. Save your files for important information.

- Mark the item for a file, if no immediate action is required. If you need it later, you'll know where to find it.

- Answer the correspondence right away with a handwritten note on the original memo. Your customers and your salespeople will appreciate a prompt response jotted on a copy of their letters or memos more than a delayed formal letter.

4. Develop an appropriate filing system. Keep a listing of your file names and file everything somewhere. It is much easier to look through 20 organized filed folders than 200 randomly stacked pieces of paper. Some typical file categories are as follows:

- Keep a file on each of your salespeople and your major customers.

- Keep a file for each major project that is "in the works."

- Your sales bulletins, along with the home office's pricing and other policy statements (whether formal or informal), should be in their own files.

- You may find a "Day File" helpful. This is a chronological (as opposed to subject) copy of all your outgoing correspondence. Review this every two or three weeks to keep your activities in perspective and to be reminded of things to be done.

- Keeping a file system doesn't have to be difficult. Just think about what you may need again, catergorize it, and file it under that category. Do this even if you're convinced you'll need the document tomorrow. The "tomorrow" documents have a way of causing clutter and making your paperwork problems seem worse than they are.

5. Stay on top of it every day. Designate a portion of each day to deal with the little chores before they become big ones. You might even have to set aside a portion of each week, such as Sunday afternoon, to make sure everything (marked "Later") is caught up. Once again, you have a full-time job in the field and a full-time job in the office.

6. Make use of time-saving devices, such as a dictating machine. Fewer than 20 percent of executives who have to handle paperwork use this tool. With

their typical orientation action to, sales managers probably use it even less than other similar groups. Keep this tool handy:

- Have it in your car to dictate follow-up letters and reports or to capture ideas when you are stalled in traffic or on the highway.
- Keep it in your briefcase to use when the plane, train, or person with whom you are meeting is late.
- Take it home with you to capture those great off-hour ideas and to catch up.

If you don't have a transcriber or transcriptionist in your office, get a secretarial service to do this for you.

The telephone is another timesaver. In many companies, every piece of paper you send out seems to fetch a piece of paper in return. Don't play this game. Call people back with answers to their memos, keep a brief record of your calls on the documents, and mark them for the file (or waste basket).

If you spend more than 20 hours a month in a car, consider getting a cellular phone installed.

HOW YOU CAN GENERATE SALES THROUGH THE EFFORTS OF OTHERS

There was once a field sales manager who always kept a bag packed. He prided himself on the fact that he could fly to a trouble spot on a moment's notice. His readiness and ability to jump into a problem and save the day made him a legend.

That kind of problem-solving approach makes good legends, but not effective field sales managers. Instead of reacting to individual problems, he should have been coaching regional managers on how to handle these problems themselves. The manager was truly a star, but a poor manager and a poor developer of people.

As a salesperson, perhaps your response to a customer complaint or difficult sale was the same—jump in and save the day. You were probably a star in this respect (or you would not have risen to your present position). Your customers invariably responded favorably to your presentations and it is hard for you to see why your managers cannot accomplish as much as you did. Some of your district and regional managers who used to seem so competent and self-reliant now require your constant support. Some of them want you with them on every call; they cannot seem to operate without your holding their hands. Other managers never call you when they really need help—and they lose big sales. So you are pulled in two directions. The excitement of the field is very tempting, but your sense of duty tells you that your place is behind the desk, in control. In such situations the strong temptation is to step in and handle the situation personally. Why not? Most field sales managers can run rings around the typical salesperson. Being a manager, however, means directing the performance as opposed to playing in the band. You have to recognize that you can't do it all yourself, no matter how good you are. The more you outshine your managers, the more you will be called upon to perform, and the less incentive they have to properly handle their responsibilities. If you continue to let this happen they will eventually be delegating their responsibilities to you.

1. Teach your people how to do what you are good at, but don't get in their way unless your role is clearly defined.

2. Tell your people to "stratify" their accounts according to their size and importance. Emphasize that you want to be involved only in their major accounts, unless a smaller one has the potential of growing quickly, perhaps because of a possible deal brewing.

3. Specify the circumstances in which you may be called in: A client's purchasing department changes management; a new catalog is being prepared; the purchasing agent is demanding to speak with someone higher about a pricing request; and so on.

4. Make sure your people do *their* homework and take the problem as far as they can before calling you (stopping short, of course, of losing the account). When requested to intervene, ask questions of your people. Get a review of what has happened, including what they have tried. Recommend other approaches if possible. Be certain that your presence is truly necessary. If there are several problems insist on a complete itinerary for your trip, prepared by the person requesting help, with objectives for every call or meeting to make sure that your time is used wisely.

In general, change your perception of the position. Recognize that you are now a manager, not a doer. Stay in the background and, if necessary, let your people make small mistakes. You can correct them later and have your people learn from them. You can do so if your reporting system is accurate and timely enough to give you advance warning of trouble spots, thereby enabling you to ask the right questions before situations blow up.

Intervening When You Are Really Needed

While some of your people always want you with them, others fail to call you in when you are *really* needed. For example, one of your managers could have a big one on the line and decide to keep everyone else out of it so as to get all the credit. Sometimes, however, the field salesperson *can't* handle it. This situation calls for the kind of help that you can provide.

Here are some ways to avoid losing sales for the want of someone asking for your help:

1. Set guidelines for what you want to be involved in: new product introduction, catalog suggestions, a major new system proposal, and so on.

One sales manager *budgets* his time with each territorial manager. He even goes so far as to allocate it according to sales volume produced—the $500,000-per-year person gets three days a quarter, the $1,000,000-per-year person gets six days per quarter, and so on. (Whether you take it this far or not, the concept is worth considering.)

2. Constantly review the activity reports from the field salespersons for such situations. Ask your people about situations you feel may be developing during your review sessions and stay on top of them.

3. Read your trade journals with pencil and paper or scissors in hand. Note or clip anything that might indicate a move by a customer or prospect, such as a new building if you sell lighting fixtures. Ask your people what they are doing about it. If necessary, start an Account Profile Sheet (see Figure 2.2) *for them*, and make sure they make some activity entries in a week or so.

4. Talk to your industry colleagues who call on similar accounts but who are not competitive. For example, if you sell lighting fixtures make friends in the carpeting or office panel business. Friends with private telephone companies are also a good source of information on who is doing what.

5. Let the market research people at headquarters know that you welcome any information they might have on sales opportunities.

THE KEY TRADE—HOW TO DELEGATE, NOT DO

Each of us has unique skills and relationships. Yours are not the same as those of your managers. They will probably, in fact, be more effective than you in some areas. So when you ask why they cannot handle a certain situation as you would, the answer is that they aren't you. If you want something handled exactly as you would, you have to do it yourself. Yet that is not your job. As a result, you have to delegate some of the responsibility. In so doing, you have to give away some of the ownership of the problem.

That key tradeoff in delegation typifies the difference between the relationships you once had with your customers and the relationship you now have with your manager. You can't interfere with the managers' approach, except when you have to so as not to let the customer go down the drain. Here are some tips to make delegation a little easier:

1. Realize that your people will handle things only 80 percent as well as you were able to. So, unless you must absolutely get involved, give your people the room to make mistakes. Remember that if five people do things only 80 percent as well as you could, you are still way ahead.

2. Wean your old customers away from dependence on you. One good way to do so is to take their phone calls, tell them that something new on the subject has come out recently and that someone will get back to them. Then have the appropriate district or regional manager get back to the customer. Generally after a

couple of exchanges like this the customer will get the message and call your district or regional manager directly.

3. Find special reasons to call your old key customers—you don't want to cut off the relationship entirely. Ask their advice, for example, on a new freight or cooperative advertising policy that your company is considering. Besides flattering them by asking for their help and advice, you'll keep your relationship with them. You make the point that, in your new management role, you are above the day-to-day activities but still available to discuss important issues with them.

4. To keep your salespeople responsible for your former accounts, tell them about these contacts. Make sure you communicate all important conversations and their results with these accounts.

5. Don't make important decisions, such as granting credit for a damaged shipment, without checking with the manager responsible for the account.

6. Be the heavy and let your people be heroes. Handle the bad news yourself and let your people communicate good news. Your customers will then learn subliminally to deal with your managers.

GETTING YOUR MANAGERS TO MANAGE

What is true of the sales force is true of the district or regional managers. Like the salesperson, these managers need ongoing positive reinforcement and supervision. Their need for feedback from you—even when a new account gets away—should be source of gratification for you, not irritation (even if you have to conceal a bad reaction to give them what they need). What you should be wary of is, again, being manipulated—however inadvertently—into doing the managers' work for them. In addition, their need for positive reinforcement should not deter you from showing them where they went wrong. You must tell them at the right time and in the right way, but tell them you must. Then you work on not allowing the mistake to happen again.

Here are some specific ways to handle those requests for help or attention and to distinguish between the two types:

1. *Use your quota as a criterion:* You and your people have a quota to meet. Salespersons don't "meet people"—they meet quotas. All your activities and theirs have to be directed toward this objective. The question is then, "Is the activity that the district or regional manager wants you to engage in the best way you could spend your time meeting the quota?" Decide whether the activity has a direct bearing on attaining your goal. Could you be doing more to meet your quota by helping your salespeople or managers, or by being in your office planning and directing?

2. *Use the manager's job description as a guideline:* Is the requested action their job or yours? Are your managers delegating their work to you? Also avoid situations in which you find it comfortable to do a job someone else should be doing.

3. *Use the size of the account involved as a deciding factor:* Don't become involved when your importance is not recognized, such as on a call on a small account whom your district managers want to impress for reasons of their own. You are an important person. Make sure that your salespeople always use you wisely.

Given these admonitions, you might still indulge yourself occasionally by doing something you enjoy—even if it is not the most effective thing you could be doing. For example, dropping in on a small account with the responsible salesperson accomplishes these things: It motivates the salesperson, impresses the client, and gives you a chance to do something enjoyable.

HOW TO MEET THE NEEDS OF THE HOME OFFICE

If the home office is doing its job, it is exerting constant pressure to submit reports, attend or hold meetings, and respond to specific inquiries. (If you are a national field sales manager, then your staff peers are the culprits.)

Many activities related to home office requests may seem unrelated to your quotas and sales-related efforts. You may even have found yourself asking whether the people at the home office appreciate your workload and goals.

No matter how unrelated you feel they are to selling, home office or staff inquiries are part of your job. Remember, first, that you want to be promoted to this level. Second, the questions may very well be important and useful to your present position. Third, you have a full-time job in the office and another full-time job in the field. You have to decide how to get 75 percent of each job done. You have to treat the home office request as an important part of your job, learning and benefiting from it as best you can, regardless of your feelings. Your answers make their wheels of business go round. And your response to their needs may well determine how suited your superiors or colleagues feel you are for more responsibility. Look upon your responses as an opportunity to show your ability.

Here are a couple of specific devices for making these requests work to your benefit:

1. *Buy time to respond properly:* If you are really overloaded when you get a request, suggest to the staff person than an upcoming meeting with a customer may shed some new light on the issue raised. Thus you buy yourself some time to handle the request properly.

2. *Use the request to your advantage:* Most of your responses will relate directly to your "mission." Research what you need to know to handle your territory with what other people feel they need to know.

For example, you may have received a request from the home office for the number of your current customers who have mini- or microcomputers. This request may be an indeliberate signal that this area is important to your company and that getting into it before you get a directive to do so would be to your advantage. By preparing a report on the minicomputer population in your territory and its potential for sales of your product, you identify yourself as someone with foresight. Also underlying the inquiry could be a new sales opportunity that you and your people should be pursuing.

3. *Keep the home office in perspective:* A good way to handle the frustration that sometimes results from having too much to do is simply to concentrate on the positive things about your job, perhaps just before you go to sleep. You'll sleep better and wake up better prepared for the next day's demands and rewards.

Above all, don't "cop out." At times you'll have to enforce policies and procedures with which you may not agree. If, however, you cannot persuade your boss to see it your way, your boss's way is the *only* way to go. Console yourself with the possibility that you might be missing some essential information. When you get a directive that makes you uncomfortable *do not* put yourself in the weak position of saying, "I know this isn't the right way to go, but it's what 'they' want." Instead, simply present the boss's decision as the only way to go and *sell it* to your people. Your people will respect you for doing your job professionally, without moans and groans. You'll also set a precedent for them: They have to support you, even when they don't agree.

IN CLOSING...

Perhaps you have met people who seem to walk on water. They don't. They just know where the rocks are. Having read this chapter, you know where some of the rocks are, too. Other chapters will show you more.

3

Proven Techniques for Increasing and Accelerating Sales Revenues and Profits

STRATEGIES FOR ORGANIZING TERRITORIES AND ASSIGNING QUOTAS

Organizing territories and setting quotas are intermingled processes, difficult to examine separately. Yet both determinations lie at the heart of the salesperson's chance for success. Is a territory "rich" enough to warrant a higher-than-average quota? Is the quota for another territory so low that it is a place for a low-producer to "hide"? Could a large territory be more productive if divided and shared by more than one salesperson? These and many other similar questions make territories and quotas one of the most important decisions that a field sales manager has to make.

DO GEOGRAPHICALLY ORGANIZED TERRITORIES DO THE JOB?

Most territories are set by geographical determinations. In some cases, this makes sense:

1. It's an easy way to define the exclusive area within which the salesperson is entitled to sales credit.
2. It facilitates home office and regional recordkeeping since little research is needed to determine what accounts belong to whom and what leads go where.

3. Industry sales figures and other indices are based on geographic boundaries—state, county, metropolitan buying area, etc.

4. Call-frequency patterns can be easily established by overlaying a territory map with locations of key customers and prospects.

It's obvious, however, that not all territories are equal in terms of sales potential. You would have to cover three or four Rocky Mountain States to get the potential of Nassau County in New York, so another dimension is required—past actual sales in the area and/or sales potential in the area. Let's look at a step-by-step checklist for setting up national or regional territories:

TEN STEPS TO REVENUE-GENERATING
TERRITORY ORGANIZATION

1. Rough out the territories based on geography. Nationally, this could mean four regions—Northeast, Southeast, Midwest, and West. It could also mean five regions, adding a central region and pulling back the borders of the other four.

2. List the total sales for each territory defined, averaging the last two or three years to smooth out any annual fluctuations.

3. Express each region's sales as a percentage of the country as a whole, adding up to 100 percent.

4. Develop overall market figures for your product line or service and add these up by region.

5. Express each region's market figures as a percentage of the country as a whole, adding up to 100 percent.

6. Average the two figures computed in steps 3 and 5 so that your determinations will take into account potential sales as well as past activity in each region.

   Note: If you are a new company or are organizing to sell a new product line, you have only market figures to work with and will skip steps 2 and 3. We'll cover this in more detail in "How to Set Quotas for the New Company or New Product Line" section.

7. Make territorial adjustments to come up with uniform territory sizes to the extent that this is practical. Consider a different alignment from your rough, such as adding a central region to a national territory or giving the Pittsburgh area to the Ohio territory in a regional determination.

8. In most cases the Northeast, as a territory is conventionally defined, will be the largest. Make adjustments. Consider, for example, giving Virginia or even the District of Columbia to the Southeast. Include Texas in the Southeast or midwestern (or central) territory as the numbers indicate.

9. Make adjustments for territorial potential such as the "Sunbelt" or the "Silicon Valley" and "Route 128" potential if you are selling to computer manufacturers.

10. Test your adjusted figures for travel and other logistical factors. It may be easier for your western manager to get to El Paso, for example, than your central or midwestern manager.

Save the figures you developed and the reasons for the adjustments. We'll use them later in setting quotas.

HOW TO DETERMINE WHEN NONGEOGRAPHIC TERRITORIES ARE THE PROFITABLE CHOICE

Most of the discussion in this chapter and the cases in Appendices A and B assume some type of geographical alignment. By making adjustments for actual sales and sales potential in our final determination we've eliminated most of the objections to geographical boundaries.

There are, however, some circumstances where geography should *not* be the sole criterion. Here are some other factors and possible situations to consider:

1. You have an unusal product with customers and prospects located in specific areas and the overall market figures are not a reliable indicator of *your* potential:
   — If you are selling to the garment industry New York, Miami, and Los Angeles have to be key areas.
   — If you are selling to the furniture industry, North Carolina will be far more important to you than overall market figures would indicate.
   — If you are selling equipment or services aimed specifically at farmers, overall industry figures will be of little value.

2. The number and location of key customers may distort the territorial alignment for other reasons. If you are selling a piece of materials-handling equipment, Memphis, as a distribution center, will be much more important than any broad industry figures would show.

3. Your product or each of your products may be so technically specialized that a country or region-wide salesperson for each product may be appropriate.

4. Pre-sale work and post-sale service may vary so greatly from customer to customer or from one month to the next that a roving group of specialists would make sense.

5. Travel costs may be prohibitive in some territories for your product, so "skimming" the easy-to-get-to territories may work. In this case, independent manufacturers' representatives (IMRs) should be considered. (This possibility is covered in detail in Chapter 16.)

These exceptions aside, a weighted geographical division is usually the most appropriate structure. It is easier to sell an established customer with whom a salesperson has developed rapport a new product than for a product specialist to sell a new customer an existing product.

Finally, territorial profitability is the absolute determinant of how to structure your organization. The first step toward this goal is in the setting of equitable quotas. Let's look first at some of the mistakes that are made.

In over 20 years of sales management experience, I've met two people who felt that their quotas were set fairly, and only one was independently wealthy. You have a quota of your own to work with and you have to parcel it out to your people.

HOW TO SUCCESSFULLY SIDESTEP THE PITFALLS
BETWEEN YOU AND INCREASED SALES

Let's first look at some of the interesting ways sales managers set quotas and suggest some reasons why these may not be appropriate.

1. My increase is 12 percent over last year, so I'll just increase the quota of all my people 12 percent. (Is that 12 percent over their last year's quota or 12 percent over their actual performance? Was last year's quota determined in an equitable way?)
2. I'll take a look at what my people have been doing and assign quotas based on what I think is fair. (What's "fair"? Will it depend on how you feel that day or on your last phone call to or visit with your salesperson?)
3. I'll come up with an appropriate index of what the territory should be doing and assign the quota based on each salesperson's share of that index. (Does this mean assigning portions of the index regardless of how well the territory has been developed up until now?)

Obviously, we have to find some other, more equitable way to assign quotas. The rest of this chapter will suggest some of these ways. But first let's examine some of the pitfalls of these three choices:

1. If your choice is 12 percent over last year's quota you may be compounding errors. There is no assurance that last year's quota was fair or bore any resemblance to marketplace reality.
2. If the choice is 12 percent over last year's actual sales, you could be wrong for different reasons. What did last year's sales really represent? How do you compensate for the people who really worked their hardest versus those who coasted? Is it fair to assign equal increases to both groups?
3. If your choice is a "fair" quota, you might think about nominating yourself for sainthood and be prepared for some legitimate challenges to your saintly status. Equitable quota-setting involves more objective

thinking about your plan and what your territories and their components are worth.

4. Finding an appropriate index is much closer to the right track and assigning quotas based on each salesperson's share of the index is approaching the quota-setting job in an intelligent manner. There are, however, some pitfalls in using indices.

   Territories are always in different stages of development. You may have a fantastic salesperson wringing out everything possible from a dead (for your company) territory who is underacknowledged. Conversely, your president may have been born in another territory so you have a natural advantage and the salesperson in this territory may look like a hero just by being there. The index method does not work equitably by itself, given these situations.

CHECKLIST FOR SETTING PRELIMINARY QUOTAS

Obviously, there are no completely right answers. There are, however, some ways to approach the challenge of setting quotas fairly that come pretty close to as right an answer as you're going to get in this world. Let's look at a checklist of standards and parameters we want to use and objectives we want to achieve in our quota-setting:

1. Make sure that the quotas you set have a direct relationship to the business potential in the territory. We'll discuss how to arrive at this below.

2. Take into consideration the present stage of developement of the territory, measured by last year's (perhaps the last two or three years') actual sales figures in the territory.

3. Factor in unusual circumstances—new company products applicable to a given industry or geographic area, recent business conditions in a geographic area, special windfall business, the impact and treatment of "home office" accounts, etc. These should all be considered in arriving at the final figure.

4. Consider your company's marketing plans, particularly as they relate to a geographic or industry area. (If, for example, you have a new computer software package for the garment industry, it may help New York, Miami, and Los Angeles but won't thrill the folks in Nebraska.)

5. Make sure that the total of all quotas assigned will bear a reasonable relationship (not more than 5 percent or 10 percent higher) to the actual company or regional plan.

6. Set up your territories to be as even as possible, given the geographic, logistical, and concentration business realities. (The Rocky Mountain

States account for 25 percent of the area of the country, but only 2 percent to 3 percent of the business for most industries. Obviously, you would look at this area a little differently than you would look at New York City.)

7. Don't let personalities or past relationships affect the setting of quotas even though they may have a bearing on communication processes. No breaks to old friends or penalties to nonfriends!

8. Since the amount of business created or serviced and the performance against quota are both factors which should affect your people's income, take this assignment very seriously and make a special effort to see that it is performed conscientiously.

9. Since one of your major tasks is the motivation of your people, *communicate* the quota-setting methodology as well as the actual numbers to them to ensure that they recognize its fairness and equitability.

CHECKLIST FOR SETTING FINAL QUOTAS

Now that we have set our objectives for defining and selecting the right answer to quota-setting and are in agreement that this is *what* we want to accomplish, let's look at *how* we will go about doing it and see if this method of setting quotas makes a lot of sense. (We will work through this checklist with actual numbers in the practice examples in Appendices A and B.)

1. Look at the past year's sales figures territory by territory. List the *actual performance* of each territory based on actual sales for last year (last reporting period) and compute the percentage of your territory as a whole that each represents.

2. Using an appropriate index (to be discussed further in our practice example in Appendix A) list the *potential* of each territory, expressed as a percentage of your territory as a whole.

3. Average the two percentage figures, apply this percentage to your total territory figure (it's OK to add a 5 percent to 6 percent "fudge factor") and this becomes the raw quota figure for all of your people.

4. Adjust this figure based on what you know about local circumstances that may influence the final quota determination. You may, for example, have a situation where some of your Chicago customers sell into Michigan, Illinois, and Wisconsin.

   If these areas are in different territories and you are giving sales and quota credit, you may knock off a few percentage points from the outlying territories and add them to the Chicago (Cook County) territory to make things equitable.

There could be a large national account in a territory, causing this area to account for a disproportionate amount of sales. How much credit the territory salesperson should get for this is a matter of history and a judgment call.

5. After you have made this careful analysis and determination, discuss the figures and the reasons for them with your territory managers who will have to make the quotas. You probably won't change your mind, but you will get more support if they have the opportunity to comment before you cast the figures in stone. (It's also possible that they may come up with a factor for adjustment you haven't thought about which is a legitimate reason for an adjustment.)

6. Give everyone the *complete* listing of quota assignments. This is, admittedly, a departure from the conventional wisdom. There are two reasons for this:
   a. If there are questions about the fairness, they exist anyway. Don't assume that you can keep secrets. Give your people the facts so the questions are raised based on legitimate and real information, not guesses on their part. To paraphrase C. Northcote Parkinson's last law, "Rumors will arise to fill communication gaps."
   b. If you can't adequately defend the figures, they shouldn't have been developed. Publishing everyone's quota for all to see communicates the message that you have confidence in the equity and fairness of the quotas assigned.

7. Discuss your methodology and the final figures with your boss. You want the boss on your side to support you and you don't want any second-guessing when the territory manager who graduated from training school with your boss, or is a brother-in-law of the comapny president, goes to your boss with a complaint about the unfairness of the quota assigned.

8. Try to arrange to introduce the new quotas at the same time you introduce your new sales and marketing program. That will show all your people how easy it will be to make those increases.

9. If you can't arrange to do this at a national or regional sales meeting, at least have the two pieces of information coincide—start with the new plan and end up with the part (the quotas) your people will play in it.

10. Don't do this in a facetious "good news—bad news" way. Your people won't think their increases are funny.

11. Stress the positive aspects and show everyone how much more money they will make with the new plan and new quota, using actual, individually tailored figures for each person. (This last part, unlike the quotas themselves, should of course be personal.)

HOW TO SET SALES-ENHANCING QUOTAS FOR
THE NEW COMPANY OR NEW PRODUCT LINE

Most of the preceding discussion was meant for the regional or national sales manager who was in or was moved into a responsibility with some past sales history. Let's see how the same principles apply if you are in a new company, a new division of an established company, or handling a new product line.

The big difference in applying the above formulas and principles is that you *don't* have a past sales history to work with. Everything else fits. Let's look at how to proceed under these circumstances:

1. Since there is no sales history, you have to rely on *potential* figures defined by industry association or industry publication indices. Obtain these and plot them on your planning sheet. (You'll find editors of your industry publications very helpful.)

2. Determine the total market for your product. In the case of a truly unique and significantly new product you may have to find a surrogate.

    That is, if you have invented a brand-new computer software package that does something that none of the existing 10,000 plus packages do, you may have to look at an existing, successful product like Wordstar ™ Lotus 1-2-3 ™, or Framework ™ and interpolate, extrapolate, or employ any of the other techniques market researchers use to come up with a "total market" figure.

3. Determine what percentage of this market you want to or can hope to (realistically) capture. Multiply this percentage by the total market and this becomes your national quota figure.

    Granted, this is a less finite figure than we have dealt with in the other situations and examples in this chapter but you will have a useful tool, meaningful goal, and solid starting point.

4. Using the territorial percentages expressed as a share of the country as a whole, assign quotas by geographic region. The total figure may be suspect until you have some sales history under your belt but the relative performance figures will enable you to effectively manage your sales force.

    (You may have been wildly optimistic about the total or desperately pessimistic, but if one region is at 20 percent of quota and another at 130 percent, it doesn't take a lot of thinking to determine who is doing the job and who should be given career relocation guidance.)

5. Monitor the figures and circumstances behind the generation of the figures more closely than you would in an established environment. Adjust quotas quarterly based on the empirical information you derive. Otherwise, follow the above guidelines and principles, using the practice examples you will find in Appendices A and B.

CHECKLIST FOR COMMUNICATING QUOTAS
TO YOUR PEOPLE

If you think setting quotas and making those judgment decisions (that will be detailed in Appendices A and B) about the adjustments is fun, you're going to have a ball with this step.

You have to convince your regional managers that:

1. The total quota figure is realistic.
2. The total has been fairly apportioned by territory.
3. You have some programs that you will work out with your people that will make these quotas (and possible increases) seem easy.

This is one of the most important jobs you will have to do successfully since it will set the tone for the year. No one is going to perform effectively who doesn't believe that the overall goals are realistic. Here's how to proceed:

1. Prepare yourself. Go over all your notes, charts, and figures and work out in your head how to make an effective presentation to your people. Pretend that it's the most important presentation you'll have to make all year because it probably is.
2. Be honest. Don't kid yourself that there are any secrets in any large or small organization. Your people will know what you are dealing with and respect you as a manager if you share everything and treat them as the "partners" you would like them to be.
3. Tell your people what your quota is. Sell them on the justification (for a 20 percent increase, for example) even if you don't totally buy it. Go through the process you went through to arrive at the quotas step by step.
4. Listen, listen, listen even if what you're hearing may sound like excuses for not wanting to make the effort required. Your people will support your objectives a lot better if they feel they have had a chance to participate in the setting of them. (See Point 10 in the "Checklist for Setting Preliminary Quotas" section.)
5. Try to find ways *their* ideas get woven into your statement of objectives. If some of your people think that developing a cooperative advertising program is *the answer* to their doubling of sales, pursue it and get back to them with a report on your progress.
6. Remember that you went through a lot of travail to arrive at those equitable quota figures, so stand your ground—calmly and patiently— while explaining why the figures are what they are.
7. In the unlikely event someone brings up a legitimate reason to modify the figures, be prepared to negotiate a change, but only as a last resort and only for a truly significant reason.

HOW TO GET YOUR QUOTAS ACCEPTED
WITH OBJECTION-STOPPING ANSWERS

Remember that your regional managers are expert at this kind of negotiating so don't accept specious reasons. Some of these less-than-convincing arguments with suggested answers include:

— *"But, we may lose that big mail-order house that generated so much business last year."*

ANSWER: *(Whether you say it this way or not) Sorry! When you got the windfall last year, you didn't offer to have it deducted from your performance figures or to give back your bonus commissions on the sales.*

— *"My statistics show that the economy will be down 5 percent to 6 percent next year, so my quota should be reduced."*

ANSWER: *Sorry! Your quota is 20 percent higher. This just means that you'll have to be 25 percent to 26 percent better instead of only 20 percent. (You will, of course, first have explained how the quotas were set and how equitable they are.)*

— *"We just lost the best district manager in the territory who will be hard to replace."*

ANSWER: *Sorry! It is the regional managers' job to provide for succession of people, to have candidates ready to go to work, and to make sure that no one is indispensable.*

— *"Davidson Enterprises is making a real move on us and cutting prices, causing us to lose business."*

ANSWER: *Sorry! There will always be someone out there who will be cheaper than we are. It is our job to be 10 percent better, not 5 percent cheaper. Our programs, with the regional managers' active support will ensure that we lose little old business and add new business.*

— *"My quota went up a lot more than anyone else's. You should reduce it so it's more in line with the average."*

ANSWER: *Sorry! Your quota went up more for good reasons, as we discussed. Every territory is going to have to pull its weight with the gravy accounts being looked upon as mostly gravy. No more coasting on windfalls—develop the rest of the territory.*

— *"I can make this quota, but I need promotional allowances, more travel money, more money to entertain customers and prospects, and more literature from the home office."*

ANSWER: *Good! You have been assigned a budget based on what the company can afford for your quota level. You will have the ability to determine how you will use it. (See Chapters 6 and 7.) Exceed your quota and your expense budget will be raised. In the meantime, come up with a plan for how you would use this additional money and what benefits this would generate for the company.*

> — *"I can make this quota, but I need more administrative back-up. I need an answering service, secretarial help, and a dictating machine."*
>
> ANSWER: *Good! It looks as if all these things will fit in your expense budget. You decide how to allocate this budget and let me know how I can help. In the meantime, come up with a plan and budget with cost-effectiveness justification.*

The objections could go on forever. Make up your own list of anticipated questions ahead of time and decide how to handle them. The "Sorry's" given above are the final stopping point after you have patiently explained the reasons for the quotas.

Even with this tough stance, you should be sympathetic and concerned. In this kind of discussion there are no bad ideas and no dumb suggestions from your people. Just remember where your stopping place is.

IN CLOSING...

Setting fair and equitable quotas is no easy job. But it is a manageable task if you approach it systematically:

1. Determine the percentage of the total quota each territory should represent as defined by an appropriate index or indices.
2. Determine the percentage of the total actual sales each territory actually represented the previous year.
3. Average 1 and 2 to come up with a basic or "raw" quota figure that is subject to adjustment.
4. Adjust the "raw" quota figure based on real (versus specious) circumstances to come up with a final quota figure.
5. Test the figures to make sure you haven't overlooked any significant factor and that you can justify all of the numbers used to determine the quotas.
6. Communicate, really communicate, the figures and the reasons for them with your regional (district) managers.
7. Get your people committed to the objectives and minimums by listening, having them participate, and incorporating their ideas in the final plan.

The rest of your management job in this area is monitoring and, as always, motivation. You should be able to communicate your commitment to your regional managers, and they should pass on this spirit of commitment to their district managers.

4

Spending Time
Where It Counts —
Account Stratification

You are probably familiar with the Pareto Time Rule, also known as the "80-20" rule. In an inventory, about 20 percent of the items account for 80 percent of the value of the inventory. Conversely, 80 percent of the items account for only 20 percent of the total inventory value. Correspondingly, in an accounts receivable context, 20 percent of the customer accounts usually account for 80 percent of the total outstanding amounts, and 80 percent account for only 20 percent of the total accounts receivable.

This rule also applies to your customer base. Specifically, 20 percent of your customers usually account for about 80 percent of the total sales volume. Most salespersons and managers already know this intuitively, but few apply the rule to their activities directly and systematically. In this chapter we'll show how to apply and implement this principle.

SIX TIME-WASTING ACTIVITY PLANNING
MISTAKES TO AVOID

1. Calling on old friends and acquaintances more often than their sales volume merits.
2. Calling on accounts closest to the salesperson's home base of operations.
3. Calling on accounts on a planned and logical basis, but ignoring the actual or potential value of the

account. (This is one of the biggest dangers. The salesperson who does this kids himself that he is "organized" but wastes time and misses opportunities by treating all accounts as equally important.)

4. Having no pattern or plan, but waiting to see who needs something and then reacting to situations that develop instead of "proacting" to make things happen.

5. Ignoring large potential prospects in favor of smaller accounts who can be counted on for an order. This reinforces the salesperson's ego but doesn't do enough to help make quota or *your* sales plan.

6. Conversely, ignoring existing customers while looking for the "big score" with a large prospect who is not at all likely to buy from the company.

Except for number 3 above, all these mistakes or problems are indicative of a lack of *planning*. The person identified in 3 is doing the *wrong* kind of planning and may, therefore, be harder to change than a nonplanner.

Let's look at the right way to assign the proper value to accounts to pave the way for the "Call Frequency Planning" steps covered in the next chapter that will help guide the planless as well as the improperly-planned salespeople.

FOUR EASY STEPS TO IDENTIFYING THE BIG TICKET ACCOUNTS

We'll discuss the steps necessary to develop an account stratification plan, an organized and systematic way to ensure that the important accounts are accorded their proper importance and called upon more regularly than the less important (lesser volume) accounts. We'll then fill in the outline and provide a plan with specific examples that can be implemented.

1. *Capture your customer list.* This sounds simple and elementary, but many sales organizations lack this basic information tool. They don't have a real grasp of who their customers really are. Develop a list with the names of all your customers in some kind of identifiable order— geographic, descending order of sales volume, classified by products purchased, or any other kind of logical order.

2. *Capture your prospect list.* Today's prospects are tomorrow's customers, so they deserve equal importance—in terms of identification if not of call frequency.

3. *Stratify the list.* We'll discuss this in more detail below. For now, recognize that some customers *really are* more important than other customers, and prospects have to be blended in an organized way. Identify customers and prospects in terms of importance as A, B, C, or D.

Analyze your categorization to be sure your stratification is at least nominally accurate. Make adjustments. Determine the appropriate "weighting" for prospects. Review your work to make sure that the stratification has been done in accordance with your sales goals rather than some arbitrarily accepted standard that was used in the past and may not still be valid.

4. *Be ready to communicate your stratification plan.* Make sure the information is captured in a way that will be useful to any future effort. You may set up a computer database or use 3 × 5 index cards. In either case, the information should be organized and available.

Recognize that a salesperson has only three (you can argue that this is two or four) hours per day of time actually spent in front of customers doing a selling job, so maximization of time is one of the most important responsibilities of an effective field sales manager. Sell your people on the value of doing this to maximize their time and increase their income.

EIGHT TIME- AND MONEY-SAVING WAYS TO CAPTURE YOUR PROSPECT LIST

The first step is to make sure you have, in one place, a listing of all your customers. Make sure the customer list is in descending order of volume with their present year's volume and last year's volume.

1. If your company has a well-organized data processing department, all of the information you will need will be captured somewhere in the computer as part of the invoicing and accounts receivable routines.

2. If you don't have this luxury, start accumulating the information for this valuable management tool *now* even if you have to dig out and sort copies of the invoices and run adding machine tapes. You can't run an organized and effective sales organization without this information.

3. If the job looks formidable, start with that 20 percent of the number of accounts that account for 80 percent of the business. This, of course, is a chicken-and-egg situation. How do you identify those 20 percent if you don't have the sales figures?

4. The answer is to *guess* . . . and work with your salespeople. If they can't come pretty close to identifying those customers, you could have more problems than you were initially aware of.

5. Capture this information in an organized way. Figure 4.1 illustrates one kind of 3-ring-binder sheet, card file, or visible card record that could be used.

KYLE RYAN TRUCKING

	Total	A	B	C	D	E	Remarks
1985	3231	—	126	2178	286	641	
1986	4768	—	241	1864	1021	1642	
Jan.	361	—	—	181	180	—	
Feb.	484	—	220	—	64	200	
Mar.	—	—	—	—	—	—	Purchases On Hold
Apr.	1120	816	114	—	190	—	Furniture Job
May							
Jun.							
Jul.							
Aug.							
Sep.							
Oct.							
Nov.							
Dec.							
T							

Figure 4.1

It provides a summary sales history by product category (A, B, C, etc.) for previous years, monthly sales figures by product for the current year, and enters reasons for unusual patterns—"new building installation," "on strike this month," etc.

This record will be valuable in reviewing an account's history and tip you off to any decreases which may indicate that a competitor is moving in, or increases which may indicate a new application for your product(s) that could be used with other customers.

If you have access to a computer or your computer department, you can use this form and others in this chapter to set up your data base or tell your Management Information Systems Manager what you need.

6. You may not have to start from scratch to develop this. Check with your salespeople or managers to see if they have this kind of information in some form. If they don't, they *should* to manage *their* territories effectively.

   Having them compile the information will help them to become familiar with their territories and make the point about the kind of recordkeeping you feel is vital to effective territory management.

7. Arrange the cards (record) in order of sales volume and develop your summary listing arranged in descending order based on the previous year's sales volume. It could look something like Figure 4.2.

CUSTOMER VOLUME LISTING

No.	Customer Name	Volume 1985	Volume 1986	% Change	% Total	Cum. % Total
12	Cardinal Books	220685	210496	- 5	19	19
23	D&B Wholesale	180424	178323	+ 10	18	37
78	K. Lisa, CPA	110626	165127	+ 50	15	52
52	Deewen Acad.	80424	181726	+ 26	9	61
47	S. David, M.D.	75476	80625	+ 7	7	68
149	S.H. Stationery	50143	40917	- 18	4	72
4	Ace Trucking	40637	32936	- 20	3	75
96	Krisan Toys	25128	28629	+ 16	3	78
184	Stuart Hdw.	20812	27926	+ 35	2	80
209	Wendall's	10486	19814	+ 80	2	82
162	SWK Doors	11718	5224	- 41	1	83
175	K. Ryan Trk'g	3231	4768	+ 48	—	83
	All Others	169710	183799	+ 8	17	100
	Total	1000000	1100000		100	

Figure 4.2

The customer number name and sales volume columns are obvious. The next column would indicate the percentage change, plus or minus from the previous year. You will probably want to circle in red and investigate all changes over 20 percent.

The "percentage of total" column is the previous year's sales volume divided by the total previous year's sales and tells you just how important that customer is.

In the next column, you accumulate the percentages. This will give you a handle on how few customers account for 10 percent, 20 percent, and 50 percent of your sales. (To keep the illustration simple, we've only listed a few customers.) A possible stratification might be:

    A Accounts: Up to 10% in the cumulative column
    B Accounts: From 10% to 20% in the cumulative column
    C Accounts: From 20% to 50% in the cumulative column
    D Accounts: All others

8. Now that we have the part of the basis for the call frequency pattern planning and implementation that will be discussed in the next chapter, add your prospects to the pool of information.

SEVEN STRATEGIES FOR CAPTURING YOUR PROSPECT LIST

In almost 30 years, I've met only two salespeople who didn't have "tons of prospects" that they were developing. (Only one was ready to retire.) Ask for an activity report, a history of calls, or even an organized list, however, and the tons magically turn into ounces.

Yet, the constant cultivation of prospects developed through cold calls, referrals, or any other means is very important. Even the most effective salespersons will experience some attrition in their customer bases. Customers do move, may be in declining industries, go out of business, and—perish the thought—sometimes start buying from competitors.

1. In a small industry with a limited market base, list everyone in the geographic territory who is not now a customer. Get the list from the yellow pages, national trade association directories, local directories, or the "drive-by" method.

   That is, if you are selling office products in Koochiching County, Minnesota, you would look for the stationery signs in Grand Falls (provided that it's August so they're not covered with snow) and add the stores to your prospect list.

2. In a larger industry, the problem is a little more complicated:

   a. Identify who your company is.

   b. Determine and write down what you have to offer in terms of product and anything else that makes your company unique.

   c. Construct an "ideal account" profile that will match your strengths with perceived needs. (You wouldn't have developed the product unless *someone* perceived a need out there.)

   Chapter 4 shows an example of this part of a marketing plan for FSM Computer Software Company.

3. Rank your prospects by relative importance. So far, except perhaps for figuring out just who you are (Step 2.a, above) and matching these capabilities with assumed customer needs, it has been fairly simple to come up with your list. But, how do you weight it?

   This involves another piece of homework which, at least in some form, should already have been done. As a start, the prospects who are able to buy the most of your product/service are the most important prospects.

4. Estimate potential volume by guessing (call it empirical prediction if you wish) based on the *assumed* size of the company and what a similar-sized company from whom you get all or most of that type of business, purchases.

If one chair manufacturer orders 100,000 casters a year from you and does $1.4 million a year in business, it's a fair bet that a manufacturer who does $3 million a year is in the market for around 200,000 casters.

5. Use an industry index and apply it to that prospect's statistic. That is, it may be an accepted office products industry standard that a company will spend $240 per year on office supplies for every clerical employee. If you are selling office supplies and know a prospect has 120 employees, you can estimate the office supplies potential at $28,000 per year.

6. Estimate the potential based on the prospect's end product and the part your products play in that product.

    For example, let's assume you sell LEDs (light-emitting diodes—those green, amber, and blue lights on computers and other machines) to manufacturers at $.14 each and your prospect makes computer monitors that he sells for an average of $50. His sales are $5,000,000 per year, so he produces about 100,000 monitors which use two LEDs each. This means you could sell him 200,000 LEDs at $.14 each or $28,000.

7. Ask the purchasing agent. You don't have to do this directly. You could allude to a volume discount program your company has and offer to put together a proposal on how he could save money. Obviously, you have to have the volume figures to do this properly.

HOW TO FIND THE PROSPECTS WHO WILL BECOME MAJOR ACCOUNTS

Another factor needs to be considered before you can properly weave these accounts into your customer listing and your call frequency planning—that is, how likely they are to buy from you. Of course this is a judgment call, but you can quantify this qualitative judgment by assigning a likely value.

Your present customers are close to 100 percent likely to buy from you, unless you know something that would suggest a risk, so their previous year's sales can be taken at face value. For prospects, this simple formula will help you determine relative importance:

Possible Sales Volume × Likelihood = Relative Weight

1. If you feel that a customer can buy $70,000 a year from you and the likelihood of getting this $70,000 is 10 percent, the "relative weight" is 7,000 and we'll add this to our list as though the prospect were a $7,000-per-year customer.

2. If a prospect can buy $50,000 from you and you feel you have a 30 percent chance of getting this business, this prospect is worth $15,000 and is more important, in terms of attention, than the larger prospect.

3. Assume the likelihood of the prospect in number 7 above buying $28,000 from you is one in ten, so he gets a 2,800 ($28,000 × 10%).

Since he probably wants more than one supplier, you may feel your chances of getting 30 percent of the business are about 50-50, so give him a weight of 4,200 ($28,000 × 30% = 8,400 × 50% = 4,200).

4. Integrate these prospects into your (simplified) customer list to give you an account stratification list that would look like Figure 4.3.

CUSTOMER VOLUME LISTING— STRATIFIED

No.	Customer Name	Volume 1985 $000's	1986
"A" Accounts			
12	Cardinal Books	221	210
23	D&B Wholesale	180	198
"B" Accounts			
78	K. Lisa, CPA	111	165
52	Deewen Acad.	80	102
47	S. David, M.D.	75	81
"C" Accounts			
4	Ace Trucking	41	33
96	Krisan Toys	25	29
184	Stuart Hdw.	21	28
209	Wendall's	10	20
"D" Accounts			
162	SWK Doors	12	5
175	Ryan Trucking	3	5
	All Others		

Figure 4.3

Note: Don't let the simplicity of this formula fool you. I've talked with literally dozens of sales managers about this, many of them quite effective. No one, of course, denied the importance of prospecting. That would be like denying the importance of the automobile in Detroit (or Los Angeles). Many had good solid plans and procedures for identifying and qualifying prospects including, in some cases, quotas and rewards for such work by field salespeople.

None, however, could explain how to make an objective choice on whether to ascribe more importance to a particular prospect than to a particular customer or group of customers.

Also, none could come up with any semblance of a plan to call on prospects based on perceived importance or sales volume. They had rules like, "Twenty percent of our salespeople's time should be spent on prospecting and they have to report their prospect or cold calls on their call report sheets," but nothing like the specifics above.

So, again, don't take this section lightly. Unless you're a lot better-read or know a lot more smart people than we do, you won't find this subject dealt with so simply and specifically anywhere else.

HOW TO WEIGHT YOUR PROSPECTS BY HOW MUCH THEY CAN CONTRIBUTE TO SALES REVENUE

We have our stratification about worked out by having gone through the steps of capturing, in an organized way, our customers and prospects.

It usually works out this way. William James said a long time ago, "A problem well-defined is half solved." In sales and marketing, as in most business activities, a problem well-defined is probably 80 percent solved.

You'll spend 20 percent of the total project time you might have spent in another way to accomplish this 80 percent of your results by working in this planned, organized way.

All that is left now is to identify our customers and prospects in a way that will accommodate the call frequency pattern planning steps discussed in the next chapter. Before we develop our stratification list, let's agree on some general ground rules that will carry us through the entire planning process and be useful in future chapters:

- 50 percent of the salespersons' (district managers') time will be spent on A accounts (customers *and* prospects).
- 20 percent of the time will be spent on B accounts.
- 20 percent of the time will be spent on C accounts.
- 10 percent of the time will be spent on D accounts.

Unless your territories are unusual in some way (flat, with no really outstanding accounts, or heavily concentrated in two or three "key" accounts) your determination of the time division for your salespeople shouldn't deviate much from the above suggestion. Also, by now you should have become a Pareto disciple and a devotee of the 80-20 rule. As you can see, the allocation of salespeople's time suggested above comes pretty close to matching the provisions of both.

What is left to do, at this stage, is to develop a listing, in order of priority, of the customers and prospects. Such a listing might look like Figure 4.4.

CUSTOMER/PROSPECT LISTING

No.	Customer Name	Volume Value $000's
12	Cardinal Books	210
23	D&B Wholesale	198
78	K. Lisa, CPA	165
52	Deewen Acad.	102
47	S. David, M.D.	81
4	Ace Trucking	33
96	Krisan Toys	29
184	Stuart Hdw.	28
209	Wendall's	20
	Prospect B	15
	Prospect A	7
162	SWK Doors	5
175	Ryan Trucking	5
	Prospect C	3

Figure 4.4

FIVE PROVEN TECHNIQUES TO
MAKE YOUR STRATIFICATION PLAN STICK

As with other plans and procedures suggested, *doing it* is only part of the task for a manager. For it to be really effective, your people, your peers, and your boss have to buy it. Some ideas:

1. Discuss the plan with your boss or peers at the home office, getting their agreement that it is a good way to go, if not the *only* way to go.

2. Have your boss or at least one of your peers contribute an idea or two that you will incorporate with your ideas so the final plan becomes *theirs* as well as yours.

3. Make the positive aspects of what you are doing look like *their* idea. You'll give up some credit if it works, but you'll have some markers you can call on later. If something you try doesn't work and you've done this, you have other people on the hook with you and they'll make sure you don't go under because (if you've set it up properly) they'll go under with you.

4. Here's the recurrent theme throughout the book. Discuss your plans with the people who work for you and have to implement all those bright ideas you came up with. Better yet, let it be their idea.

Their "mediocre" idea will work much better in the field than your "brilliant" idea. It will also help when the home office people quiz your people about an idea. If they have participated in and contributed to it, it will be defended and the home office person will go away saying something like, "Well, I still don't see how it can work, but the field seems to have taken to it."

For example, a district manager in San Francisco once had a dealer who had a "fantastic" idea about how to use his cooperative advertising money. He didn't want to send out direct mail flyers. He didn't want to use newspaper advertising. He didn't want to do any of the conventional things that our home office marketing research department told him were right.

His idea was to parade a bikinied model up and down Montgomery Street with the company slogan on the front and his "Buy from . . ." message on the back of a sandwich board sign. A crazy idea! And we had a lot of problems with the home office when they found out about it. There was no way this ridiculous, undignified idea could work.

But it did! The dealer who liked the idea made it work. San Francisco is really a small part of the California market, but this little dealer bought more product during the period of the promotion than anyone else. His mediocre idea worked better than all our brilliant ideas because he made it work. After looking at the sales figures, the home office decided to back off even though they "knew" it was a dumb idea.

5. Look at your list, considering your sales objectives, and make sure it makes intuitive sense to you and is consistent with what you want to do with your territory. At this point, there is no good substitute for sound, informed field sales empirical judgment. Just double-check to make sure it's in line with your "new market" or "new product penetration" or any other objectives.

IN CLOSING. . .

There was once a sales manager who came across as being totally uninvolved. He didn't seem to understand anything about selling; he was a decent person who was always ready to listen to the salespersons' ideas. He always invited the sales and managerial staff to participate in meetings. And he was always there with a compliment if something that the staff had done worked well and made money for the company.

Yet he never seemed to contribute anything. He just listened, asked a few questions, and let the staff put their ideas into effect. They even wrote his management reports for him. When a board meeting required a detailed discussion of a particular project or market penetration effort, he had someone on the staff present the idea. His only contribution was to introduce them.

The staff came to know that they had to present understandable action plans, with clear and specific objectives and timetables, or their manager wouldn't comprehend what they were trying to do and wouldn't approve the money. Every marketing or sales idea we came up with was theirs. Yet he had the title of "Executive Vice President, Marketing."

One day he decided to go out in the field, honor customers with his presence, and "get a feel" for what was going on. He asked the staff for a listing of the most important accounts by territory and city. He obviously wanted to spend his time only with the biggest accounts. He also wanted a listing of the biggest prospects in each territory with brief analyses of why they had not been sold so far.

After the trip, to the surprise of the staff, the manager really didn't do a great deal of harm. In fact, in spite of his "interference," most of the customers he called on were doing more business a few months later, and two of the six prospects identified for him started to order.

Was this manager really lazy—or a very foxy people manager?

5

Success-Proven
Call Frequency Planning
That Brings in
Increased Sales Revenues

Given the customer information as compiled in Chapter 4 the next question is, "What number of calls per year is appropriate for each type of stratified account?" This chapter attempts to answer that question.

EIGHT CALL FREQUENCY PLANNING ERRORS
THAT STEAL SALES
WITHOUT YOUR KNOWING IT

1. No planning at all. This may sound obvious, but most salespeople really don't have an advance plan for how they will spend their days.

2. Planning calls based on specious reasoning. This could mean calls based on a so-called plan that doesn't meet the goals established or a plan that is based on circumstances that existed 30 years ago.

3. Planning calls based on the volume done by present customers, ignoring what those customers can do versus what prospects in the territory can do.

4. Not differentiating between what current customers and currently identified prospects can do compared with the whole big world out there.

5. Assuming that all customers or prospects are more or less equal and not assigning more weight to those who can do a lot more than they are presently doing.

6. Forgetting about former big customers who have not been called upon recently for whatever reason.

7. Not keeping in touch with former customers or prospects who may have changed in terms of buying patterns or business volume potential.

8. Not getting to see the A accounts often enough by planning sales calls only between the hours of 9:00 A.M. and 5:00 P.M. Monday through Friday and not taking advantage of the extended workdays and workweeks many customers have.

The most important and debilitating issue is that of assuming that all customers are equal or that they all buy for the same reasons and stop buying for the same reasons. This just isn't true! We will take the lessons we learned in Chapter 4 and apply them to a Call Frequency Planning scheme that will produce the kinds of results we want to produce.

HOW TO PLAN EFFECTIVE CALL FREQUENCY PATTERNS

Here are some ground rules for producing effective field sales management results in terms of call frequency patterns:

1. Identify the 20 percent of your customers who will account for 80 percent of the results you will obtain.

2. "Capture" this list in a finite form for your district (regional) managers and get it to them.

3. Set up a reporting system that will allow you to monitor the results from (at least) this critical 20 percent. (The other 80 percent can be dealt with on an exception basis.)

4. Make sure that your district (regional) managers understand the rules you are playing by and realize that their performance and promotability will be measured by these rules. You will, of course, have involved them in the planning process in developing the goals.

5. Develop a listing of *all* territory customers/prospects with your district (regional) managers like that in Chapter 4 that you all agree upon.

6. Agree—*really* agree—on the ground rules. Agree that this isn't a school exercise where you agree on MBOs or other objectives and then forget them as soon as the meeting is over. *Make it clear that this is not a theoretical exercise but the development of real plans and real operating tools where real operating results are expected.*

7. Make your people know that you're serious about this. Discussions are good. Firing someone who doesn't do what has been agreed upon is a

pretty good indication of how serious you really are. Rewarding those who do follow the plan *they* have agreed to is even better, especially in the long run. (Incidentally, before you decide to fire someone, check out Chapter 10 and pay special attention to the "three-month plan" outlined there.)

8. Follow your own rules. You are trying to get your people to buy Vilfredo Pareto's ideas. Make sure you set the right example. The only way I know to get people to work hard for me is to convince them that I'm working at least as hard—and doing it in the right 80-20 way. Check out the 75-75 rule which will be discussed in detail in Chapter 8. (You have a full-time job in the field and a full-time job in the home office. You have to figure out how to get 75 percent of each job done.)

9. Work with your people in setting up the call frequency patterns (we'll deal with this in more detail below) and make sure that they see the possibility of some really positive results in their income in developing and following this plan.

10. Set the plan down in specific terms. Don't assume that because you and your people have agreed, philosophically, on a course of action that they will implement it without some guidance (or even remember it) when they walk out your door. It's a lonely world out there for your district managers and they are more likely to seek help from their old favorite customers than from you—unless you have set up the reward structure so that they receive benefits as a result of following the plan that you and they have agreed upon.

11. Have your marketing colleagues in the home office and/or your boss agree with your plan. Have them contribute an idea or two that can be incorporated in the plan, use it and make sure they get the credit for it.

12. Encourage your field people to identify the nonconventional times to see accounts, especially A accounts. Most of these people didn't get to be A accounts by working only conventional hours.

In Appendix D, a guide is provided using a typical salesperson's day. This will help to deal with some specifics in defining call frequency patterns by illustrating just how little time your salespeople (district or regional managers) have to work with.

In this illustration we suggest that two to four hours a day is all the effective time that is available. Let's see how this scarce time can be most effectively used.

HOW TO SET HOUR- AND DOLLAR-SAVING CALL FREQUENCY PATTERNS

We found that even our well-planned, exemplary salesperson has only three hours a day for effective selling. Let's assume we're going to create such an improvement that this can be increased by one-third and plan 20 hours effective selling time a week. This gives us 1,040 hours per year.

Or does it? The best-laid plans can get abandoned quickly if there is no allowance for reality. ("You wanted me to follow up on that hot prospect, didn't you?" "His machine was down and she was screaming. Of course I had to be there." "You can't get anything done there the week before Christmas.")

Let's add up some of the reality elements in terms of the 1,040 hours per year or 20 hours per week:

Vacation time (3 weeks × 20 hours)	60
Holidays (10 × 4 hours)	40
Personal or illness days (5 × 4 hours)	20
Prospecting time (20%)	208
Crisis-resolving and other necessary but unplanned time (10%)	104
Sales meetings and other training or home office activities (10%)	104
Other time (to allow for Murphy's Law and other calamities (5%))	52
Total	588

Only 452 hours left! It was bad enough that our salesperson was only able to do an effective face-to-face selling job for 25 percent of a 12-hour day. Now we find that more than half of that is gone, too. Is it any wonder that sales managers throw up their hands in despair when they try to plan in an organized effective way?

Remember, too, that the above numbers were based on a 33-1/3 percent increase over our model salesperson to get four hours a day. (You may quarrel with some of our time-allocation percentages, so figure out your own and see how many selling hours or days *you* come up with.)

We'll discuss stretching the days or weeks below. For now, let's work with the 452 figure and assume that we have an average (rounding up) of 10 hours per week or 40 hours per month (rounding down) and that each sales call, exclusive of travel, waiting, or shooting-the-breeze time will take an average of one-half hour. This gives us 20 calls per week or 80 per month. This begins to look a little better since we're concentrating on only *quality* time and have allowed for special situations.

To keep things simple and consistent, let's use our stratified customer list (Figure 4.3) to work out the frequency. We'll make some assumptions:

1. We won't call on the D accounts personally at all. They will be handled by mail and, when necessary, by phone. If they do require a visit we'll consider this "prospecting" time.

2. The A accounts will have twice as much importance as the B accounts and four times as much as the C accounts. This starting point can be modified if, for example, the biggest A account is many times the size of the account in second place.

3. We'll try as much as possible to handle the C accounts by mail and telephone but "fit them in" with the others.

To make it a little more realistic, we'll multiply the number of accounts in Figure 4.4 by 10. The accounts then break down in number as follows:

A Accounts	20
B Accounts	30
C Accounts	40

Let's weight them according to the importance we ascribed above:

A Accounts	20 × 4 = 80 points
B Accounts	30 × 2 = 60 points
C Accounts	40 × 1 = 40 points
Total	180 points

By dividing the points in each category by the total number of points and then applying the result to the available 20 calls per week and 80 calls per month, we get the following table:

Stratum	%	Calls per Week	Calls per Month
A	44.5%	9	36
B	33.3%	7	27
C	22.2%	4	17
D	0%	0	0

Dividing the number of accounts for each category by the number of calls per week available gives us the following call frequency pattern:

A Accounts:	Every 2.2 weeks
B Accounts:	Every 4.3 weeks
C Accounts:	Every 10 weeks (as convenient)
D Accounts:	As needed

Looking at it another way, dividing the number of calls available per month for each category by the number of accounts in that category gives us the following call frequency pattern:

A Accounts:	1.8 calls per month or about twice a month
B Accounts:	.9 calls per month or about once a month
C Accounts:	.4 calls per month or about every two months

Naturally, geography will play a part in the actual routing, and you may decide that you have some A or B accounts that are more important than others, but you now have a rough guide that matches our idea that A accounts are twice as important as B accounts and four times as important as C accounts since the plan is for them to be called on with that degree of frequency.

HOW TO PLAN CALLS SO THAT THEY PRODUCE ORDERS

Pinning down the actual day that your salespeople call on accounts may be a lot simpler than it sounds:

1. Many customers prefer to see salespeople only on certain days anyway and may have a day in mind already.
2. Many will appreciate the orderliness of your sales force in being so well-organized that they can pick a day.
3. Many are disorganized themselves and you will be a hero for bringing this little bit of discipline into their otherwise less-organized lives.

Of course, if you are selling Boeing 757s, your strategy will be somewhat different. However, even for sales of items like mainframe and minicomputers, the above could be a guide on how often to follow up with prospects. It certainly works well with an established customer/prospect base.

To illustrate how this would work, let's take the simplified and stratified customer listing from Chapter 4 (Figure 4.4) and expand it to show the frequency before we illustrate the final steps in this effective sales management planning tool (Figure 5.1). You can see that we took a couple of liberties since some of our B

CUSTOMER VOLUME LISTING—STRATIFIED

No.	Customer Name	Volume 1985 $000's	1986	Call Freq.	Best Day
"A" Accounts					
12	Cardinal Books	221	210	2 weeks	Tue.
23	D&B Wholesale	180	198	2 weeks	Wed.
"B" Accounts					
78	K. Lisa, CPA	111	165	3 weeks	Fri.
52	Deewen Acad.	80	102	4 weeks	Thu.
47	S. David, M.D.	75	81	5 weeks	Tue.
"C" Accounts					
4	Ace Trucking	41	33	8 weeks	Mon.
96	Krisan Toys	25	29	8 weeks	Fri.
184	Stuart Hdw.	21	28	8 weeks	Mon.
209	Wendall's	10	20	10 weeks	Wed.
"D" Accounts					
162	SWK Doors	12	5		Thu.
175	Ryan Trucking	3	5		Fri.
	All Others				

Figure 5.1

Week	Mon.		Tue.		Wed.		Thu.		Fri.		Sat.		Sun.	
No.	AM	PM	AM	PM	AM	PM	AM	PM	AM	PM	AM	PM	AM	PM
1.														
2.														
3.														
4.														
5.														
6.														
7.														
8.														
9.														
10.														
11.														
12.														
13.														

Figure 5.2

Week No.	Mon. AM	Mon. PM	Tue. AM	Tue. PM	Wed. AM	Wed. PM	Thu. AM	Thu. PM	Fri. AM	Fri. PM	Sat. AM	Sat. PM	Sun. AM	Sun. PM
1.			A18					A7						
2.														
3.			A18					A7						
4.														
5.					SALES MEETING—ALL WEEK									
6.			A18					A7						
7.														
8.			A18					A7						
9.					VACATION									
10.			A18					A7						
11														
12.			A18					A7						
13.		SEMINAR												

Figure 5.3

accounts were obviously "more equal" than others. The real account listing would be 10 times as long to match our above figures, but we wanted to keep it simple.

Also, K. Lisa, C.P.A. is a very attractive woman and our salesperson wanted to see her a little more often. Well, some frivolity is allowed as long as the job gets done. Remember what we said earlier in this chapter about making the job fun if you want to get that 33-1/3 percent increase in effective selling hours?

CHECKLIST FOR FILLING OUT THE CALL PATTERN SCHEDULE

1. Set up a chart like that shown in Figure 5.2 for a quarter (13 weeks) with days divided into mornings and afternoons.
2. Block out those times that you know will be unavailable for calls—vacations, sales meetings, etc.
3. Start filling in the days that it is best to call on some accounts as far as you already know this, using their strata designation (A, B, C) and their account numbers. Your chart might now look like Figure 5.3.

   In a larger geographic territory, the geography itself may be the dictating factor. One of our objectives is to reduce nonselling time during prime hours, so you don't want to go from Atlanta to Birmingham to Augusta if you can avoid it.
4. Call the A accounts and see if there is a day that is best for them. If not, suggest a day that fits your salesperson's schedule and try to group accounts geographically. With your B accounts, try to fill up Mondays and Fridays first since these will be the most difficult. Tell your salespeople that their customers won't resent this, they will respect it.
5. Fill in the schedule with the C accounts, using mostly geographic considerations like being in the same industrial park as an A account.

HOW TO ANSWER TYPICAL OBJECTIONS TO CALL PLANNING

The above steps to organizing time and planning call frequencies seem so logical and right that it may be hard to imagine any objections to such a scheme. A lot of salespeople and regional managers, however, feel that planning is inhibiting, and they may need further convincing.

I had a rep once who really fought this concept. He would do anything to avoid becoming organized. He was effective in his territory by telling taller Texas tales than anyone else. He felt that it took the mystique and art out of the profession to sit down and "plan." Let's look at some of his reasons for resisting planning and find some answers to suggest:

COMMENT: *Customers don't want to be pinned down to a specific time. They want to "play it loose."*

ANSWER: *Aren't you "pinning them down" when you set up an appointment? If you don't set up appointments, aren't you pinning them down if you show up in the lobby or even the barn?*

COMMENT: *Something always comes up to get in the way, no matter how well you plan. You have to see what is going on in the real world* today.

ANSWER: *When you plan, you can avert 80 percent of the crises. Also, the schedule allows for these crises with "loose" time.*

COMMENT: *I like to be creative (always the key word cop-out) and plan (plan?) to deal with the immediate situation.*

ANSWER: *This isn't planning. It's reacting. "Creativity" comes from* controlling *the situation rather than waiting for it to happen and then shooting from the hip in reaction.*

COMMENT: *You never know what kinds of opportunities may come up, so you have to kind of hang loose so you can jump on them when they come.*

ANSWER: *You don't* wait *for opportunities to come up. You can* create *your own opportunities by deciding what you want to happen and then planning to make it happen. Nothing ever turns out exactly (or even close) to what you want, but planning gives you at least three times better odds that you can make happen what you want to.*

COMMENT: *But, you Easterners don't understand my people and the way business is done down here. (In the West, Easterners don't understand. In the East, Midwesterners and West Coast people don't understand.)*

ANSWER: *Your people, more than anyone else know how to plan. They plan crops, they plan feed for the spring foals, and all those other things we city people don't pretend to understand. (When you hear "you don't understand my people," you know he's beginning to weaken. That's always a dead giveaway to having no more argument.)*

COMMENT: *But how are we going to put all this together?*

PUTTING A "LIVE-FIRE" CALL FREQUENCY CHART INTO ACTION

How? Good question, indeed. The task of scheduling even for a week is formidable for most people. Now we are asking salespeople to schedule a month or a quarter in advance.

Let's wrap up this section by showing you a completed theoretical scheduling plan (that could be a real plan) which accommodates the parameters we discussed above in terms of call frequency planning and pins it down to dates. Further, it pins down the calling schedule to early morning, mid-morning, and late morning. Same for the afternoon.

Remember that early morning could mean breakfast and late morning could mean lunch. Early afternoon could mean lunch and late afternoon a 5:00 p.m. sales meeting, cocktails, or dinner. This is discussed further in the "Stretching Your Time" section below.

Figure 5.4 shows the scheduled appointments for 90 accounts—20 A accounts, 30 B accounts, and 40 C accounts. D accounts are not shown since it is assumed that they'll be reached by phone or mail. All 90 accounts are scheduled for a quarter, 13 weeks, close to the ideal time identified above. We've also assumed, in this quarter, two holidays, a week for the salesperson to be on vacation, a week at a sales meeting, and attendance at a two-day seminar.

At first glance it looks a bit bewildering. Let's look at the strategy behind it and then go into a little detail about how it was constructed. Then we'll go back and analyze it and try to criticize both the chart and the thinking behind it.

The letters on the chart refer, of course to our A, B, C stratification. The numbers represent different accounts within that category of account from our master listing. Let's review how we assembled this array of alphanumeric information and what it all means:

1. First, we blocked out the time we knew would be unavailable for calls— holidays, sales meetings, vacation, and seminar attendance. We also threw in every second Wednesday afternoon as free time. This could be used to catch up, grab some midweek recreation, handling special customers, prospecting, or any other reason.

2. We provided six spots for each day—three morning and three afternoon —recognizing that not all three would be used every day because some accounts take more time and because we wanted to leave time for prospecting and problem-handling without disrupting the rest of the schedule.

3. Next, we filled in the A accounts based on the day that was best for that account, a day we suggested or because of geographic considerations.

4. We went on to fill in the Bs and Cs based on the planned frequency of calls and geography—important even if your salespeople cover only a single city. It could be the difference between traveling one hour or more to the next call or ten minutes.

5. We went back and double-checked to make sure that our A accounts, whom we wanted to call on twice a month, weren't skipped for three weeks or more because of holiday or other conflicts, and made the necessary adjustments.

6. In order to stretch our time and create a longer workweek, we were able to schedule some people who think Saturday morning is their best time. Also, one of these salespersons has a fairly regular Sunday morning golf game with two customers who, to justify their country club dues, just love to discuss business at this time.

Week No.	Mon. AM	Mon. PM	Tue. AM	Tue. PM	Wed. AM	Wed. PM	Thu. AM	Thu. PM	Fri. AM	Fri. PM	Sat. AM	Sat. PM	Sun. AM	Sun. PM
1.	HOLIDAY		A18 B 1 B21	A 6 A16 C 3	B 8 C 7 C25	A 3 B12 B23	A10 A17 C 1	A 7 B11 C12	A19 B 4 C24	A11 A14 B29	A 9 B 3 B26		A 4 B27	
2.	A 1 A 5 B27	A12 B13 C11	B 2 B 5	B10 B20 C34	A15 A20 B28	B16 C12 C20	B18 B30 C27	A13 B 1 B25	B15 C22	B19				
3.	A 8 B14 C19	A 2 B 6 C17	A18 B17 C13	A 6 A16 B24	B 7 C18 C21		A10 A17 C30	A 7 C16 C38	A19 C40	A11 A14 C10	A 9 B 9 B22			
4.	A 1 A 5 C23	A12	B21		A15 A20 C31	A 3 B12		A13 C 5	B 4				A 4 B27	
5.	SALES MEETING—ALL WEEK													
6.	A 8 B14 B27	A 2 A12 C 4	A18 B 1	A 6 A16 C39	A15 A20 B28	A 3 B16 B23	A10 A17 B30	A 7 A13 B25	A19 C 8 C 9	A11 A14	A 9 B 3		A 4 B27	
7.	A 1 A 5 C26	B 6 B13	B 2 B 5	B10 B20	B 7 B 8		B18 C14 C32	B11 C36 C37	B15 C33	B19 B29	B 9 B26			
8.	A 8 C28 C35	A 2 A12	A18 B17 B21	A 6 A16 B24	A15 A20	A 3 B12 C29	A10 A17	A 7 A13	A19 B 4 C15	A11 A14 C 2	A 9 B22		A 4 B27	
9.	VACATION													
10.	A 8 B14 B27	A12 B13	A18 B 5	A 6 A16 C 3	A15 A20 B28	A 3 B16 B23	A10 A17	A 7 A13 C 1	HOLIDAY		A 9 B 3 B 9		A 4 B27	
11.	A 1 A 5	A 2 B 6 C17	B 1 B 2 C11	B10 B20 C34	B 7 B 8 C 7		B18 B30	B11 B25 C12	A19 C24	A11 A14 C10				
12.	A 5 A 8	A 2 A12	A18 B17 B21	A 6 A16 B24	A15 A20 C21	A 3 B12	A10 A17	A 7 A13	B 4 B15 C22	B19 B29	A 9 B22 B26		A 4 B27	
13.	A 1 C19 C23	— SEMINAR —			C25 C31 C20	C12 C18	C27	C 5 C16 C38	A19 C40	A11 B14			A 4 B27	

Figure 5.4

7. Some spots are open because we couldn't find any takers or because, logistically, it didn't make sense to fill them with existing accounts. We'll develop a prospect list of accounts near those planned, for example, in week 4, Tuesday.

So, that's how such an impossible job is put together. Of course it won't work all the time. Customers have their own vacations, meetings, and other scheduled times. They get called into meetings ten minutes before you are scheduled to be there. Having a plan that will work 70 percent to 80 percent of the time, however, is still a lot better than no plan at all.

This layout can then be translated to a calendar for the specific quarter involved, and all the planning has been done. Your salesperson can concentrate on dealing with exceptions and making sales happen instead of working day to day, hoping to connect with appointments.

When the nature of the territory is that there are few regular accounts and the prospects and customers require firm appointments for each call (as opposed to every second Tuesday afternoon), you will need more appointment-scheduling time unless this chore can be delegated so that your salespeople spend as much of their time as possible *selling*.

Incidentally, if the number of A, B, and C accounts in your salespersons' territory is between 70 and 100, this chart could be a good guide in your planning. Just substitute customer names or account numbers for those shown. Or, list the A1 through C40 codes on a piece of paper and list customer names next to them as the frequency planning chart is completed.

One question that has been asked where I have helped a client implement this kind of system: "Doesn't all this planning and laying things out specifically take the mystery and art out of selling?" The answer is "No!" It frees your salespeople for the really important things they have to do instead of focusing on all those little details that constantly get in the way of their maximum effectiveness.

FOUR PROVEN TECHNIQUES FOR STRETCHING YOUR SALESPEOPLE'S TIME TO GET ADDITIONAL ORDERS

No one can stretch time. There are, however, some ways to extend the workday beyond the hours from 9:00 a.m. and 5:00 p.m. and the workweek beyond Monday through Friday. Saturdays, for some, could be another option. Let's look at some of these ways:

1. Schedule breakfast meetings. A dealer in Chicago used to meet with his people for breakfast at 6:00 a.m. It started informally and became a company tradition. This was a perfect time to get their attention. The mail didn't arrive until 8:00 a.m. so they weren't distracted about what they could react to. They didn't start to make their planned telephone calls or personal visits until at least then (assuming they had planned their days).

It was a long day if you were staying at O'Hare and had to get up at 4:30 to get on the Kennedy to hit the loop by 5:45, but the salespeople who understood this work habit walked away with more business than those who had Cubs' tickets or Bears' seats and more respect from the dealer and his people.

2. Schedule late afternoon-early evening meetings. Some customers like to leave the office near 5:00 p.m. but also like the idea of stopping at the local pub or coffee shop to miss the evening traffic jams and welcome a business reason to do this.

3. Find out other quirks about a customer's workweek. Some like to involve their staffs in early Monday morning meetings to get the week started and would be amenable to a sales training meeting or a presentation. Others like to hold late afternoon meetings, especially on Friday to make sure their staffs put in a full week. Some like a Friday evening beer bust cap for the week where business is discussed informally and a team spirit is fostered, and don't mind having it subsidized by someone with something to sell.

4. Find out your customers' personal habits. Are they tennis or raquetball players? Someone who likes to work Saturdays but who gets lonely if no one else is around? Someone single who enjoys business dinners that need not bust the expense account?

   I had a customer in Orlando who loved his midweek golf game but had trouble justifying the time away. Also, like our Sunday morning golfers mentioned above, he liked to log in "business meetings" to justify the country club write-off. He would even pick up the lunch tab if I brought along a few golf balls since his had such an affinity for water. The balls would, of course, be imprinted with the company logo. Our brand awareness index among the Rio Pinar crowd had to be as high as anywhere in the country.

The main point is to look for those opportunities to stretch the day and week, especially for A accounts, and to find those times when your customers are likely to be the most receptive. Some of these suggestions may seem inconsistent with the ideas of scheduling family time and could seem onerous to some salespeople who want only a 9-to-5, Monday-through-Friday job.

To deal with this question you obviously have to know your people and get their commitment. In most cases, we're not talking about spending a lot more time—only spending the existing time more wisely on those activities and with those people who will make a significant difference in effectiveness and results.

MORE WAYS TO BOOST SALES BY ORGANIZING YOUR SALES STAFF

1. In this chapter and the section immediately above, we've discussed only the conventional workday and workweek. Other time-expanding and effectiveness-increasing tools like direct mail, telemarketing, and trade

show attendance are discussed in detail in other chapters. Also, we've been talking about increasing the time utilization of your salespeople more than your own, which is covered in Chapter 8.

2. All accounts are not alike. Some accounts need to be seen constantly and require a fair amount of entertainment. *You* have to decide whether their business justifies it.

Others may consider your salespeople an interruption or a bother and would just as soon send in orders, talk with your people on the phone, and know that they or you are available if they have a problem. (This happens to be one of the most important attributes most purchasing agents and other buying influences look for in a salesperson—What did you do for me when I had a problem? You can have 19 good transactions without problems and get measured, positively or negatively, only by the twentieth problem one.)

3. Some accounts want you to spend a lot of time with their salespeople (in a dealer or distributorship) or the end-users of your product (in a direct selling environment). In others, the purchasing agent guards his turf so carefully that you couldn't get near an end-user if you were selling gold for $5 per ounce. Again, you have to weigh the present and potential business against the time required to get it.

4. Despite your best selling and educational efforts, some of your sales-people may feel that you are trying to turn them into robots. You have to convince them that the opposite is true; you're teaching them how to handle the mundane details of their jobs so that they will have *more* time for the more challenging, creative, and fun aspects of selling. Your selling effort to them should concentrate on this.

On the other hand, you will have some salespeople who want to "play it loose." They are probably wrong and would benefit from giving these techniques and tools a try. If they are good, you may want to soft-pedal any changes and implement the planning steps one or two at a time until they begin to see the benefits to them. (You can put up with a prima donna as long as she sings on key.)

IN CLOSING...

With all your accounts and prospects identified and stratified, you can think about setting a budget. This management function has to be classified as "most important" inasmuch as all the sales in the world don't count for much unless they are profitable. Effective field sales managers meet sales, profit and expense budgets. Chapter 6 will enable you to present a well-prepared and thoroughly thought-out sales and expense budget.

6

How to Maximize Profitability Using Accounting Techniques to Set Your Sales Budget

In many companies the combined sales and marketing function is the most expensive and consumes more of the sales dollar than any other function. This proportion is fair because it influences the number of sales dollars more than any other. In fact, in some companies, the sales and marketing expenditures may total more than the entire manufacturing costs of a product.

CONTROLLING YOUR SALES BUDGET TO GET THE MOST FROM YOUR EXPENSE DOLLARS

Obviously, the field sales manager must be accountable for whatever percentage of the total expenses his or her area represents. It's a difficult area. Most sales managers are not trained accountants and feel uncomfortable putting numbers down on paper and trying to quantify their subjective feelings and judgments. The budgeting job may then go by default to the company controller.

The controller, however, is usually not as aware of the kind of expenditures you need to be effective and of the sales-enhancing possibilities of dollars well-spent on introducing new products, increasing the market penetration for old ones, and opening up whole new markets.

Controllers get paid to demand *facts* as a justification for budget dollars, and a lot of your reasons for wanting to make certain kinds of expenditures just cannot be factually justified in specific dollar amounts to an accountant's satisfaction. You are looking at it from two different viewpoints, if not two different worlds, so a great deal of frustration can result.

Part of the answer lies in working closely with the controller and other staff people for information, input, and support. This won't help a great deal, however, unless you have some grasp of the relationship between dollars spent and results achieved, and some idea about how to put numbers on your qualitative judgments.

This doesn't mean you have to take a course in accounting. Budgeting, as in most accounting-type activities, involves logic and good business judgment more than knowing whether a transaction requires a debit or a credit to a certain account.

This chapter will deal with how to do just that. To cover the most ground and take the broadest challenge, we'll assume a *new* product in a *new* market that will be sold nationally. We will assume that you have P & L (Profit and Loss) responsibility. That is, that you are responsible for the company making money on what your people sell and not just sales volume. This doesn't mean that you are responsible for production costs or administrative expenses, but that your area has a measureable "profit contribution" goal.

If you don't have this responsibility, you (in most cases) *should*, in order to make intelligent business decisions and avoid time-consuming conflicts with other functional areas over the differently perceived benefits of an expenditure.

The lessons from this "starting from scratch" approach should prove helpful to national or regional managers selling an established product to an established customer base. Since we dealt with setting quotas in Chapter 3, we'll concentrate mostly on expense budgets as opposed to sales forecasts. First, let's look at some of the mistakes that are commonly made in the budgeting process.

TEN BUDGETING PITFALLS TO AVOID— AND HOW TO PREVENT THEM

1. Having no budget, forecast, or plan at all, and reacting to situations as they come up.
2. Assuming that sales management is such an arcane art and so subject to the vagaries of the marketplace that it is not possible to forecast sales levels or plan expenditures in any logical manner.
3. Not matching achievement goals measured in terms of sales volume, increased sales volume, new accounts opened, etc., with expenditure levels.
4. Having a plan, but not developing timely monthly reports to match the plan with actual events in time to take corrective action when the plan

is not working or to exploit and further develop something that is working.

5. Conversely, assuming that budgeting is an exact science with the elements subject to absolute degrees of predictability based on certain parameters.

6. Not distinguishing between the level of expenditure needed for existing products in existing markets, new products in new markets, and all the possible combinations of old and new.

7. Taking overall standards such as "Sales expenditures shouldn't exceed $x\%$ of sales" as absolute rules rather than as guidelines to be analyzed and verified.

8. Using overall or specific industry standards as rules without making allowances for differences in products, methods of marketing, or desired customer base.

9. Allocating overall budgets by dividing the total by the number of regions or districts, allocating by percentage of sales, or some other method, without balancing different regional needs against profitability.

10. Not realizing that, under the right circumstances, with the right planning and monitoring, there really *can* be a causal relationship between expenditures and results.

CHECKLIST OF PROFIT-GENERATING BUDGET TECHNIQUES

We will first lay out an overall plan for this new division to which you have been appointed field sales manager to market a new product to a new market, and then fill it in with specifics and examples. Some of the steps may sound familiar. They should. The thinking process is similar to what we discussed in Chapter 3 on setting quotas fairly.

1. Define the overall market for your product. The developers of the product must have had someone in mind when they decided to create it. Who will buy it? Talk with the engineers who have lived with the product through the development stage. When they get over their shock at being asked their opionion by a sales manager, they may have some good ideas for you.

2. Quantify the market. How many potential buyers are out there who would qualify as prospects at the determined price point. (You remember from Chapter 3 that you will, of course, *capture* this prospect list in some form.) It's OK to start with a rough list and narrow it down as you gain experience selling the product.

3. Stratify the market. Divide your prospects into A, B, and C categories. (You know from Chapter 4 that you will have to do this sooner or later anyway.) When you get to determining your staffing requirements, you will want to make the distinction to maximize their efforts.

4. Decide how many calls it will take to sell the product. Is it a one-call close like vacuum cleaners or aluminum siding, or will it take several calls with presentations to several management levels and buying committees who will decide on purchasing a new computer system? You will also need a handle on this to determine your staffing requirements.

   Don't say "I have no idea." You know it's somewhere between one and two hundred. Use your best guess for now and remember the old selling maxim, "Most sales are made on the *fifth* sales call and most salespeople give up after three or four calls on a given prospect. As a result, 50 percent of the salespeople are making 80 percent of the money being made in sales."

5. Guess at a close rate. Do you feel that every prospect will buy once he understands what your product will do, or do you feel that you'll get one out of 50 because of a relatively narrow application area?

6. Estimate a selling cycle time. This will depend to a great extent on the dollar cost. It's easier to get a quick decision on a new cutting oil for drilling machines than a wave-soldering machine for circuit board manufacturers. Being realistic here will tell you the amount of time and funding that will be required until you hit the break-even point and possibly keep your product from being killed just when it is ready to take off. If you've been around for a while you've seen this happen once or twice.

7. Test your assumptions—at every step. Get out of your office and call on some of those prospects. If you already have a staff, set up a standard plan with a questionnaire form and get out and *listen*. Revise your plan according to what you hear and tabulate your results in an organized, logical, and systematic manner.

8. Determine the total market and estimate the first-year share you are likely to obtain. We'll discuss this in much more detail below.

9. Determine a probable product life cycle. If your product is a new cutting oil, you could go out five or ten years. If it's a new, state-of-the-art computer system, three to five years may be safer. If it's a new computer software package you may not have time to do any planning at all in the days that are left.

10. Develop a unit sales forecast based on the above information. You might develop minimum, likely, and high forecasts. Multiply this by the weighted average selling price. If quantity discounts are a possibility, factor them into your calculation.

11. Get unit cost information at different production levels so you can determine gross profit, which will lead later to profit contribution estimates.

12. Determine your field staffing requirements to meet these forecasts based on the information developed in the first nine steps. Unless your product is truly revolutionary, you are trying to beat a competitor to the punch, or you feel early obsolescence is inevitable, you will probably plan a region-by-region rollout.

13. Estimate the cost of the people you want to hire, starting with salary, incentive compensation, and if appropriate, relocation costs. You will not hire one hundred people at once so determine how many you can absorb at one time and plug this into your monthly sales forecast and expense budget plan.

14. Add in the other costs for which you will be responsible starting with travel, lodging, office space, if appropriate, clerical support, telephone, and your own home office expenses.

15. Develop a pro forma profit and loss statement for each volume assumption level. (This isn't as scary as it may sound, even if you have never balanced your checkbook. We'll illustrate below how to take things out of your head in an organized way and develop information in such an organized way that your controller will be envious.)

16. Obtain approval and start to implement your plan according to the timetable you have laid out or been given. It is assumed that you have heeded the advice in previous chapters and have had your staff colleagues, especially the controller, involved in every important step so that their support and approval is assured.

Skim briefly through the Practice Example in Appendix E, since much of the following discussion refers to this "work-through" example.

HOW INCREASED SALES BOOSTS PROFITS

In the pro forma P & L statement illustrated by Figure E.1 in Appendix E, we show a net return on sales of 15 percent and, presumably, a more acceptable return on investment.

But sales could be lower or higher than estimated. A complete discussion of breakeven points and fixed and variable (or semifixed and semivariable) costs is really the subject of a complete book. For now, let's look at the impact on Cost of Goods Sold on a sales volume 30 percent higher or lower than the $10,000,000 estimated.

HOW JUST 30 PERCENT HIGHER SALES
CAN DOUBLE NET OPERATING PROFIT

In Figure E3 in Appendix E, we show four categories that represented the *Cost of Goods Sold* total of $6,000,000:

Material Costs	$ 223,000
Labor Costs, Software Packages	46,000
Labor Costs, Installation/Customization	900,000
Overhead Costs	4,831,000
Total Cost of Goods Sold	$6,000,000

We will review each of these components to determine the effect of a 30 percent increase in sales (from 2,700 units to a rounded-off unit sales figure of 3,500).

1. *Material Costs* are probably going to increase in direct proportion to the sales increase. It's true that there will be some decrease through volume buying of the diskettes. It's also true that the per unit cost of the documentation and packaging will decrease somewhat since the costs include setup and printing plate costs (the "fixed" element of this cost).

    On the other hand, unexpected increases may upset carefully laid purchasing plans and require purchases to be made at a *premium*. We will assume, for purposes of simplicity, that the net effect will be to leave this expense at the same amount of $82.59 per package ($223,000 from Figure E.3 divided by 2,700 units).

    This gives us a new Total Material Cost of $289,000 (3,500 units times $82.59 cost per unit).

2. *Labor Costs, Software Packages* also are assumed to increase in direct proportion to sales volume. There may be economies of scale through specialization and the use of lower-paid employees because the extra volume and supervisory time will be spread over a greater base.

    On the other hand, sales beyond the plan could mean overtime premiums and/or training expenses. We'll assume that the per unit cost of $17.04 ($46,000 divided by 2,700 units) remains the same.

    This gives us a new Total Labor, Packages cost of $59,640 (3,500 units times $17.04 cost per unit).

3. *Labor Costs, Installation/Customization* will increase somewhat in proportion to sales volume increases since more volume will fill in the gaps of idle time. We have hired people to do the work to provide a high service level so we know there will be peaks and valleys. More volume should smooth this out to some degree.

    Our present Labor Costs, Installation/Customization unit cost is $333.33 ($900,000 divided by 2,700 units). The "smoothing" should produce some unit cost savings which we will estimate at 10 percent.

This brings the per unit cost for Labor Costs, Installation/Customization to $300.00 and our total cost for this category to $1,050,000.

This is an introduction to the concept of "semi-variable" costs. Doing twice the business, for example, doesn't mean a doubling of installation people since we have assumed that our present people are not installing or customizing packages one hundred percent of the time, so we may need to increase the force by only 50 percent to 80 percent.

In this case we've assumed, with some validity, that while sales increased 30 percent, Labor Costs, Installation/Customization will increase only 17 percent. ($1,050,000 new total cost minus $900,000 old cost equals $150,000 which, divided by $900,000 equals 16.67%). This reflects the lower unit cost ($300.00 versus $333.33) and the higher sales volume (3,500 units versus 2,700 units) and shows the impact of sales volume on a "semivariable" cost area.

4. In *Overhead Costs* we have (in this particular example) a fairly close example of costs that are more than 90 percent "fixed." That is, sales volume changes will have little impact on the amount of these costs.

It's true that some indirect manufacturing costs like tape for the packaging machine, shipping labels, and other miscellaneous costs not included in Material Costs will increase somewhat, but the impact will be insignificant on the overall total.

Sales increases (or decreases) have a dramatic impact on this cost area. Our present unit cost of Total Overhead Costs is $1,789.26 ($4,831,000 divided by 2,700 units). We are going to assume that the 30 percent sales volume increase will result in *no* additional costs in this area. Over 90 percent of the costs are in the "Amortization of Research" area and this amount has already been spent.

(We are assuming no new research for the purposes of this example, unrealistic though that may be. Sales volume may make new research possible but still doesn't affect what has already been spent.)

This figure of $4,831,000 for Total Overhead Costs, therefore, will remain the same and our unit cost will drop from $1,789.26 to $1,380.29 ($4,831,000 divided by 3,500 units).

Our total cost at the $10,000,000 sales volume or 2,700 units was estimated at $6,000,000 from Figure E.3 with a unit cost of $2,222.22. Here is what the new costs look like with a sales volume increase of 30 percent:

Total Material Costs	$ 289,000
Total Labor, Packages	59,640
Total Labor, Installation/Customization	1,050,000
Total Overhead Costs	4,831,000
Total Cost of Goods Sold	$6,229,640

Our total costs have increased $229,640 or less than 4 percent on a 30 percent increase in sales volume. And, our unit cost has dropped from $2,222.22 to $1,779.90 ($6,229,640 divided by 3,500 units) or a decrease of 20 percent. This is the magic of spreading fixed or relatively "fixed" expenses over a greater sales volume.

Here is a new, simplified version of the Pro-Forma Profit and Loss Statement shown in Figure E.1, showing only the impact of the increase in Sales Volume and Cost of Goods Sold:

Gross Sales		$12,962,950
Less Returns and Allowances		130,000
Net Sales		12,832,950
Cost of Goods Sold		6,229,640
Gross Profit		6,603,310
Total Administrative Expenses	566,000	
Total Sales Expenses	1,848,000	
Total Expenses		2,414,000
Net Operating Profit		$ 4,189,310

This shows an increase of almost $3,000,000 or almost *three times* the profit from a 30 percent increase in sales volume. Some impact! Again, this is the "magic" of spreading fixed costs over a larger sales volume. The fixed costs were already absorbed by the first $10,000,000 in sales and since our fixed costs are so high relative to total costs, most of the extra $3,000,000 in sales went straight to the bottom line.

We've used this extreme example to illustrate a point. Most businesses, especially trading businesses like retail stores or wholesale distributorships will have a much lower ratio of fixed costs to total costs (higher ratio of variable costs to total costs) since the goods are *purchased* and there is little fixed research and development cost or other (besides building and equipment) fixed costs.

A complete restatement of the Profit and Loss Statement would have to recognize the impact of the increase in sales on the Administrative Expenses and Sales Expenses categories. Administrative Expenses would not increase in anything like a direct proportion of 30 percent, but there would presumably be more telephone calls, more stationery, and possibly another person needed to process orders. Sales Expenses would also increase, especially in the Incentive Compensation and Bonuses category.

Even if we added an additional 20 percent or approximately $400,000 to these expenses, the impact of a 30 percent increase in sales volume is still a dramatic doubling of Net Operating Profit.

In the next section we'll flip the coin over and look at the terrible consequences of not making your sales volume numbers.

Case: How 30 Percent Lower Sales Turns a Profit into a Loss

We will continue to use Figure E.3 as a base for the example and deal only with the impact on Cost of Goods Sold to make the point. The four categories that represented the Cost of Goods Sold total of $6,000,000 were:

Material Costs	$ 223,000
Labor Costs, Software Packages	46,000
Labor Costs, Installation/Customization	900,000
Overhead Costs	4,831,000
Total	$6,000,000

We'll take a look at each of these components to determine the effect of a 30 percent decrease in sales (from 2,700 units to a rounded-off 1,900 units:

1. *Material Costs* are assumed to decrease in direct proportion to the sales decrease. There will be some increases in unit costs since our purchasing agent may not be able to buy as favorably and the fixed or set-up costs of the printing will be spread over fewer units.

    For simplicity's sake, however, we will assume the same unit cost of $82.59 per package ($223,000 from Figure E.3 divided by 2,700 budgeted units). This gives us a new Total Material Cost of $156,921 (1,900 units times $82.59 cost per unit).

2. *Labor Costs, Software Packages* are also assumed to decrease in direct proportion to sales volume. There may be some dislocations in the labor force since our manufacturing manager geared up for a higher level of sales and may have to lay off some people, our unemployment contribution will increase and we will have to retrain when sales volume increases.

    However, we're going to assume that our manufacturing manager will work out these problems and that the unit cost will remain at $17.04 ($46,000 divided by 2,700 units). This gives us a new Total Labor, Packages cost of $32,376 (1,900 units times $17.04 cost per unit).

3. *Labor Costs, Installation/Customization* will not decrease to any significant degree since we want to maintain our high service level and keep those people on the payroll. About the only decrease might be in their travel expenses because there will be fewer jobs and fewer locations to travel to, so we will ignore this and keep the $900,000 figure.

4. Similarly, the *Overhead Costs* are not going to decrease much. Fewer shipping forms will be used and we may be able to turn off the lights an hour or so sooner, but the bulk of the expense will remain whether the sales volume is 10 units or 10,000.

The 30 percent decrease from budgeted sales volume has an equally dramatic impact on this cost area. Our present unit cost of Total Overhead Costs is $1,789.26 ($4,831,000 divided by 2,700 budgeted units). Since there is no way to decrease the $4,831,000 by any appreciable amount, our unit costs for this cost category have skyrocketed to $2,542.63 from $1,789.26—a *42 percent increase*, because of the sales volume decrease.

It could be argued that having most of your Cost of Goods Sold made up of amortization (allocating cost over a period of time) of research costs is a bit unusual.

This is true. However, most companies have similar investments in plant, machinery, and equipment that also represent fixed costs for depreciation (also an allocation of cost over a period of time) that go on at about the same rate irrespective of sales volume.

Note: In their impact on the financial statements, "depreciation" and "amortization" are, for our purposes, the same. An accounting purist could argue the point, but they both represent the allocation of the cost of an "asset" (any property that is owned and has cash value) over the estimated useful life of that asset.

Depreciable assets are those that are presumed to benefit the business over an extended period—like buildings, machinery, and office equipment as opposed to short-term or "current" assets like accounts receivable or inventory.

While the terms "depreciation" and "amortization" are often used interchangeably, depreciation usually refers to the allocation of cost over a period of time of *tangible* assets like buildings and equipment. Amortization usually refers to the allocation of cost over a period of time of *intangible* assets like patents, copyrights, goodwill, or research and development costs of things like software packages.

Intangible assets get on the books by "capitalizing" (making an asset out of) expenditures that will benefit the company long-term. Oil companies, for example, may *expense* (charge to current income) drilling costs, or they may *capitalize* them and *amortize* the cost over the estimated life of the well.

The decision to do one or the other usually has little to do with accounting theory. A profitable company wishing to reduce income taxes will expense (charge against current income) as much as it can. A new company, eager to have its financial statements look as favorable as possible, may choose to capitalize as much as it can, especially if it intends to go into the captial market for money to finance new product development or is planning a public offering of its stock.

Back to our example of the impact of a 30 percent decrease in sales volume. You remember that our total cost at the 2,700-unit or $10,000,000 sales volume level was estimated at $6,000,000 with a unit cost of $2,222.22. Here is what the new costs look like with a sales volume decrease of 30 percent:

Total Material Costs	$ 156,921
Total Labor, Packages	32,376
Total Labor, Installation/Customization	900,000
Total Overhead Costs	4,831,000
Total Cost of Goods Sold	$5,920,297

Our total costs have decreased about $80,000 or a bit over 1 percent on a sales volume drop of 30 percent from the budgeted amount. Our unit cost, however, has increased from $2,222.22 to $3,115.95, a 40 percent increase! The magic, you see, works both ways.

When you opened the doors the first day of this budgeting period, you were faced with almost $500,000 a month in fixed overhead costs ($6,000,000 divided by

12). This is in addition to the commitments made to selling and administrative costs of close to $200,000 per month.

While you might be able to effect some reductions in everything but the amortization of research costs because of sales volume, you were stuck with most of the costs, at least for the first month or two.

Here is another simplified version of the Pro-Forma Profit and Loss Statement shown in Figure E-1, again showing only the impact of the decrease in Sales volume on Cost of Goods Sold. Again, we have assumed that the Administrative Expenses and Sales Expenses remain the same even though we know that some expenses in these two categories will decrease and that you might postpone hiring some salespeople.

Gross Sales		$7,037,037
Less Returns and Allowances		70,370
Net Sales		6,966,667
Cost of Goods Sold		5,920,297
Gross Profit		1,046,370
Total Administrative Expenses	566,000	
Total Sales Expenses	1,848,000	
Total Expenses		2,414,000
Net Operating Profit (Loss)		($1,367,629)

What a swing! From dreams of early retirement to thinking about a second mortgage on the house.

Sales managers are often accused (justly, in many cases) of seeking volume at any cost. The above examples show that extra volume or the lack of it can, indeed, have a tremendous impact on a company's profitability.

This is not to make a case for the "sales at any price" argument, but it suggests that the application of the above budgeting and "what if" exercises will enable you to effectively gauge the impact of any price changes or discounts granted on the Profit and Loss Statement. It should also enable you to communicate with your controller like you may never have before.

KNOWING WHERE PROFITS END AND LOSSES BEGIN— THE BREAKEVEN POINT

It was suggested earlier that a full and complete discussion of budgeting is the subject of another whole book. A complete discussion of break-even analysis could be yet another book. However, no discussion on budgeting would be complete without at least a mention of it, however fleeting.

The breakeven point is usually illustrated on a chart which looks like that shown in Figure 6.1. The horizontal line represents fixed expenses which stay

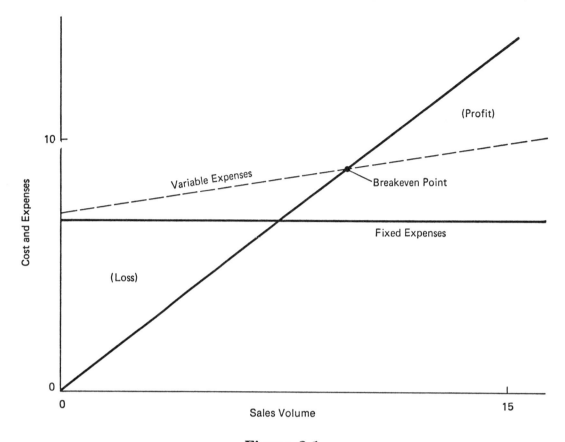

Figure 6.1

constant, regardless of sales volume. The steep southwest-northeast line starting at the left-hand corner represents sales volume and the less steep southwest-northeast line starting at the fixed expense horizontal line represents variable costs. The point at which the latter two lines meet is the break-even point—the point at which there is neither profit nor loss.

There are almost as many ways to arrive at this point as there are practitioners of the art. (The term "art" is used deliberately here, since dividing expenses into their fixed and variable categories is a subjective exercise which relies on the judgment calls of the person doing the computations.)

Accounting practitioners and my management-consulting colleagues could poke a lot of holes in this shortcut way of determining the breakeven point and I've never seen it explained this way in any accounting or management textbook, but here's the shortcut:

> Divide the total estimated fixed expenses by the reciprocal of the variable expenses expressed as a percentage of total estimated sales volume.

Don't let this formula throw you yet. It was expressed in as few words as possible. Let's use Figure E.1 again to illustrate what we mean and work out the breakeven point for FSM Computer Services Co.:

1. First determine what expenses are fixed and which are variable. As mentioned above, this is a judgment call, but we'll estimate as follows, taking each major category of the Pro-Forma Profit and Loss Statement:

   Cost of Goods Sold: We have already determined in working through our 30 percent increase and 30 percent decrease exercises that most of the expenses wouldn't change a great deal with changes in sales volume, so we're going to estimate these at 90 percent fixed or $5,400,000 ($6,000,000 × 90%).

   Administrative Expenses: Without a major change in our business plan, most of these expenses will go on, regardless of sales volume increases or decreases. Fewer telephone calls may be made, less stationery and supplies will be used, and we may decide to get along with one less person, but most expenses will continue. We'll estimate this category at 90 percent or $500,000 in fixed expenses ($566,000 × 90% and rounded off).

   Sales Expenses: Here we have some options whether or not we choose to exercise them. We don't *have* to hire a full complement of salespeople with their attendant expenses. We don't *have* to spend the entire advertising budget or attend *all* the trade shows—we have a good deal of discretion over these expense items. Also, Incentive Compensation and Bonuses will vary directly with sales—a true, almost 100 percent variable expense item.

   To stay in business, however, there has to be at least some semblance of a sales organization with fixed expenses attached as soon as we make this decision. Rather than overanalyze, let's estimate these expenses as 50 percent fixed and 50 percent variable. This makes the fixed portion $924,000 ($1,848,000 × 50%).

2. Add up the fixed portion of the costs and expenses:

Cost of Goods Sold	$5,400,000
Administrative Expenses	500,000
Sales Expenses	924,000
Total Fixed Expenses	$6,824,000

3. Add up the total costs and expenses:

Cost of Goods Sold	$6,000,000
Administrative Expenses	566,000
Sales Expenses	1,848,000
Total All Expenses	$8,414,000

4. Determine the variable expenses:

Total Expenses	$8,414,000
Less Fixed Expenses	6,824,000
Variable Expenses	$1.590,000

5. Determine the variable expense reciprocal. First divide the total of the variable expenses by the originally estimated and budgeted sales volume. $1,590,000 divided by $10,000,000 equals 15.9 percent. The reciprocal is .841 (1.0 – .159).

6. Divide the total fixed expenses by the variable expense reciprocal. $6,824,000 divided by .841 equals $8,114,150 and *that* is our breakeven point.

To prove that this simple (or not so simple) formula works when books have been written about nothing more than arriving at where we have come in the past couple of pages, let's go back to our simplified Profit and Loss Statement and see how it works out:

Gross Sales		$8,114,150
Cost of Goods Sold		5,700,150
Gross Profit		2,414,000
Total Administrative Expenses	566,000	
Total Sales Expenses	1,848,000	
Total Expenses		2,414,000
Net Operating Profit (Loss)		$ -0-

We made some assumptions in the Cost of Goods Sold area above and ignored the sales returns. The adjustments and assumptions are not really worth going into here. Instead, let's illustrate the breakeven formula and computation with a simple example:

You own a small clothing boutique and have estimated (by going through steps very similar to what has been outlined in this chapter) your fixed expenses at $100,000. You also figure that you have variable expenses of 60 percent of sales.

Dividing the fixed expenses by .40 (the reciprocal of .60) we get a breakeven point of $250,000. Our Pro Forma Profit and Loss Statement would then look like this:

Sales		$250,000
Fixes Expenses	100,000	
Variable Expenses @60% of sales	150,000	
Total Expenses		250,000
Net Operating Profit (Loss)		$ -0-

Figure 6.2 shows how this would look on a breakeven chart.

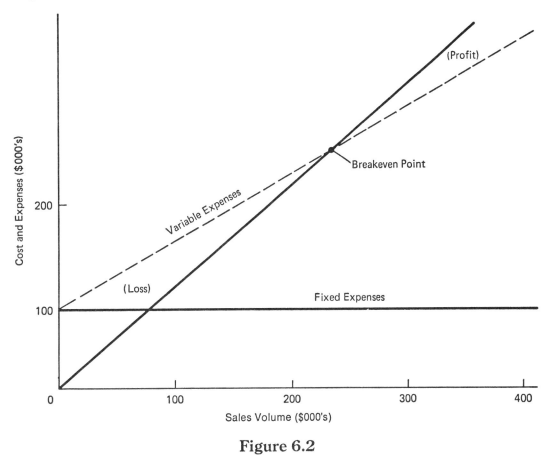

Figure 6.2

So, the shortcut formula works and you are now, in addition to being a budgeting expert, at least somewhat conversant with the concept of fixed and variable expenses as they apply to breakeven analysis and breakeven points.

IN CLOSING...

Given the simple measures in this chapter, you should feel confident and comfortable when discussing your budget. You should be able to address such questions as the real profit impact of additional volume at a lower price, or the wisdom of spending money on advertising to meet and exceed your budget objectives. In some companies, the sales management function is often viewed as "outside" the company management structure, or the sales manager would need too much help from the controller's office—it is thought—to put together any meaningful numbers. In other companies, control of the budget is the route to power, so the development of this management mechanism is not shared with the sales manager. Whatever the reason, too often field sales managers are excluded from budget preparation. Yet they still have the responsibility of meeting the sales budget and of not exceeding the expense budget. As an effective field sales manager, you should have an important role in the process, starting from the preliminary budget discussions several months before the fiscal year begins and continuing through the entire revision process.

7

Allocating Your Total Budget to Spend Dollars Where They Count

Given your total budget, you now have to allocate portions of it equitably. Allocating too much or too little can be as wasteful as not having a budget at all.

EIGHT BUDGET-ALLOCATION MISTAKES THAT WASTE EXPENSE DOLLARS

1. Being "smart" and assuming that you know more than the people out there in the field who have to do the work.
2. Thinking that your salespeople are "dummies" (or worse) and assigning budgets on this basis.
3. Assuming that the home office wouldn't have assigned you the responsibility for expenses and budgets if they knew what they were doing and, therefore, don't expect inputs from you in this area.
4. Assigning quotas based solely or mostly on historical perspectives.
5. Assigning quotas based on predetermined (by whom?) percentages is equally as bad as mistake #4.
6. "Nit-picking" expense accounts as, for example, requiring receipts for tolls.

7. Not examining expenses carefully enough and letting salespeople determine how much they will add to their income by "padding" their expense account statements.

8. Not setting and adequately communicating the standards you expect to be followed.

TECHNIQUES FOR ASSIGNING ACCOUNTABILITY FOR EVERY DOLLAR ALLOCATED

As we've discussed a number of times before, there is no "the" answer to any problem—management or personal. But now, we're going to come up with something approaching "answer," if not "the" answer:

> Deciding how your salespeople should spend the budget you have allocated to them is *easy. You don't!*

So far in this book we have discussed a lot of very sophisticated ways to run your organization. We have worked out a number of detailed formulas for developing prospects, evaluating customers, quantifying their worth, and plugging them into a calling schedule. You learned how to prepare budgets and Profit and Loss Statements like an accounting pro.

Now, we're about to depart from this completely disciplined accounting-like approach and suggest something different based on an intuitive and an empirical approach that throws the ball to your people.

Lee Iacocca suggested something like what we are going to suggest when he said "To a certain extent, I've always operated by gut feeling. I like to be in the trenches. I was never one of those guys who could just sit around and strategize endlessly." Most people like Lee's style, but tend to forget his penchant for having plans put *in writing* so that there is some assurance that they are well thought through. Let's see how we can apply both elements of this philosophy to *our* situation.

The suggestion is that we give our salespeople *complete* responsibility for what happens. We give *them* the budget and let *them* work out how they will spend it to make happen what we, as home office or regional managers, need to have happen. This makes our job easy and (at least as important) gives them the feeling of self-respect and pride. The first step is to make sure we determine an equitable allocation by territory so that we produce the maximum results for the money spent.

CHECKLIST FOR DOLLAR-WISE BUDGET ALLOCATION

1. Before looking at the numbers, review your goals for the coming budgetary period:
   — Is the emphasis just on increasing sales?

— Is one of your goals a more profitable sales mix at the same sales level?

— Are there new market areas you want to penetrate?

— Are new product introductions scheduled?

— Is a district or regional test scheduled for a new product before it is rolled out nationally?

— All of the above?

Any of these factors will affect your allocation of resources to a region or district since we want the allocation to be consistent with the goals and objectives we set in our planning sessions.

2. Review the past history of expenses versus sales. If gross margins are your responsibility and improving these margins is one of your goals, you might want to also compare expenses to gross margins to provide an additional input to the allocation decision.

   You could, for example, afford 10 percent in expenses for a region producing a 50 percent gross margin if the average for the country was 8 percent in expenses with a 40 percent gross margin. The more sparsely populated areas of the country will probably cost more to cover, but discounting or large volume purchases at lower prices should be less prevalent in these areas. Figure 7.1, Sales Expense Analysis-A, shows an example of how this might look.

SALES EXPENSE ANALYSIS—A
$000's

No.	Region	Sales	Gross Margin	Expenses	% Expenses To Sales	% Expenses To G.M.
1	Northeast	5817	2154	406	7.0	18.8
2	Southeast	3859	1610	340	8.8	21.1
3	Midwest	4416	1827	314	7.1	17.2
4	Central	3234	1329	297	9.2	22.3
5	West	4138	1582	393	9.5	24.8
	Total	21464	8502	1750	8.1	20.6

Figure 7.1

Since FSM Computer Services Co. is a new venture with no past history, we have used the sales figures from the example in Chapter 3 to complete our analysis.

3. Look at your own expense budget as a percentage of sales and recognize that the individual budgets assigned to your managers have to average out to this figure. We will assume that you have $2,000,000 or 8 percent of your $25,000,000 sales budget, including district managers' salaries but not regional managers' salaries which are included in *your* budget, as your salary is included in your manager's budget.

4. Complete a worksheet like that shown in Figure 7.1 showing the historical expenses as a percentage of sales and as a percentage of gross profit. Then, compute an average of last year's figures against your 8 percent of sales to come up with a raw figure.

   Do this for expenses as a percentage of sales and expenses as a percentage of gross margin so that you have the complete picture in front of you on the worksheet. (You may recall that this technique is similar to our quota-setting method from Chapter 3.) This will give you something like the worksheet shown in Figure 7.2, Sales Expense Analysis-B.

SALES EXPENSE ANALYSIS—B
% EXPENSES TO SALES

No.	Region	% Last Yr.	Budget @ 8%	Average
1	Northeast	7.0	8.0	7.5
2	Southeast	8.8	8.0	8.4
3	Midwest	7.1	8.0	7.6
4	Central	9.2	8.0	8.6
5	West	9.5	8.0	8.7
	Total	8.1	8.0	8.1

% EXPENSES TO GROSS MARGIN

No.	Region	% Last Yr.	Budget @ 8%	Average
1	Northeast	18.8	20.0	19.4
2	Southeast	21.1	20.0	20.5
3	Midwest	17.2	20.0	18.6
4	Central	22.3	20.0	21.2
5	West	24.8	20.0	22.4
	Total	20.8	20.0	20.4

Figure 7.2

The constant figure in column 2 at the top of the worksheet is your overall expense budget figure of 8 percent of sales that the $2,000,000 represents. The constant figure in column 2 at the bottom of the worksheet is your overall expense budget figure of 20 percent of gross margin. This number hasn't been used before but we got it from our controller. It is based on a 40 percent gross margin. ($25,000,000 in sales × .40 = $10,000,000)

5. Take the final quota figures by region from Chapter 3 and enter them in column 4 of the worksheet. You recall that the quotas assigned by region were:

Northeast	$ 7,680,000
Southeast	4,560,000
Midwest	5,000,000
Central	3,900,000
West	4,800,000
Total	$25,940,000

6. Multiply the "Average" expenses as a percentage of sales from column 3 by the sales quotas in column 4 to arrive at a "raw" sales expense budget by region in column 5. Again, this technique of arriving at the raw (unadjusted) figure by averaging what happened last year with what we want to happen this year is similar to what we did to arrive at our raw quota figure in Chapter 3. This gives us an unadjusted starting point for the expense budgets we will assign to our regional managers.

Our total adds up to $2,091,000, a bit over our budget of $2,000,000. But the regional quotas on which it is based add up to $25,940,000, about the same percentage above *our* actual quota of $25,000,000, so we'll leave this as it is for now.

Let's examine each regional figure to compare with last year, see how close we come to our overall objective of 8 percent of sales, and look at the gross margin section of the worksheet to see how affordable the budgets are:

1. *Northeast:* We've provided a healthy 42 percent increase ($576,000 compared to last year's $406,000) and the Northeast has a 32 percent increase in quota (from figure 5.6). We know that the Northeast has a windfall account that doesn't require much in the way of support or expenditures, but we also want this region to go after even more new accounts than we expect from other regions and this takes some money.

   Despite the discounting that is prevalent in this area, the expenses as a percentage of gross margin are the second lowest in the country. Let's compromise and give them $540,000 and enter this figure in column 6 of our Sales Analysis-B worksheet.

2. *Southeast:* This area has only a 13 percent increase in the expense budget figure using the "raw" determination. They have an 18 percent increase in quota. Their expenses last year at 8.8 percent weren't much out of line with our 8.1 percent average determined in Figure 7.1, Sales Expense Analysis-A and their expenses as a percentage of gross margin are OK.

   But we want them to operate more efficiently this year, so let's give them $380,000 and enter this in column 6 of the worksheet.

3. *Midwest:* This area has a 21 percent increase compared to a 13 percent increase in quota. They were close to the Northeast in operating at 7.1 percent of sales last year and had the best ratio of expenses to gross

margin, so we'll leave this figure alone and watch carefully to be sure the money is spent wisely on sales and profit-increasing programs.

This will give them the same amount of money as the Southeast but they have to produce almost $500,000 more in sales as the Southeast, so we're not being overly generous with this allocation.

4. *Central:* This region is our lowest sales volume producer and runs a close second to the West in expenses as a percentage of sales and as a percentage of gross margin. We've given them only a 13 percent increase in budget to come up with a 20 percent increase in sales, so let's round this figure up to $350,000.

At 9 percent of sales ($350,000 proposed expense budget divided by the $3,900,000 quota), this is still at the high end of our expenses-to-quota ratio range, but there are some basic expenses ("fixed" expenses) that apply to a territory whether the volume is $3,000,000 or $8,000,000.

5. *West:* This was our most expensive territory last year in terms of expenses as a percentage of sales and as a percentage of gross margin. Working with the district managers has convinced us that there are a lot of ways to cut expenses. This region has the most expensive offices and

SALES EXPENSE ANALYSIS—B
% EXPENSES TO SALES

No.	Region	% Last Yr.	Budget @ 8%	Average	Quota ($000's)	Expense Budget ($000's)	Final Budget ($000's)
1	Northeast	7.0	8.0	7.5	7680	576	540
2	Southeast	8.8	8.0	8.4	4560	383	380
3	Midwest	7.1	8.0	7.6	5000	380	380
4	Central	9.2	8.0	8.6	3900	335	350
5	West	9.5	8.0	8.7	4800	417	400
	Total	8.1	8.0	8.1	25940	2091	2050

% EXPENSES TO GROSS MARGIN

No.	Region	% Last Yr.	Budget @ 8%	Average
1	Northeast	18.8	20.0	19.4
2	Southeast	21.1	20.0	20.5
3	Midwest	17.2	20.0	18.6
4	Central	22.3	20.0	21.2
5	West	24.8	20.0	22.4
	Total	20.8	20.0	20.4

Figure 7.3

SALES EXPENSE ANALYSIS—C
SUMMARY

	Total	Territory				
		NE	SE	MW	C	W
Goal ($000's)	2000	614	365	400	312	384
% Sales	8	8	8	8	8	8
Last Year ($000's)	1750	406	340	314	297	393
% Sales	8.1	7.0	8.8	7.1	9.2	9.5
Average ($000's)	2091	516	383	380	335	417
% Sales	8.1	7.5	8.4	7.6	8.6	8.7
% Expenses to Gross Margin—Last Yr.	20.8	18.8	21.1	17.2	22.3	24.8
Final Budget ($000's)	2050	540	380	380	350	400
% Sales	7.9	7.0	8.3	7.6	9.0	8.3
Increase (Decrease) From Last Year—$000's	300	134	40	66	53	7
—%	17	33	12	21	18	2

Figure 7.4

pays more to support people than any other region. Their expense accounts also disclose a penchant for the good life.

We decided to make a point and round their budget figure *down* to $400,000, still a small increase over last year and attainable with the needed cost reduction program we intend to implement this year in this profligate region.

We're still a little over our budget with a total of $2,050,000, but the $2,000,000 was based on $25,000,000 in sales and we've assigned more than that as quota. Actually, our goal of keeping the expense budget to 8 percent of sales would give us $2,075,000 ($25,940,000 assigned quota × 8%) if we made the entire quota, so we're in good shape. Our Sales Expense Analysis-B now looks like Figure 7.3.

We know that when we present these expense figures at the national sales meeting, our regional managers are going to come armed with dour predictions for their respective regional economies and statistics on how travel and lodgings expenses have increased in the past year.

Just to be sure we know exactly where we are when the inevitable screaming and gnashing of teeth begin as we communicate these budgets (along with an explanation of the way they were reached), let's summarize (Figure 7.4) the steps we went through as the final test to be sure we have equitably assigned our $2,000,000.

APPLYING THE FINAL TEST—DOES THE BUDGET MAKE SENSE?

1. The *goal* figure was our starting point with the total at 8 percent of the $25,000,000 national quota and each region at 8 percent of its assigned quota.
2. We then compared this with *last year* and computed, as a starting point to this year's allocation and assignment, an *average* of the *goal* and *last year*.
3. To be able to explain the reasons why, in some cases, the expense budget did not increase in proportion to the increase in quota, we analyzed the percentage of expenses last year to *gross margin*.
4. Making adjustments, we arrived at our *final budget* figure with an overall total of 7.9 percent, just within our goal of 8 percent:

   - The *Northeast* is low at 7 percent for the reasons discussed above, but still got a substantial 33 percent increase over last year's actual expenses to implement the plan to go after those new accounts.
   - *Central* is still high, but we'll have to increase sales to cover the region's fixed expenses before we can control this further.
   - The *West* got the smallest increase for the reasons mentioned above. The defense to the Western Regional Manager is that he was the highest in terms of percentage of sales and, more important, expenses as a percentage of gross margin. Unless margins improve, you can't afford expenses of more than the 8.3 percent of quota allocated.

Now that we're satisfied that we've been fair and equitable and have the figures to back up our contention, let's go back to the discussion on "the" answer to field allocation problems by looking at how we'll check up on the actual results produced by our district or regional managers during the year.

HOW TO MONITOR THE EXPENSE BUDGET
AND SAVE DOLLARS

Earlier, we suggested that you shouldn't decide how your regional managers and their salespeople should spend their budgets. We went through a lot of analysis to determine what we could afford for each territory's assigned volume and used our "gut feeling" to make appropriate adjustments.

Now, except for guidance, we'll keep our hands off *how* the money is spent as long as the total stays within the guidelines as a percentage of sales. That is, if a region is producing at 90 percent of quota, they will have to watch expenses carefully to spend at less than 100 percent of budget. If a region is over quota, you should have no problem approving $50 to $80 in additional expenses for every $1,000 they are over quota.

How your regional or district managers spend the money, however, will be their responsibility as long as they meet the quota numbers. If a regional manager wants to add two telephone salespeople instead of filling a vacant district manager slot, let your manager do it. If the manager wants to cut down on travel expenses to provide more money for dealer promotional support or to rent hotel rooms for preparation to prospective end users of your product or services, let the manager do it.

By operating in this way you have:

1. Pulled the rug out from under half of the excuses for not meeting quota.
2. Put the budget-meeting responsibility where it really belongs—in the hands of the people closest to the money-spending situation.
3. Simplified your job so you can spend more time on creative and planning aspects.

Because your regional managers are truly acting as managers of budget money as well as of people, they should also be more motivated to produce.

For example, make it possible for people to do what they want to do and they will find a way to accomplish what you need to get done. A few years ago, 20 district managers worked for me directly, and I decided to groom some of them for regional manager positions. One district manager covered Texas and Oklahoma and lived, for some strange reason, in Waco. I thought it would be a good idea to split the territory roughly along Route 20 with Dallas and Oklahoma in the northern section and Houston, Austin, and San Antonio in the southern section.

The district manager was offered his choice of sections with the understanding that a junior person would be brought in for the other section who would be responsible to the district manager. He chose the South. He wouldn't get a lot more money, but would have the best shot at the Central Regional Manager position if it came to be. I figured that, after the initial training period, the senior manager would need to spend a couple of days every three months in the North and be available for telephone consultation.

The senior district manager disagreed. He felt he needed at least two days a month in Dallas. After an hour of discussion about the impact this would have on the budget and on coverage in the South, I finally said, "Billy, this doesn't make sense. What are you really looking for?" It turned out that Billy had a girlfriend who was a salesperson for one of our smaller distributors.

So we made a deal. Billy could spend his two days in Dallas as long as he stayed above quota in the territory he was primarily responsible for and we increased our business with this distributor by 30 percent a quarter for the next year. Of course there was much grinding and gnashing of teeth, but Billy finally agreed to give it a try.

Billy stayed over quota, his junior district manager finished in second place for the year, our business with this distributor skyrocketed, and Billy and his girlfriend were happy. This may not be a typical motivational strategy, but it illustrates that point about people getting done what you need to get done if you make it possible for them to do what they want to do. The principle is less colorful but no less effective in letting salespeople decide how to spend their budgets to accomplish the sales volume you need.

CHECKLIST FOR AVOIDING MONEY-WASTING MISTAKES

Now let's go back to the budgetary allocation mistakes we listed earlier under the heading "Common Budget Allocation Mistakes" and develop a checklist to be sure we've covered all the bases in this important aspect of your job.

1. We didn't try to be "smarter" than the field people who have to do the work. We told them what we could afford and left the actual expenditures (with a little guidance) up to them.
2. Doing this meant that we treated them with the respect and confidence a territory manager deserves.
3. You now know clearly what you are doing in this area and know how to prove this, so there should be no problem with the home office having confidence in you to handle this important responsibility.
4. We used history to a degree in setting quotas and allocating expense budgets, but effectively combined past history with current, objective reality.
5. The only predetermined percentage we used was our total budget figure, something we had little control over. And, we used this only as a guide.
6. Since we have determined that our people are primarily responsible for achieving their quota results within their expense budgets, the onerous nit-picking chore of detailed checking of expense reports has been lifted from our backs.
7. Our "monitoring" of the expense budgets need only consist of a monthly review of actual expenses and comparison with budgeted amounts, casting an eye on the salesperson's or manager's performance level.
8. The entire process, particularly with the worksheets developed that led up to the final numbers and the tests performed on those numbers, indicated that we are, indeed, serious about what we are doing. The monthly reviews will be the final standard-implementing step.

8

How to Manage Your Sales Management Time Effectively

NINE TESTED WAYS TO TURN COSTLY TIME-WASTERS INTO REVENUE-GENERATING TIME-SAVERS

Managing time effectively is very important for any manager, yet it is typically the most neglected skill. As a field sales manager you are responsible for two full-time jobs: field management and office administration. Time management is a particularly important skill for you to master.

17 TIME MANAGEMENT MISTAKES THAT MAY BE COSTING YOU MONEY RIGHT NOW

1. Not having clearly defined goals—personal or business.
2. Spending too much time on things unrelated to the goals and not enough on things important to the goals.
3. Not identifying the really important tasks and not developing specific plans to accomplish them.
4. Not knowing where and how time is spent.
5. Not reviewing in a planned and logical manner how much time was spent in what areas.
6. Not using commuting or waiting time effectively.

7. Forgetting things that should have been written down so that the effort has to be made all over again.

8. Spending too much time searching for notes on napkins, coffee coasters, and airplane sickness bags.

9. Having to painfully reconstruct details of meetings or thoughts because a need has arisen.

10. Planning travel time too loosely or too tightly with no clear-cut objective for each hour.

11. Ignoring office activities when traveling so that problems pile up for your return to the office.

12. Handling "emergencies" in a panicky way with no logical prioritizing.

13. Not delegating and not clearly spelling out expectations and limits to the delegatees.

14. Letting your people panic and get you involved with the details of the crisis situation when they delegate their work and responsibilities to you.

15. According home office visits or colleagues' requests too much or too little quality time.

16. Failing to recognize the importance of the right timing in decisions, actions, or requests.

17. Forgetting the importance of, and not planning, family and recreational time.

We'll provide answers to most of these problems in this chapter—some by example or illustration and some by step-by-step guidelines and suggestions. Some of the broader issues will be covered more than once throughout this book. Let's look first at the question of where priorities should be.

HOW TO ARRANGE YOUR PERSONAL GOALS FOR GREATER CAREER EFFECTIVENESS

Let's do some thinking and soul-searching before we get to the more "scientific" aspects of this phase of your management responsibility. You're a manager, not a doer or "star." More and more of your time should be devoted to these kinds of planning activities.

This would be a good time to sit down and decide what it is you really want. Is your business career or other activities and interests the most important thing in your life? Do you want to do the best job on your current assignment or do you want to do everything you can to advance? This is a political world so the two don't necessarily go hand-in-hand.

Get a piece of paper and write down your answers to the following questions:

1. What do I really want?
2. What am I willing to give up to get it?
3. What are my alternatives?

Don't let the brevity or simplicity of the questions fool you. Even if your answers are only a few lines long, you will have to do a lot of soul-searching to answer them accurately and you should have the answers before you can set your goals. Pay particular attention to question 2 and remember, "There's no free lunch." You may decide to go back to question 1 after answering this accurately.

Also, don't be dismayed if you have to go back and restate some of the "what you really want" question because of the conflict discovered when you begin to consider the alternatives.

CHECKLISTS OF BUSINESS AND PERSONAL GOALS

What *do* you want? Spend some time thinking this through before you go any further with this chapter or even this book. (You recall that this is consistent with suggestions made in previous chapters, so it shouldn't be out of place with such an important aspect of your job as time management.)

The first step in managing time even more effectively is to determine just what it is you feel you should accomplish with your time—what your real goals are.

List your goals on a sheet of paper in two sections—Business Goals and Personal or Lifestyle Goals. Naturally, there is some tie-in and overlapping but the exercise of dividing the two will help clarify how your business goals will help you meet your personal goals. Your sheet might look something like this:

BUSINESS GOALS

Date _____

1. Surpass my quota and profit and loss budget for the year by 20 percent and become the leading sales manager.
2. Obtain a promotion to national sales manager (Vice President of Sales, President) within two years.
3. Increase my salary and bonus to $100,000 within five years.
4. Develop at least two people now working for me who will be able to take my place within two years.

5. Develop at least three new programs to enhance sales that can be duplicated across the country or in other divisions of my company.

6. Learn how to manage my time so effectively that most crises are eliminated or minimized and I have the time for a minimum of five hours a week for creative thinking and planning activities.

7. Attend three sales and/or marketing management seminars a year for the next two years.

Your personal goals sheet might look something like this:

PERSONAL GOALS

Date _____

1. Purchase the home in Vielgeld Lakes that my wife has always wanted within two years.

2. Build my net worth to $250,000 in ten years to have financial independence. Have one year's salary in liquid assets within three years.

3. Take flying lessons and obtain a pilot's license within one year and have my own plane within four years.

4. Take a two-week vacation with my family to Egypt and Israel next year. Have at least half the cost paid for before we leave.

5. Spend at least one day plus one evening of "quality time" with my family each week.

6. Play racquet ball three times a week and get in ten days of skiing during the winter season.

7. Take one course each semester toward my M.B.A.

Well, this is a pretty full business and personal life that will require a lot of time management discipline to accomplish all the goals. Notice, however, how the goals were specific and pinned down to a definite time period. Without this, the thoughts are not goals—just good ideas.

There may also be some conflicts and choices to be made. Can you travel as much as you should to be successful in your work and still do the personal things you would like to do? Will the leisure time activities get in the way of the necessary homework?

There are no right answers to these questions, but you must decide what it is that you really want when you begin to reconcile possible conflicts in the business and personal goals. Perhaps you could travel midweek and take courses on Monday. You might combine customer entertainment with sports activities.

The important thing to do is to plan and allocate limited and finite time resources and decide on your priorities as the first step in your time management program.

Finally, make sure that your family is in accord with these goals and have perhaps developed their own goal sheets. Conflict here could waste a lot of time and energy that could go to more productive use.

STRATEGIES THAT WORK
FOR CONTROLLING THE USE OF YOUR TIME

About 100 years ago, one of the early management consultants came up with the idea that we all spend 80 percent of our time on the things that account for 20 percent of our effectiveness or results. Conversely, said Vilfredo Pareto, we spend 20 percent of our time on the things that account for 80 percent of our results or effectiveness.

Your job is to do things for you and your people to narrow this gap. In this chapter we'll deal with some of the ideas and techniques that will enable you to become a gap-narrower.

Unless you're one of the few of us who should be nominated for sainthood, you're making mistakes in time management. You're spending too much time on the wrong things and not enough on the right things that will get you your *next* promotion and help you achieve those goals you listed. Appendix F covers this in more detail. For now, let's look at some aspects of this gap-narrowing business and explore some specific exercises:

NINE PROVEN TECHNIQUES
FOR SPENDING YOUR TIME MORE PROFITABLY

1. Get a spiral-bound notebook. Use this one book for every note, every draft memo you write instead of dictating, every memo of a phone call and thoughts on things to do that occur to you during the day.

   Use it to record notes of meetings with customers, conversations with your managers, and staff meeting notes. Avoid the temptation to scribble notes on scraps of paper that get lost or have little meaning out of their original context.

   You must have had the experience of wondering in what suit you put that phone number of the person you met on the plane who knows somebody who can use your product, and finding out that the suit is at the cleaners. Or, you wind up at the end of a week with a lot of memos, reminders, notes on business cards, napkins, and hotel stationery, half of which got lost, and then you have a reconstruction job to do.

   This spiral notebook system won't guarantee that you'll remember the significance of those notes to yourself that you scribbled in a taxicab or surreptitiously at dinner, but it at least gives you a decent shot at staying ahead. Sometimes, of course, it is inappropriate to take out your trusty bible. Just remember to post your notes to this bible as soon as possible.

One client who has taken this advice to heart does a lot of entertaining. It probably wouldn't be proper to prop up the notebook against the bottle of Pouilly Fuisse, so he uses a small notebook as a subledger. Periodically, he excuses himself and, while in the men's room, makes notes to be transcribed later into his master book. It's effective.

2. Set aside the first few pages for your "To Do Now" and your "To Do Long-Term" lists. The first section would include phone calls you want to make or return, memos to dictate, errands to run, supplies to buy, and projects to get started on. These are the day-to-day reminders that we usually keep on assorted scraps of paper and matchbook covers. This section in your notebook keeps them organized and all in one place.

3. Use the second section for a list of those quarterly or annual projects that will help you attain your goals. It might include courses you want to take, books you want to read, new customer or market areas you want to explore, long-term market direction proposals to the home office or board of directors—anything that doesn't have to or can't get done this week or this month and doesn't fit a normal timetable of activities.

4. Use the last three or four pages for appointments. If you need a daily or weekly calendar for appointments, use those pages for a daily summary —one day per line. This will help you plan ahead and tell you in a quick way where you've been when you do your monthly "What did I accomplish?" summary.

It's also a bit impressive when you turn to the last page of the notebook you've been scribbling in during a meeting and have a list of appointments laid out and try to find a way to "fit in" the person you want to meet with again. (Everyone has calendars; *you* have a complete system.)

5. As you complete your "To Dos," draw a line through the item. When you finish the page, draw a line diagonally across the page. There's something psychologically satisfying about looking at a page of mostly crossed-out lines and finally drawing that diagonal line. Review the notes you've taken frequently.

6. Draw a diagonal line through completed items, but don't tear out the page. Paper-clip completed pages together, but leave them in the book as a historical record. This will come in handy when a "completed" item comes up again, when you can't remember where that phone number is or if you get involved in any kind of litigation that involves remembering what happened when.

Don't take this litigation issue lightly. Sales managers increasingly get involved in antitrust and unfair competition cases. A client of mine actually used some pages from my spiral notebook covering our discussion and a discussion with his sales rep as an exhibit in a case involving commissions owed the rep. My deposition stating that everything of substance that I did was written in the book in chronological sequence added the needed credibility. The client has been using her book religiously ever since.

7. When a book is finished, place the dates the activity covered on the cover and file it. You'll be surprised how often you go back to an old book if you keep it properly. You may find that a new book each month works and provides a convenient method of organized filing.

8. To make sure your system works properly, keep the book with you at (almost) all times. Chain it to your wrist if you find this necessary.

9. Don't dismiss this as too simplistic until you've tried it. The best ideas really are the most simple. (I can remember a client questioning a $400 bill for a 10-page marketing plan. I told him I could have given him 20 pages for $250. It took a few hours of working with the plan that was developed, but he finally agreed that the 10-page plan did the job effectively.)

The spiral-bound book is only one means of accomplishing the proper end. One client has a loose-leaf book with printed "To Do" lists, appointments, and blank pages to handle all the notetaking. He's so enamored of this system that he won't talk to me on the phone at home unless he has his book in front of him.

Another client uses the basic system recommended, but supplements it with a notation in the upper right-hand corner of the name of the file in which he wants to keep a copy of the page. This may be going a bit far for some of us, but this file-happy nut increased his sales over 35 percent last year. *I'm* not going to tell him his methods are wrong.

HOW TO USE MONEY-WASTING TRAVEL TIME TO GENERATE SALES

Have you had this happen to you yet? You planned (over a month ago) a three-day trip to work with your manager in Los Angeles. You really did this right. You identified the major customers you wanted to see, as well as the major prospects with whom you are doing little or no business. You have your manager prepare an itinerary that included breakfast and dinner meetings with customers and prospects. You reviewed this two weeks before your trip and made appropriate changes and modifications.

You know that nothing ever really goes off like clockwork, so you had a back-up plan for any plane delays, last-minute cancellations (where you went to Plan B cold calls or an increased market penetration discussion with your manager), or anything else that could go wrong. However, with all this back-up planning (and this is usually the case when you have a Plan B and a Plan C), everything came off as it should have for a very successful trip which you could write up as a "How To" for every other effective field sales manager.

When you *plan* for Murphy's Law, and have an adequate and appropriate Plan B and Plan C and have done all your homework ahead of time, nothing goes wrong. It gets discouraging when you count on things going wrong and have an alternative plan and then things go exactly as you planned, but consider the alternative.

Now you come back to the office and all hell breaks loose. You have eight calls to make to the home office, some of which will require an hour or two of preparation since they're mad about not talking to you last week. Three other managers have crises that they insist are life or death situations. Your office manager was out for a day and forgot to turn on the answering machine that you, wisely, provided for such circumstances.

You spent two hours on the plane trip back doing your dictating and recording notes in your spiral notebook like a good, effective time management manager. You had a whole scenario of what your first day or two back in the office would be like. Now, it's all turned upside down. What to do?

Well, before addressing what *should* have been done to avoid this situation, let's address the emergency with some emergency measures that will get you out of this hole.

HOW TO STOP THE POST-TRIP CRISES
FROM STEALING YOUR TIME

1. Issue a "stop panicking" order to your office manager and your people. Assure them that it's going to work out. Appear, whether you feel this way or not, calm, cool, collected, and confident. Don't talk about your successes or anything else about your trip. Your people won't be listening.

2. Compile a list of those so-called emergencies that have to be handled all at the same time. Give each staff person the opportunity to briefly (30 seconds) describe the nature of the emergency and to propose a solution (see the section on "Delegation"). *Don't* let them off the hook on a proposed solution and don't let them delegate the problem-solving effort to you.

3. Allow some time for the normal histrionics. Cut them off at the appropriate time. This will be about one-half hour *after* you think it

should end and about one-half hour *before* your staff thinks it should. Remember that one of the things you want to accomplish (and this is as good a time as any to do it) is to get your staff out of their bad habit of delegating their work and their decisions to you.

4. Declare a restroom and coffee break—one of the rights you still have left as a manager of this panicked group. Plead an emergency phone call of your own and make it a full 15 minutes so you can't possibly reconvene until then. Your panicky staff will certainly understand this emergency and most members of your staff will undoubtedly have emergencies to resolve, so you can stretch this to 30 minutes.

     Your people will calm down during this period, a lot of the unsolvable problems will get solved, some will turn out not to be problems at all, and you have a chance to plan your strategy.

5. During this half-hour, forget the restroom and the coffee pot. Look at the list you've made (in your spiral-bound notebook) and find the one emergency you know you could solve with a phone call. Do it! If there is time, find another and record the results in your book.

6. Call the staff back in, exactly one-half hour later. One person will still be on the phone and will be told that the meeting is reconvening, so it will probably be 32 minutes. Now tell your staff that you can't do everything at once or even by yourself. You are going to, with their help, assign priorities and people to all of these "emergencies."

     You will rank them A, B, and C and will assign someone to handle the task or tasks; with the agreement and consent of your staff, you're trying as much as possible to toss the ball back to them, where it belongs.

7. All the emergencies will be discussed and categorized with assignments given. Can you guess what will happen? Right! All of a sudden, the emergencies are only little issues that can be dealt with with a minimum of trauma. (You are, of course, making a list of assignments in your spiral to be dictated and confirmed later.)

8. Tell your people to turn on the answering machine (have assistants take calls) until all the emergencies have been resolved satisfactorily. They are not allowed to take phone calls or have meetings until they have addressed all of the situations they have called emergencies.

     Call a staff meeting for 4:30 this afternoon to review assignments and resolutions. This means that your staff has to do what is needed instead of what they like to do, and the needs somehow will be quickly resolved so that they can get back to the "like to do's" of their jobs.

9. Some things will remain unresolved: more information is needed, one staff member needs to discuss the solution with you, the person called is on vacation, etc. Schedule another staff meeting for the end of the week to resolve the leftovers and get back to the scenario you worked out on the plane.

OK, you resolved the panic situation well. Do you feel good about this? You shouldn't. It shouldn't have come up. Let's review some "dos" about travel that will avoid the nonproductivity that existed while you were gone and allow you to put your plane scenario into action as soon as your feet and briefcase pass over the office threshold.

FIVE SHREWD TACTICS FOR HEADING OFF TIME-CONSUMING PROBLEMS WHEN YOU'RE OUT OF THE OFFICE

1. Always let your secretary, administrative assistant, or office manager know where you will be 24 hours a day. This way there is no excuse for your being out of town and not in touch. Make it clear that you are always reachable within an hour or two except when you are flying from Boston to San Francisco. (Even this is being changed with telephones aboard aircraft.)

    Since you have planned your trip well, you can leave customer phone numbers, your manager's office number (here's a way to check up on how well your managers' communications systems work), and your hotel number, as well as the best times to call, based on your itinerary.

2. Spend some time with your Number Two before you leave, two days before you leave, so you are not subject to the last-minute syndrome where you forget most of the really important matters. (You remember that the practice example rated doing this an "A" on the effective time management scale.)

    Provide a list of assignments to be accomplished. Anticipate problems that might develop and provide guidelines on how to resolve them including those things that you want him to resolve and those things that you want to be contacted on.

    Your Administrative Procedures should have already spelled out a degree of latitude your Number Two has to make decisions in your absence, according to your guidelines. Assure your Number Two that your management style encourages results rather than measuring mistakes and that you understand that doing things involves occasional mistakes. You expect him to make decisions during your absence.

3. Don't accumulate "baggage" on your trip. This has nothing to do with any shopping excursions. It refers to the lists of "Things to do when I get back" a lot of field sales managers keep. Forget it. Do it now.

    If a letter needs to be dictated, do it in the car on the way to the next call or in your room at night. If you must make a phone call, do it while you are waiting for a customer or from your salesperson's or regional manager's car. Mail in your cassettes so your correspondence will be waiting for you when you return (or already mailed out).

4. Reserve an hour a day for phone calls and communicating your directives to your office. It seems that the afternoons always get you involved in something, so the ideal time of 4:00 to 5:00 p.m. or 4:30 to 5:00 p.m. probably won't work. Even if you didn't get involved, you would have to spend precious customer-call hours to get back to your hotel or your manager's office to make your calls.

Better to settle for 8:00 to 9:00 a.m. This may make you suspect in the minds of your managers—they may assume that you just want to sleep late. This should disappear when they find out what you really do.

You'll get your people back at the office started early, plan what you want them to do for the day, and catch up on yesterday. This will also make it clear that you expect full days to be put in whether you are in the office or not.

Things that need specific and immediate follow-up attention will get addressed within a day, just as if you were in the office. Calls that came in after 2:00 p.m. yesterday when you checked in with your office can be answered and new directions given to your staff. You will create the impression of being in your office, more available and more reachable than most people are when they really are in their offices and still get your field sales management job done.

(Remember the 75-75 rule? This is how you manage to get 75 percent of your full-time job in the field and 75 percent of your full-time job in the office done. Forget the other 25 percent of each one. The tasks in this category probably would be classified "D" or, at best, "C."

5. Handle situations that can be dealt with right away as soon as they arise. Keep a dictating machine in your briefcase. When you are traveling from one call to another, tell your manager to keep his eyes on the road and his mind on driving and do your dictating on the spot while you still remember what needs to be followed up on.

There is also a side benefit; you'll be giving your manager a lesson on the value of time. If your trip lasts more than a day or two, send the cassettes back to your office. The people you called on will be pleasantly amazed to get a follow-up letter before you get back to your office and your manager will be astounded. The home office may not even realize you've been gone if you handle things this well. Speaking of the home office, let's deal with their demands on your time in the next section.

HOW TO TURN HOME OFFICE'S DEMANDS ON YOUR TIME
TO YOUR ADVANTAGE

If you're a regional manager, you have already learned how much "help" the home office people want to give you. If you are headquartered in Cleveland, you'll get it over the phone. If you are headquartered in Los Angeles or San Francisco, you'll get help year round. Miami offices usually get the most help during the months of January and February and are not allowed to have problems come up in August.

If you're a home office national field sales manager, you might be a travel ticket for your staff colleagues. This subject is dealt with in more depth in the section of this book on using home office resources. For now, let's just deal with the time-management aspects of this problem/opportunity.

Here is where you realize that however effective your own time-management techniques are, you are going to have some obstacles thrown in your path. Your time is not your own. This is a problem, but it can also be an up-the-ladder opportunity.

The people at the home office are, of course, measuring you on your performance against quota. But they are also looking at you in terms of how you "fit" the corporate or management style that has already been established. We'll assume that your management is very capable, so they're always looking for talent that can be promoted and exploited.

So, think really hard about what you want. (Remember that exercise in the beginning of this chapter. You not only had to decide what you wanted, but what you were willing to give up.) This may be one of those times for "giving things up." Like it or not, you may have to make some compromises. We're not suggesting that you do anything that you're ethically uncomfortable with—just that sometimes, you do what the boss wants (or even what your lateral colleagues want), even if you know that you have a better idea or a more appropriate and businesslike way of doing things.

For example, suppose you have an appointment set up with one of your people with a key account. The appointment was made weeks ago and it's important that you be there because your salesperson needs some extra back-up.

The day before the appointment, your boss or one of those marketing people from the home office or one of your home office colleagues calls you to tell you that he will be in town. He wants you to pick him up at the airport and wants to "see some customers to get a feel for what's really happening" out there and thinks that you are the only person who can really act as a guide to this kind of determination.

What do you do? Tell the home office person you're busy and that he should reschedule? Tell him that he really should have known better than to call you on a day's notice because you're so well organized that your month is planned? Or forget your appointment because your standing with the home office is more important than any field sales activity?

None of these answers are completely acceptable! Here's where compromise to effective time management comes in. First, let's look at the possible reactions:

1. Tell the home office person you're busy. This has the advantage of making him aware of the value of your time and that you place a high value on it. A good answer in the best of all possible worlds. Not a good answer in the real world.

Your home office people have to think that what they are doing *has* to be more important than anything going on in the field. After all, they are the people who make everything happen. Dispute this and you could wind up handling the Sioux Falls, South Dakota branch office.

2. Lecture the home office person on the niceties of dealing with important field sales managers like yourself and explain to him how valuable your time is.

How far do you think you would get with this approach? The fact that the person who wants (wittingly or not) to change your schedule *is* in the *home office* or has a staff position. That, in the minds of some, automatically puts them in a superior position.

He might have a wedding, class reunion, family get-together, or even a girlfriend and is using the trip as a company-paid excursion to this activity. This may not be fair or right, but, remember that we're dealing with the real world, not the way we both know things should be.

3. Cancel your appointment, let down your salesperson and your customer and put the home office visit on the top of your priority list.

Now you're giving several messages. You're telling your people that you're a home office patsy and you don't care about all their hard work in setting up the appointment. You're setting the example of being politically oriented instead of performance-motivated.

As you have no doubt guessed by now, there is *no* right answer. You're going to be in some kind of trouble no matter what you do. You can say "the heck with my people, my job is to get me promoted and I'll take care of them when I get to the home office." You can say "the heck with the home office, I have a responsibility to my people and my customers, and those clowns are not going to get in the way of my doing my job as I see it."

Your're a manager and you have to compromise—for the sake of your own career, for the people who are working for you, and for the company. And, this is only one of the many time-management decisions (read compromises) you'll have to make along the way.

This may seem to be a bit away from the time management subject we have been discussing, but this is the real world. In it you may have to deal with the real issues, the ones that are people-motivated. And, it's an important issue in your time-management efforts and your learning to live with the political realities of a real-life corporation.

Let's look at a possible, admittedly nonfoolproof way, to deal with the above situation:

1. If you have been given a message to call the person back, it's a little easier—you have some time to think. If you happen to be in the office when the person calls, you have a bigger problem.

When dealing with *anyone* from the home office, don't respond right away without giving yourself time to think. Plead a meeting, an irate customer who is on the other line, a fire in the basement, or any other reason. Don't talk to the home office on anything but routine matters without giving yourself time to think, strategize, and plan.

Remember that you're being evaluated for a promotion all the time, no matter how long you've been in your present position.

2. Call the home office person back and start with (very polite) questions about what his "mission" is. He may not know, but you'll gain points for thinking things through as long as you don't make the person you are talking with feel foolish.

3. Tell him that you're already booked for that day without closing out the possibility of getting together. You'll gain points for being organized and thinking ahead if you don't blow it as we'll discuss below. Ask if the trip can be made on a different day. Feel out the person about the reason for the visit being made on that particular day.

It may be that he is on his way to a convention, or on the way back from another trip. Valid reason. It may also be that visiting you may just happen to fit in with a wedding or family reunion. This may not be a valid reason in your mind, but you won't do yourself any good by judging and pointing this out.

If it is the former reason, think about rearranging your schedule, explaining that you will have to do this (rack up some points). If it is the latter reason, unless you're a purist who believes that all management decisions and actions are based solely on what is good for the company, play ball. Work your schedule around to accommodate the home office person.

(Incidentally, if you really believe that *all* management decisions are made solely on the basis of what is good for the company without any consideration of personal needs or wants, I still have that land about 60 miles west of Fort Lauderdale and I would still like to talk to you about it.)

4. If you can't get the home office person to reschedule that trip, call your salesperson and tell him that something really critical has come up and that you have to have an "executive" meeting with the HOP. Depending on your relationship with the customer, you should call or have your salesperson call and reschedule the appointment, pleading a home office meeting that you've been called to on a subject that is near and dear to the heart of your customer. ("It looks like they now want to deal with that prepaid freight issue you raised and they want my input.")

Even if you are convinced that the reason for the home office's trip is specious, play ball. You may need a friend in headquarters and this isn't a bad way to make one. Also remember that home office staffers are people too—they have their own needs and wants and are as sincerely (in the right kind of company) interested in the success of the company as you are.

We've dwelt a lot on the home office interference with your job under the heading of time management. This is not accidental. If we dealt only with your own time management problems, and the home office got in the way, you might just decide to abandon this as something that was a good idea but not worth following through upon. Don't! This is just another facet of your job in this political world that you must deal with effectively.

5. Whatever you've worked on in terms of timing and your scheduling or rescheduling, meet the home office person at the airport, personally. It will give you time to talk at the baggage-handling area and in the car and show that you feel he really is a very important person.

6. At the gate (or as soon afterward as possible), ask if he has an agenda. Do you see how this puts you several points ahead and reinforces your image as a well-organized manager? If the visitor doesn't have one, produce yours and get agreement on it. Set a businesslike tone right away and keep some degree of control over your time-management program.

If there is a serious discussion about the agenda (and this just might be possible) try to hold the talks on the way to a meeting or a major call (just like your meetings with your managers).

This way you'll kill three birds with the same stone:

a. You will have the discussion, provide your input, and find out what is really going on. (The trip could be completely innocent and innocuous. This doesn't stop you from subtly pumping your home office person [or staff colleague] for information.)

b. You will impress the home office person or colleague that you are, indeed, a businesslike person who places a lot of value on your time.

c. You might really accomplish something. This person could have something that your customer is interested in. Also, he may have a budget that could be used for "our" customer's (read "your") interests to do something like establish a test marketing program on co-op newspaper or trade press advertising, provide salesperson spiffs or any other logical or not so logical reason. Also, the visiting staffer has to have some gossip from the home office that your customer would like to hear.

The essential point is that you, by nature of your assignment, are stuck with this kind of "interference" . . . you can look at it as a disruption of your planning and fuss a lot over it or you can plan ahead and just assume that it's going to happen and fit it into your schedule.

The more constructive approach would be to plan and then "plot" to see how you could get the most advantage (for your people and your company, of course) from such interruptive visits and activities.

We'll discuss this further in the chapter on using home office resources. For now, let's not look at this as an interruption or disruption of our time-management planning, but as an opportunity for further growth that, properly utilized, could help us get where we want to go faster. After all, isn't this one of the goals of any time-management exercise?

TIMING WHAT YOU DO FOR THE GREATEST PAYBACK

Just as going efficiently down the wrong path doesn't accomplish much, doing the right thing at the wrong time may be equally unproductive. Shakespeare's famous lines from Julius Caesar make a point:

> "There's a tide in the affairs of men that taken at the flood leads on to fortune. On such a sea are we now afloat and we must take the current when it serves . . ."

This quotation points out the qualitative dimension of time management.
Let's look at two simple ways to become more effective in this area:

1. Think about where your people are before deciding how to approach them on any subject. Your manager who just closed a big account doesn't want to be lectured about his expense account. You won't get far motivating an under-quota performer when he's down because of not closing an account. Nobody wants to hear about effective time management after being snowed in overnight in Terre Haute.

2. Think about where your bosses or managers are before you decide to present your brilliant proposals. If budgetary control is the buzzword at headquarters, it's not the right time to suggest a costly program. Similarly, if increased sales is the demand on everyone, your program to cut costs will get lost. Also, you have another thing to deal with. Your proposal should be in response to a request that makes everyone look great.

CHECKLIST OF TIME- AND MONEY-SAVING QUESTIONS
TO ASK YOURSELF

Here are some questions you should be asking yourself every day. Since, for most of us, it takes a long time for good habits to become ingrained, you might photocopy these pages and prop them up in front of your first Monday morning cup of coffee. Remember Ben Franklin's admonition that we need to be reminded about four times as often as we need to be taught.

1. Is my week planned with allowances for crises and interruptions or am I going to react to what happens? Do I have a plan for where I will be and what I will be doing every hour?

2. Granted that there will be disruptions, is my weekly plan consistent with my monthly, quarterly, and long-term goals? Have I assigned priorities?

3. Have I delegated everything I can? Have I provided guidelines and procedures for the delegated tasks? Is there a positive feedback reinforcement mechanism in place to reward the delegatees for handling things properly?

4. Am I remembering that my people shouldn't be delegating their work to me? Have I provided the right kinds of ground rules and parameters for their independent action with the right kinds of controls to be sure I haven't let this get out of hand?

5. Is Vilfredo Pareto (you remember, the 80-20 rule) my shadow? Am I constantly striving to spend my time on the "A" tasks, or am I doing what I feel comfortable doing to the detriment of what will really help me accomplish my goals?

6. Am I using my commuting time and waiting time wisely? If there is a flight delay or a traffic jam, do I know what constructive activities I will engage in during this time? Can I cost-justify a phone in my car?

7. Have I adequately communicated to my people the value of their and my time so none of us spends hours on a $100 account to the detriment of a $10,000 opportunity? Have I taught them how to tell the difference between the possibly productive long-shots and the time-wasters?

8. Have I provided for time to think and plan so I will spend two hours heading off time-wasters by doing fire prevention work instead of ten hours putting out the fires the lack of planning caused? Is there really a specific time or just a vague hope that this will somehow happen?

9. Are my paperwork systems under control and are my dictating machine batteries fresh?

10. Have I left some personal, family, and recreational time in my schedule so I won't lose perspective of what my real values are and so I will stay fresh and alive? Did I discuss this with my family so it is a mutual agreement and common plan, especially if I have to be out of town this week?

9

Hiring Salespeople Who Will Produce the Results You Want

TEN TECHNIQUES FOR HIRING THE RIGHT SALESPERSON THE FIRST TIME

Hiring the wrong person can cost your company from $20,000 to $100,000, depending on how quickly you correct the mistake and how much training, time, and other expense you invest. While aggressive screening, interviewing, and selecting methods do not guarantee success, the lack of such methods pretty well assures poor hiring choices. In sales, selecting the right person for the job is especially difficult since most experienced field sales managers will admit that they don't really know why one candidate succeeds and another does not. Past experience, testing (properly used), and hunches can all help. Yet there are no absolutes. The realistic approach is to avoid as many mistakes as possible, and to correct the ones that you cannot avoid.

TEN COMMON MISTAKES THAT CAN TRAP THE WRONG SALESPERSON

1. Having a rigid set of criteria about the "ideal" candidate and not recognizing that selling success is a subjective thing which doesn't lend itself to any known set of conventional rules.

2. Over-reliance on the Personnel (Human Resources) Department to find the "right" candidate. Most personnel departments screen out

candidates who may fit predetermined criteria rather than look for the slightly flawed gem in the pile of resumes.

3. Putting too much emphasis on a salesperson's success in past positions and being overly impressed by the companies the person has worked for. (Not every IBM salesperson is necessarily right for your computer products company.)

4. Putting too much emphasis on a salesperson's past lack of outstanding success. Everyone has a proper niche. Some candidates may not have found theirs yet.

5. Relying solely on the recommendations of customers or other business acquaintances who may be trying to do your candidate a favor, or who have their own axes to grind, or who don't understand your sales staffing needs.

6. Putting down, at least in your own mind, the lack of past specific selling experience. Only about 20 percent of the salespeople selling today started in sales.

7. Not having a clear-cut definition of the position and your expectations of what excellent performance means in the position.

8. Spending more than half of the interview time talking instead of listening to the candidate.

9. Not having a definite outline for the interview, or specific questions you want answers to, or a precise idea of what you want to happen during the interview.

10. Not checking credentials and references, not "reading between the lines" when you call references, and stopping short of thorough checking.

Make sure you know exactly what it is *you* are looking for in a salesperson. You can't rely wholly on what buying influences *say* they are looking for in a salesperson, so the listing that follows is a combination of what purchasing agents and other influences *tell* you they want and some empirical experience which has helped determine what they really want:

SIX REASONS TO LISTEN TO WHAT YOUR CUSTOMERS WANT IN A SALESPERSON

1. *Problem-solving ability.* You probably won't find this in any survey on what purchasing agents think, but the ability to come through when the customer has a problem is what distinguishes the successful salesperson from the also-ran. And it isn't the big technical problem that is usually the issue. It's usually the little things like a sample that didn't arrive or a special request that the factory overlooked that PAs focus on.

As we discussed in another chapter, you can have nineteen successful transactions with a customer and a problem with the twentieth. The twentieth will count for more, positively or negatively, than the previous nineteen. "What did you do for me when I had a problem?" is what buying influences really think of when they are considering placing an order, regardless of what they tell the pollsters.

2. *Reliability.* Your salesperson doesn't have to have all the answers as long as he listens to the customer's problem and gets back with an answer within the time period promised.

   This point involves honesty and credibility, but the judgment will be based less on the absolute value of the salesperson's help than on the salesperson's doing what was promised. PAs, like other people, don't like surprises, especially unpleasant oncs, like not getting answers they counted on.

3. *Understanding of and empathy for the customer's problems.* A lot of successful salespeople don't sell—they let their customers buy. They are able to do this because they don't focus on *their* need to sell a product or service but on the *customer's* need to solve a problem.

4. *Professionalism.* Most purchasing agents today think of themselves as professionals and want to be treated this way. They can hear jokes on television, be adored by their dogs, entertained by their families, and conned on the boardwalk. They want *help* from the salespeople who call on them and they want it delivered in a professional way.

5. *Industry and product knowledge.* This is deliberately listed next to last, since most of the above points describe an *attitude* toward problem-solving that is more important than the actual product knowledge. The knowledge of the product and, more important, the customer's industry and application helps a great deal in enabling the salesperson to provide solutions, but it's the "Let's both get on the same side of the table and look at the problem" attitude that earns the PAs respect in the long run.

6. *Personality.* This is deliberately listed last since it really is the least important of the traits listed and because purchasing agents will tell you that it is not important. Don't believe it. Given a choice we would all prefer to give the order to someone who is easier and more pleasant to deal with.

   This doesn't, however, mean being a delightful charmer or coming across slick and smooth as silk. These attributes are as likely to turn off the PA as they are to make a good impression. "Personality" in this case means openness, humility, obvious respect for the purchasing agent, and the willingness to listen.

Now let's look at some of the likely or not-so-likely places to find these paragons, recognizing that the conventional human resources department is not likely to agree with many of our sources or choices.

WHERE TO GET LEADS ON GOOD SALESPEOPLE

1. *Your own company.* This doesn't necessarily mean sales trainees or customer service people who have been intentionally groomed for a territory. It could include sources from the assembly line to the accounting department. If good old Joe from the line makes it as a salesperson for you, you'll have more candidates than you can use, better relations with manufacturing, and, by providing a career path, a happier company.

2. *College drop-outs who want to sell.* The fact that college was not for them is no indication that they will not make it as salespeople. I've interviewed a lot of recent graduates who feel that the world owes them a return for their years of study and who expect to run the company (at two to three times their starting salary) within a year or two. Most drop-outs I've met really do have something to prove and are grateful for the opportunity to do it.

   I once had a personnel director ask me what percentage of my salespeople had degrees. He was shocked that I had no idea. Intrigued, I found out and tried to correlate degrees to performance. My top person was a drop-out. The number two had a high school education and numbers three and four had degrees—no correlation at all with education.

   It's true that there are some technical selling jobs that require specific training, but after five years out of school the specific training is a lot less important. Too many graduates stop learning the day they get their degrees while non-degreed people have had an extra four to six years to gain experience and learn skills that could be valuable to you.

3. *Colleges, universities, and specialized training schools.* Despite the above comments, having a degree doesn't necessarily make one a bad person or indicate that he won't do the job. Just look for the person who wants to sell and who is drawn to sales not because it looks easy or like a comfortable social environment. Look for the person who realizes that salespeople don't meet people—they meet quotas.

   This source gives you the opportunity to grow your own talent and mold the people to meet your and their needs. A particularly good candidate would be someone who worked before going to college or who found out what the real world was like by holding down a job while attending classes.

4. *Your competitors.* This is always a tricky area and depends a great deal on the ethics and practices of the particular industry. Without a clearly understood prohibition, it is a source to be pursued. If a person is really happy and really fits his present company, you are unlikely to be able to lure him away, so you shouldn't feel badly about making the effort. You

might find an unrecognized star who just happens to be in the wrong firmament or who is uncomfortable with the company style or some other situation.

5. *Same industry sources.* A computer hardware salesperson could make an ideal candidate for a computer software opening. An HVAC salesperson might fit a plumbing supplies company. Being active in trade shows and getting a reputation for being receptive to inquiries will help develop this source.

6. *Referrals from your own company or your own sales force.* For some reason the candidate's peers-to-be are often the last people asked for ideas. These people know the job, its requirements, and the company. In industries where there is a real shortage of sales talent, some companies pay a recruiting bonus for referrals, with good results.

7. *Newspaper or trade journal ads.* You could wind up with a lot of paperwork, but can minimize it by being very specific about the requirements of the job, the job environment, and geographic location in your ad. Running the ad in vertical industry trade publications will also help to qualify your resume-senders. Besides being a source of qualified candidates, the ad can also be used to get exposure for your company and make future recruiting efforts a little easier.

8. *Search firms and employment agencies.* Some of my best friends are headhunters and I would agree that the best headhunters can perform a useful service. Too often, however, the search firm merely processes paperwork and still leaves it up to the Human Resources Director and sales manager to do all the work.

   If you have a search firm that really will interview, check references in detail, and screen candidates for you, you might use this source to save you time that could be better spent leading your salespeople and increasing company sales. Give some of the other methods a shot first, however.

9. *Outplacement centers for other companies.* Corporate restructuring, layoffs from business reductions, and other reasons put a lot of good candidates on the market. By listing your requirements with some of the companies in your area, you could get first crack at the best candidates if and when there is a workforce reduction at those companies.

10. *Your own circle of friends and acquaintances.* This doesn't necessarily mean hiring your friends, but using them as a vehicle to spread the work that you are:

    a. presently looking for someone, or,

    b. always interested in talking with someone with the qualifications you have defined.

TESTED, TIME-SAVING TECHNIQUES
FOR SCREENING APPLICANTS

One of the most frustrating and time-consuming chores of an action-oriented sales manager is combing through piles of resumes to find the best candidates to interview. Here are some ways to make the job easier and faster:

1. Make sure you have defined exactly what you want in a salesperson in terms of experience, education (if appropriate), traits, and other criteria. Develop a checklist to help you and others who will assist you.

2. Delegate the initial screening to your human resources department or administrative specialist with instructions to pass on any questionable resumes so you have the chance to see a possible gem and have the final word on who gets eliminated.

3. "Batch" the resumes. Don't try to look at them each day as they arrive. Take a week's worth of responses to your recruiting efforts (or the human resources department's screening) home with you for the weekend and go through them all at once when and where there are no interruptions.

4. Do a rough sort into three piles: "Yes," "No," and "Maybe." At first, until you really know what you are dealing with, don't be too judgmental—it's OK to wind up with a big "Maybe" pile.

5. Further sort the "Maybes" into "Yeses" and "Nos." This should move more quickly because of your experience in the screening process so far.

6. Rank the top five or six of your "Yeses" by preference. Use this exercise to test your assumptions on any "No" you may have rejected on the first pass.

7. Have someone else go through your top choices (including some of the "Yeses" you did not consider in your top ranking) and give you an evaluation. This will let you test your assumptions and judgment a bit further.

8. Give the "Nos" back to Human Resources—they might fit another opening in the company. Hold on to all of your "Yes" resumes and other paperwork in case some of your top-ranked candidates don't pan out.

9. Set aside time from your schedule three to four weeks from now during which you will concentrate on the interviews and follow-up activity. Leave some more time an additional three to four weeks from now to pick up those candidates you couldn't get together with and for second interviews with the most promising candidates.

10. Personally, call your top five or six candidates to arrange for personal interviews. Don't delegate this responsibility. No one else will handle it quite the way you will and the initial conversation is a good start in getting to know the person.

HOW TO PREPARE FOR THE INTERVIEW
SO YOU GET WHAT YOU NEED FROM IT

Effective interviewing, like effective selling, is both a skill and an art. It involves more than just talking to candidates as selling involves more than just "meeting people."

We will assume that you have talked extensively, at least once, with your candidates and have chosen at least three to meet you for a personal interview. You will have sent them some material on your company to save time and so you can see during the interview how well they read and understood it. You may have found that you have some mutual acquaintances and have already some preliminary reference-checking, protecting the privacy of the candidate, and treating the information confidentially.

If the candidate is traveling some distance (more than one or two hours) to meet with you, you will have scheduled meetings with others including Human Resources, plant tours, etc. You will be combining the first two steps in the process because of the distance and inconvenience. A candidate in the same city can easily drop in three or four times in a month, but a candidate who is flying from Dallas to your office in Chicago deserves a full day's worth of attention and activity.

Here are some additional points to consider in making sure you are fully prepared for the interviews:

1. Have a formal agenda prepared if you are going to have others talk with the candidate and make sure they know that you are taking the timetable seriously.

2. Unless the candidate is "driving over," pick him up at the airport—personally. Besides getting a possible relationship off on the right foot, you are showing respect that will pay off whether or not the candidate is eventually hired.

   If it is really difficult to make the airport trip yourself, choose the person who will do this carefully. Don't send the company driver unless he has been trained to handle this kind of responsibility well. Make sure the person chosen is briefed on the purpose of the visit and the importance of the visitor. He should express an apology for your not being able to be there in person.

3. Review the resume and any other pertinent information as close to the interview time as possible so you won't fumble in asking questions related to background.

4. Tell your people to hold all but the most important interruptions. There is a school of thought which suggests that you let business go on as usual because this is what the salesperson will have to deal with in the real world of purchasing agents. I suggest that this shows a lack of proper respect for the person and could put a damper on the interview and possible future relationship.

5. Review your checklist, outline, or form (see below) and have it handy. Rehearse in your mind your opening comments and some of the most important questions, and think about how you will react (or not) to different responses. A few minutes spent doing this will prepare you mentally for an effective interview.

HOW TO CONDUCT THE INTERVIEW—WERE YOU SOLD?

Interviewing skills come naturally to few people, especially those who have spent much of their careers trying to get along well with people, seeing mostly the good in them and being as nonjudgmental as possible. You have to do a complete flip-flop as an interviewer:

1. Your job is to look for those behavior patterns or traits that might indicate failure in the job you are trying to fill—the "knock-out" factors.
2. Besides just holding a conversation during the interview, you have to try to form a complete picture of the negatives and positives since *your* success depends on your ability to predict the success of a candidate.
3. In addition, you have to be thinking about how the candidate will react to on-the-job situations based on the reaction during the interview process. You have to put aside your natural inclination to be charming and concentrate on the objective evidence you can gather.
4. To make the process even more complicated, you also have to sell the candidate on you and your company in case you decide you do, indeed, have a gem who should be hired for the position.

As a sales manager, however, you have it a little easier than your colleagues in other fields. You are hiring a person to sell and how well this person sells you in the interview can be a good indication of how well he will do in the field. An accountant who aggressively sold himself to the controller wouldn't necessarily prove his accounting ability. You, on the other hand, can legitimately ask, "Would I buy a product from this person?"

You already know by looking at the record of your present salespeople what the technical qualifications of the position are even if they should be questioned and challenged. You already know what the person needs to know and this, to some extent, can be objectively measured. Whether or not it can be applied effectively in your company is the big question. Here are some questions to ask to help satisfy yourself on this point:

1. What was my first impression of the candidate when I first talked with him on the phone? (Your salespeople will be using the phone a lot so phone impressions are important.)

2. What was my first impression when he walked into my office (or when I met him in the lobby)? (Your customers will judge your salespeople this way, so first impressions *do* count. Put yourself in the shoes of your typical customer and record your reaction.)

3. Can I see this person fitting in well with our customers, the home office people with whom he'll be working, and with colleagues? (Chemistry is important. Some research scientists can work by themselves and therefore can be judged solely on ability; salespeople cannot.)

4. Did he start selling me before he really understood what my needs and the requirements of the job were? (Too many salespeople start selling before they know why the prospect is not buying or before they have any idea about how to satisfy the prospect's needs. Assertiveness is fine, but you don't need blind aggressiveness. This could be evidence of a large (bad) as opposed to a strong (good) ego and lack of clear-cut goal orientation.)

5. Was I asked questions about the material I sent out ahead of time or about anything else that the candidate has found out about the company? (A salesperson who doesn't do some homework about a customer's or prospect's company is less likely to make the sale. Being unprepared, uninterested, or too lazy to do the thinking and digging is a good failure predictor.)

6. How did he respond when I asked if there were any questions about the company? (This is a second chance for the candidate to show he has done the homework. It is also an open invitation to grab the ball and sell you on why he would be a perfect candidate for the job. If this opportunity is bobbled, you may have a knock-out factor.)

7. Were past accomplishments brought up at the right time in answer to a question or point I made? (In some selling situations, timing is everything. Features and benefits should be introduced in answer to a prospect's questions or in line with the prospect's thinking. Holding a key accomplishment point back until the right time could indicate a conceptual awareness of the importance of timing—a plus factor. Blurting it out prematurely could indicate that the candidate has not thought this "sales call" through clearly enough.)

8. Did I get an adequate answer on the reasons for having left previous jobs or why the candidate is unemployed now? (If there is some hesitancy, if the previous employer was 100 percent at fault, or if the candidate makes disparaging remarks about previous employers, make a note to check these references even more carefully.)

   There is a school of thought that suggests you consider only candidates who are currently employed. There is some merit in this suggestion. Your batting average will probably be higher, but you may wind up paying a higher starting salary and miss that occasional gem.

Also, it just might be true that the person is unemployed through no fault of his own or that a former boss really was impossible to work with.

9. Were there any mannerisms displayed during the interview which I found particularly irritating? (If nail-biting, lack of eye contact, yawning, nervous giggles, cigar smoking, or chewing on mints while talking bothered you, it will probably turn off your customers and cut down the candidate's chance of success.)

INTERVIEW RATING FORM

NAME _____ TEL NO. _____

FACTOR RATED	SCORE
1. First telephone impression _____	
2. Subsequent telephone comversations _____	
3. Correspondence before interview _____	
4. First face-to-face impression _____	
5. Fit with company (chemistry) _____	
6. "Selling" approach (appropriate?) _____	
7. Awareness of company (homework?) _____	
8. General presentation _____ _____	
9. Mannerisms and demeanor_____	
10. "Closing" technique _____	
TOTAL	
FINAL SCORE (Divide points by number of entries)	

Figure 9.1

10. Did the candidate *close*? Did he ask for the job? (The interview process, simulating an important sales call, is a perfect opportunity for the candidate to demonstrate selling skills and the close is one of the most important of these skills. The expression of enthusiastic desire to join your company and actually ask for the job is a big plus. The lack of it could be a knock-out factor.)

This is a lot to have going on in your head all at once and, after interviewing three or more candidates, it all tends to run together. To help keep things straight, avoid subjective judgments and have a tool to help in the final selection—a checklist form with a rating for your response to the questions asked above will prove invaluable.

Figure 9.1 shows a suggested form. It provides for rating candidates on a scale from one to ten along with a "Comments" section so you can record for future reference the reasons for the rating. Spend a few minutes *immediately after* the interview to record your impressions while they are still fresh and before anything else happens to cloud your mind.

You are now ready to go on to the reference checking and testing of the candidates you have chosen as finalists.

HOW TO AVOID A LAWSUIT

Just as pricing and terms decisions should be cleared by your company attorney or legal department, the questions you ask a candidate, especially in writing, should be similarly cleared. There really are some questions you can't ask and some that will set you up for a discrimination suit and problems with the Equal Opportunities Commission. Check with your legal advisor and, for now, consider the following list of possible questions off-limits:

1. Any questions on race, religion, color, national origin, or political preferences.
2. Any questions on age, sex, marital status, or family situation.
3. Any questions on physical or other handicaps, criminal record, or personal financial matters.
4. Any questions about the candidate that do not relate *directly* to the job.

What's left? Well, you *can* ask about education and past work history that is relevant to the job you are trying to fill. You can evaluate personality and you can test for aptitude, general intelligence, and specific job-related skills. All of this may sound a bit sticky, but check with your legal counsel. You want to spend your time leading your salespeople, not giving depositions or appearing in court.

The main point to keep in mind is that you have to treat everyone who will be applying for a position equally except when there is a good, job-related reason for the difference. If you are selling ski equipment and the position requires time and expertise on the slopes, you have a valid reason for asking about skiing ability. If the position requires lugging around two-hundred-pound diagnostic machines, you have a reason to question general physical strength and ability.

It's natural for all of us to want to hire people who are like us. It's equally natural, especially when making conversation over lunch, to ask about some aspects of a person's personal life. Natural, but potentially dangerous. As in other situations, the right documentation will protect you and your company if you run into a candidate who would rather sue than be hired. It will also help keep your thinking nondiscriminatory and give your attorney something concrete to review to make sure you aren't unintentionally breaking the law.

Documentation starts with the job description or, more specifically, the job specification listing. In this you can describe all the attributes your candidate should have, including personal attributes appropriate for the position, education, work experience, and special skills. There should be no mention of any of the "off-limits" areas listed above.

By using this specifications listing to advise your human resources department what kind of person you want and as a guide during your interviews, you should be able to steer clear of any possible legal trouble.

HOW TO GUARD AGAINST A WRONG HIRE

Elements of the candidate's background which are a matter of record—education, degrees, dates of employment, etc., can be easily checked with a form or individual letter. If time is short, use the phone for this verification.

It's far more difficult to check on performance in past positions or to verify accomplishments claimed. The candidate's former supervisor may feel guilty about having let the person go and will bend over backward to provide a good recommendation to assuage this guilt. Most people will also want to avoid any possible legal recriminations and will be less than completely open about the candidate's shortcomings.

To overcome these problems, you have to learn to read between the lines. Think about what the person you are calling did *not* say that might have been said about an outstanding performer. Ask positive questions about the candidate's greatest contribution or most outstanding accomplishment, for example. If the person being called hesitates or can't come up with an example, you may have part of an answer.

Ask questions that are a matter of fact and record and not subjective opinions. Ask where the candidate stood on the list of performance against quota. Ask how many first- or second-place contest awards were won. Ask, as sales manager to sales manager, for more information on how a particular program which the candidate professed to excel at was put together. You may get some answers through this back door.

To some skilled interviewers, the clincher is the question "Would you rehire this salesperson?" Asking "Why not?" to a "No" answer puts the former supervisor on the spot and may elicit the information you are looking for. If the answer is an unhesitating "Yes" the person may be covering himself or you may have a candidate who has checked out satisfactorily.

Finally, try to find former customers or associates, especially if you already know them even in a general way. You'll get far straighter answers from these people. However, because they have seen the candidate in a different way than you will, be careful about the credence you give to the answers. A customer could be upset because the salesperson was required to enforce a company policy the customer didn't like and wants to kill the messenger, or the customer could be interested in helping out good old Joe or good old Alice regardless of their capabilities.

If time is short or if you are trying to quickly fill a number of positions, you may go by your interview results and make the offer subject to verification of all background claimed on the application form. Just be sure to put this qualification *in writing* to the candidate.

WHEN TO STOP LOOKING AND MAKE AN OFFER

The best answer is to do it when you are satisfied that you do, indeed, have the candidate you were looking for and who measures up to the specifications you originally set. It should also feel good to you. You should be able to see this person fitting in well with you, your customers, colleagues, and the home office people.

Also weigh the cost of correcting a mistake against the value of getting a slightly-less-than-perfect candidate out there selling. If you have a six-month training program, you have to be a lot more careful than if you can get the candidate out selling and being productive after a week's orientation.

HOW TO GET THE BEST RESULTS FROM TESTING

Testing procedures are a highly controversial topic, probably because too many employers use them as a crutch or substitute for going through all the steps suggested above. It's also true that, in a sales job, test performance has proven to be a poor predictor of success in the field whether the tests involve aptitude profiles, handwriting analysis, or astrology.

Tests have certainly been oversold in too many instances and looking at test results is generally a poor way to measure motivation, maturity, and personal self-confidence. They can, however, be a useful tool *if* they are regarded as just that—another aid in the selection process that augments, but does not take the place of, the steps suggested above.

If you decide to use this tool or if your company has had good success with a set of tests, have all your present salespeople go through the same process as candidates. Correlating the test results with the actual performance of your salespeople will give you the best indication of the kind of reliance you can place on the testing process and the tests used.

17 TECHNIQUES FOR MONITORING THE NEW HIRE DURING THE CRITICAL FIRST 30 DAYS

This refers to the first 30 days of the candidate's sales career with your company— after the one-week orientation period or six-month training program you have all new salespeople go through. Even before and during this period you and your candidate will have set in motion some of the attributes, habits, and work patterns that will last for years. It's important, therefore, to get off to the right start. You did this during the interview process by following the above suggestions. Here are some guidelines for following through on that good start.

1. Establish a businesslike, get-the-job-done tone from the first day the candidate shows up for the orientation or training program. Set a specific time for the new salesperson to show up and have a specific schedule planned for the day and week and make sure your colleagues whom the person will spend time with understand how important it is to you to make the right impression by being on time.

2. Don't let the new person get away with just strolling in when it's convenient. If he is coming in from out of town, fly him in the night before (at least the first time). Sunday nights in motels are lonely, so you could ease the pain by meeting the person at the airport and having dinner together. This will establish the fact that you and your salespeople think that 9:00 to 5:00 is a time to be in front of customers as much as possible and not to be used for traveling.

3. See that homework is assigned during the training or orientation period and cover it the first thing the next day. You might pick the person up for breakfast in time to get to the office before the usual starting time. Again, you're showing that you mean business and that the job involves more than 9:00 to 5:00.

4. With the salesperson, lay out the first month's scheduled activities with particular emphasis on the first week in the field. Freedom and creativity can come later. Your own circumstances will determine whether the salesperson will be on his own or whether you or a regional manager will be along.

5. Spend at least two days with the salesperson no later than two weeks after the person starts in the field. You want him to know that he is not alone and you want to reinforce the businesslike tone you set during the training period.

6. Tell the person to plan on two full days of calls—you can talk in the car or over dinner. This will give you a chance to see how well the person plans his time and activities and to nip any bad habits in the bud. It will also give you a chance to reinforce the good feelings of being a part of a team as you play your leader role. The salesperson will have the opportunity to answer any questions or express any reservations that may have arisen that couldn't be covered in the training or orientation sessions.

7. Remember that, besides being a supervisor and leader, you are also a teacher. You will be evaluating how well your new salesperson has:
   — thought about the sales call
   — planned the sales strategy for the call
   — determined the objective for the call
   — executed the call
   — analyzed the reasons for results or lack of results from the call

8. Before each call, make sure the salesperson has the answers to the following questions from the point of view of the customer or prospect:
   a. Why should I spend my time with you?
   b. Where is the benefit in what you are proposing for me and my company?
   c. Why should I buy your product (proposition)?
   d. Why should I buy it now?

9. Make sure the salesperson knows how and when to ask for the order (or other end result).

10. Let the salesperson handle the call without interruption; you should talk only when the salesperson asks you to jump in or throws the ball to you.

11. Make sure something is left behind after each call—a specials sheet, a piece of product literature, or even an envelope stuffer. Bring some new material from the home office if appropriate to make the point.

12. Spend a few minutes after each call, analyzing the call. *Don't criticize.* Instead, ask questions. Ask, on a same-team basis why something was handled in a particular way.

13. If you feel the salesperson really blew it on some issue ask, "How do you think it would have worked if you had . . .?" instead of criticizing.

14. Continually ask "What are you going to try to do and how?" then provide suggestions only after asking questions. Remember the teacher role.

15. If possible, take the salesperson on the problem-solving call with an account you are familiar with. Explain the purpose up front and then let him analyze *your* performance after the call.

16. Don't be misled by how simple the above suggestions are. The proper execution is slow and difficult and takes time, hard work, and consistency. If you are already doing all of these things when you work with your new salespeople, count yourself among the really effective minority.

17. When you return to your office (or while on the road), dictate and send to your salesperson a listing of the strengths you observed which can be capitalized upon and the weaknesses you will offer to help correct. Put a copy in the file you keep for each salesperson so you have a basis for review on the next trip.

The main thing to remember is that you have made an investment in your new salesperson in the selection process and in the training stage. The kind of immediate follow-through indicated in this section will make this investment pay off.

IN CLOSING. . .

Mistakes in selecting people for your team can be as costly as mistakes in selecting or pricing products. Like product-related decisions, hiring decisions are either accepted or rejected by your customers—who write the orders. So be aware of what your customers are looking for in salespeople—both in what they say they are looking for and what they *really* want.

10

Using the Painless Three-Month Plan on Those Who Aren't Cutting It — And How to Tell Them

If you have any feelings or conscience, you cannot fire someone painlessly. You always wonder if you did the right thing; if you shouldn't have given the person another chance; if you did everything you should have to ensure the person's success. So, without pretending to take the pain away completely, you can try to identify the signs of a developing problem and spell out ways to save the person headed for dismissal. Failing this, you can make the parting of the ways as fair as possible and as much of a growth process for both parties as it can be. As a field sales manager, you have an objective standard that makes the task of evaluation fair—performance against assigned quotas.

TEN WAYS TO DETECT THE EARLY SIGNS OF A HIRING MISTAKE

Spotting the signs with salespeople whom you see infrequently is difficult because of the lack of day-to-day exposure and because salespeople can be clever enough to convince you that they are 100-percent committed to the job while they are spending half their time trying to find a new one or taking flying lessons. Here, however, are some tip-offs you might look for:

1. You or your inside sales people get calls from your customers asking about or questioning a policy or price change that was put into effect two or three months ago. The "tilt" sign in your brain should light up. How long has it been since the salesperson was there and what was covered during the call?

2. You stop getting phone calls and memos suggesting changes, asking for exceptions to standard terms, or complaints about delivery. This is a good indication that the salesperson isn't aware of what is going on or has stopped caring. The most productive salespeople are usually the ones with the biggest list of complaints and requests for exceptions. They usually fight as hard for the company with the customer as they do with you.

3. The salesperson is hard to get in touch with. You call and get indefinite answers from his office about where he is or when he will be back. It could be a cover-up for a golf outing or that the office person really doesn't know. Effective salespeople make sure they can be reached if a customer has a problem or wants to ask a question about an order to be placed.

4. Your calls don't get returned as promptly as they once did. If a salesperson has become disenchanted with the job, it's easy to forget to call back and more comfortable to avoid this confrontation.

5. The salesperson starts getting sloppy about dress. The person who used to show up in a pinstripe suit for Saturday morning clean-up work starts wearing sportscoats on customer calls. The casual dress is a dead giveaway of a casual attitude toward the job.

6. The travel pattern changes. There could be less travel indicating that the salesperson is less willing to put up with the strain. Or you may, for example, find your Florida salesperson spending a disproportionate amount of time in Miami and neglecting Jacksonville, Ocala, and Gainesville. Getting too comfortable in a resort city doesn't get the job done.

7. Your attempts to work with the salesperson in his territory are put off with vague excuses about personal commitment conflicts or "You wouldn't really want to be on this next trip." What is he hiding?

8. Paperwork—call reports, competitive intelligence, and even expense reports—are slow coming in. The lack of follow-through here could be an indication of a lack of interest in following through with customers.

9. You get calls or inquiries about the salesperson that don't seem to fit any logical pattern. Your product manager asks "Is Joe doing OK these days?" or your advertising manager pointedly comments "We don't seem to have made any inroads with our co-op program in Alice's territory. I wonder what's wrong." Joe and Alice may be more inclined

to share their problems with your other managers than with you and your project manager and advertising manager may be trying to get a message through to you without violating Joe's or Alice's confidence.

10. Sales are slipping. This was deliberately left to last since it is the most obvious and easiest to detect. In some industries, however, it may take a while before poor performance starts showing up, so the other indicators are something to always be on the watch for.

Now that the problem is identified, we need a plan to do something about it. The telltale signs listed above may be a reliable measure of a lack of interest in the job or an indication that your salesperson is looking for a new career opportunity.

They could also be cries for help from a competent salesperson who has gotten stale, become disenchanted, or who has personal problems that, when overcome, won't affect job performance. Let's see if we can identify the causes, but more important, *save* the salesperson for a continued effective career with your company. The next section discusses a way to do this and accomplish other objectives.

HOW TO USE THE THREE-MONTH PLAN
TO SAVE YOUR HIRING INVESTMENT

It looks as though your salesperson has gone stale. Sales are down, you get poor excuses for performance, and you've seen some of the telltale signs listed above. You could be action-oriented and fire the person right away for nonperformance. You could threaten to give the person only 30 days to clean up his act or leave the company. Or, you might just add a small fraction of time and effort to the investment you already have in the person and try to save it.

Even if this doesn't work (I've been successful only one out of three times I've used the approach outlined below), you'll feel a whole lot better about your final decision. Your people will also respect you and the company more, knowing you really made an effort and treated the person fairly. Here are the steps in the Three-Month Plan:

1. Identify the areas of nonperformance. Ranking your people monthly on their performance against quota should be a regular habit, so your first clue will come as soon as you get last month's figures and find out who is on the bottom of the list. Playing "low person out" every quarter (unless everyone is over quota) is not as heartless as it may sound. The person on the bottom is letting everyone else down and resentment on the part of the performers is bound to set in if the situation is not corrected quickly.

2. Go back and figure out when this started to happen. Did the salesperson start the year on the bottom or has there been a gradual or abrupt slippage that you can pin down to a time period?

3. Consider economic factors that have changed since quotas were set which may have affected performance. If the bottom has dropped out of the soybean market, your Kansas salesperson is probably not going to win the best salesperson award this year.

4. Once you have your facts, make an appointment to see your salesperson. Don't take "no" for an answer unless the person is going into the hospital for an operation. Then find out when the anesthesia will wear off. Rather than set up a special meeting, you could follow the usual pattern of working with the person on calls. This may give you some clues before you start your formal review and cause you to modify your approach.

5. That evening—before dinner, during dinner, or after dinner—discuss the performance and how you feel about it. Have all your facts and figures to discuss in an objective way. Let the salesperson know that you feel he's capable of doing better, rather than chewing out the person for letting you down.

6. Listen to both the poor excuses and the legitimate reasons the person has for being on the bottom. Make a list of them so they can be addressed later. Making the list also makes it finite and objective. Most salespeople, when asked if that is really all that is getting in the way, are surprised at how short the list really is. They ask themselves, "Is that all that was bothering me?"

7. This is the "What do you need from me or the company?" step. Take the list and identify specific corrective measures that can be taken. If the salesperson needs more literature, make sure it's sent the next day. If he needs to rent a VCR for presentations, authorize it on the spot. If he needs technical support for a difficult sales presentation, find a way to provide it.

8. Now ask the salesperson for a commitment: "Joan, you are at 70 percent of quota and I need you to be at 100 percent. How soon can you get there?" A typical response would be "Next month" or "Give me a month or two with the new tools and support I'll have and I'll be there."

9. Now, lay out the "Three-Month Plan" in terms of percentages of quota that will be attained. Hitting the first month's objective buys the salesperson the right to try for the second month's objective. Not meeting it is tantamount to a resignation. Make this clear.

   You will probably find that the salesperson is now less sure about his ability to get to 100 percent in the "next month or two." Fine. Get the salesperson to suggest his plan. It will now be more like 75 percent next month, 80 percent the following month and so forth. That's OK. If it takes five months to get to 100 percent it's still a big improvement and a lot better than having to replace a trained salesperson who once showed a lot of promise.

Accept the plan but make it clear that it is the salesperson's plan and any shortfall will mean the person is letting himself down and should find a more fulfilling job. Confirm the commitment and the consequences of not making it in writing as quickly as possible with copies to your boss and the personnel or human resources department.

10. Call the salesperson the following week to make sure the material you promised got there or to authorize anything else requested that you had to clear with someone else. Offer to provide any assistance you can to help the salesperson meet his goal. (Remember that a manager's or leader's job is to *assist* his people to do the best job they are capable of doing.)

11. When the next month's figures are in and the salesperson has beaten his goal, provide congratulations, offer to provide any additional help, and remind the person of the current month's objective if he is going to try for the third month.

12. If the goals are not met and there are not some really unusual circumstances (a flood or fire in the plant that held up shipments, for example), express your regret, provide career relocation guidance for the salesperson, and re-read Chapter 9.

You may save only one out of three salespeople whose performance has slipped by using the Three-Month Plan. You may save none. You will, however, have accomplished a good deal. You will have been more than fair with the person and your other people will see and appreciate that. You gave it a shot, but with a definite time period and specific performance standard that was the salesperson's own and made it clear that poor performance is not fair to everyone else. You should also be able to sleep the night you have to take the dismissal action, should this prove to be necessary.

If the plan works, you will have made it clear that poor performance cannot be tolerated, but you are willing to shoulder your share of the responsibility and help out whenever possible. Your other salespeople will respect the standards set, and if the plan works, you will also have a rededicated salesperson who should prove to be a strong performer in the months and years to come.

HOW TO FOCUS ON THE ISSUES—NOT THE PERSONALITIES

In the above discussion we talked performance numbers and other specific, objective things that were not happening and that we could make happen. Nowhere is there any indication of criticism of a person. This is no accident. There really is no such thing as "constructive criticism" that deals with the person rather than issues. All such criticism is destructive. There may be constructive *correction*, but this usually deals with issues, rather than personalities anyway.

All of your discussions leading up to dismissal should focus on the issues. You don't have the right to destroy or damage a person's perception of himself and you may have to live with that person in the future, possibly as a customer. Consider the following Dos and Don'ts:

Don't Say	Say Instead
You've really done a poor job during the last three months.	Your performance figures don't show that you are doing what you are capable of.
You don't look as sharp as you used to look.	Is there a reason why you feel dressing more casually makes sense?
You have really been getting lazy about your paperwork.	Do you understand how important it is that I get everyone's reports the following week?
You did a poor job on that last promotion.	Why do you think that last promotion didn't work well for you?
You're letting customers down with your poor scheduling.	Let's look at your call frequency planning to see how we can make sure all important customers are seen regularly.
You're never around when I need to reach you.	It's important that I be able to reach you quickly. Be sure to leave your number with your administrative assistant.
You're spending much too much time in San Diego.	Are you working on a special project in San Diego?

Personality-focused questions and comments put the person on the defensive so that he is more concerned with defending the perceived charge and thinking about what to say next. Issue-focused comments, and especially questions, put the emphasis where it belongs in a nonthreatening way.

PROVEN TECHNIQUES FOR CONDUCTING THE DISMISSAL FAIRLY

When the decision is finally made to dismiss a salesperson, you can talk about performance issues rather than the person and ascribe the reasons the relationship didn't work to a mismatching of the person with the qualifications of the job:

> "It looks like your capabilities don't match our needs."
>
> "This is a difficult industry for someone used to a long selling cycle."
>
> "The paperwork demands of the job seem to have been more than you could be comfortable with."
>
> "Apparently, doing the job successfully requires more technical skills than we thought."

This is not to suggest that you pussyfoot around about a salesperson's lack of skills or motivation in carrying out the assignments. You owe it to the person to be honest about the weaknesses so that he can make the necessary corrections in the next job. You can, however, focus on the issue involved that needs correcting rather than tearing down the person. It won't do your reputation or ability to hire good people any good to have people out there bearing scars from you.

Finally, in line with our suggestion to avoid personality issues, avoid the temptation to psychoanalyze the salesperson. Leave therapy to the therapists.

WHAT TO DO IF A "VETERAN" IS NOT PERFORMING

Much of the above discussion is related to the salesperson *you* hired who didn't work out. You may also have inherited some salespeople who have been in their positions for some time who aren't working out according to your standards. Most of the steps suggested above apply to their dismissal, if necessary, but there are some unique considerations to take into account.

Presumably, the people you inherited met the standards of your predecessor or they wouldn't still be there. It's true that your predecessor may have been unhappy with their performance and reluctant to take any action, but the fact that he didn't take any steps to correct the situation told your salesperson that his performance was acceptable.

Now you've changed the ground rules. You may still have to proceed with the Three-Month Plan for the sake of your other salespeople, your company, and your own career. It's fair, however, that these people get a chance to live up to your performance standards—even two or three chances. It's not fair or morally right to change a veteran's ground rules without bending over backward to help him make the adjustment. Your other people will be watching and judging your leadership ability. You do have to be firm, but you'll get points and more performance from your other people by bending over backward to be fair to the veterans you've inherited.

TEN QUESTIONS TO CONSIDER TO
AVOID MAKING THE SAME MISTAKE TWICE

If you followed the Three-Month Plan and handled the dismissal process well, it should have been more helpful (in the long run) than damaging to the person dismissed. Below is a list of questions you can ask yourself after the dismissal to make you a better sales manager and improve the selection process for next time:

1. Did you really know what you wanted when you developed the job specifications? Did you spend enough time thinking through what attributes really make for success in the field?

2. Are the specifications you developed really the determining factors for measuring performance on the job or do they need to be modified?

3. Was the selection process rushed because of a perceived need to fill the job right away?

4. Was the training or orientation process thorough? Should you have been able to spot potential problems before you put the person in the field?

5. Did you get this salesperson off to the right start or throw him out in the deep water (the field) to test his buoyancy?

6. Were the goals the salesperson was supposed to meet realistically set for the time period involved?

7. Was there a personality conflict with you or others? If so, should the selection criteria be changed or should your attitude be changed?

8. Did circumstances change since the person was hired that created the mismatch? If so, should you modify your selection criteria or the circumstances?

9. What have you learned about your expectations of salespeople? Were you too tough? Were you not tough enough when the problems were correctable?

10. How will this experience affect your working with your other sales-people? Should you be more tolerant? Less tolerant? Should you pay more attention to small problems so they don't turn into big ones?

Now, a degree of self-examination is good, but don't carry this too far. You really *are* partly responsible for the person not working out and, except for cases of clear-cut dishonesty or breach of ethics, there is no absolute right or wrong. However, wallowing in post mortems is not productive. If you never make mistakes, you can't be doing very much. It's a lot like skiing—the person who brags about seldom falling down isn't trying anything new, isn't testing his ability against the slopes and is missing a good deal of the joy of the sport.

Remember that a good deal of sales success depends on how well-motivated the person is. Contrary to conventional wisdom, you really can't motivate people. All you can do is provide the climate and environment where they will want to motivate themselves to reach your and their objectives.

IN CLOSING...

Although a dismissal represents a loss to both the salesperson and the employer, such an action can, if properly handled, be an occasion for growth for both people. Perhaps the key element is fairness, and to be fair you need to see as early as possible the telltale signs that the salesperson has turned off. For most people, the dismissal experience is never a pleasant one, but the measures suggested in this chapter should make it as painless as possible.

11

Holding Effective Sales Meetings

HOW TO CONDUCT MEETINGS THAT CAN SAVE TIME AND HELP GENERATE REVENUE

As soon as you think a meeting is needed, ask yourself, "Is the meeting really necessary?" Meetings take time and are often deservedly thought of as the biggest time-wasters in a company. Use meetings as a last resort. Instead, ask yourself if there is any other way to accomplish your objectives. If you call a meeting at the drop of a hat, you get a reputation for being indecisive and unable to map out a course of action. If you call few meetings, the ones you do hold seem more important.

Once you are convinced that a meeting suits your purpose, think it through. Plan it well and rehearse it on paper ahead of time, so that it's a productive, organized, and memorable event.

SEVEN TECHNIQUES TO USE TO ENSURE THAT THE MEETING ACCOMPLISHES ITS PURPOSE

1. *Fact-Finding:* What is really going on? How did this happen? How is this program going? What can we do to improve our performance on this?

2. *Problem-Solving:* How do we define and handle the current problem and how do we develop procedures that will keep the problem from happening in the future?

   A healthy exchange of ideas among salespeople, between sales and operational people, or between salespeople and management should be encouraged and promoted in this type of meeting.

When those people who are affected by the problem have a chance to take a crack at solving it, they are far more likely to implement the solutions developed and will have a much better understanding of why those dummies in the home office could let something like this happen.

3. *Reporting/Communication:* Monthly sales performance reporting could provide a format for general meetings. In other cases, like performance on a particular product line, the product manager could coordinate the meeting and have the facts and figures that compare actual with anticipated performance.

   The constant ingredient in these meetings is the sharing of information so that your sales and staff people feel involved, as though they are really part of the team. Good product knowledge acquired through effective training won't get the job done. You also have to motivate your people to use these skills. Involvement is the fastest and surest way to accomplish this.

4. *Motivational:* These are clear-cut and undisguised communication meetings with an open motivational theme that spell out objectives, welcome participation, and tell your salespeople, "Here's what's in it for you when we meet our objectives."

   Allied to these are the "atta boy (girl)" meetings that publicly applaud something done particularly well and try to find ways to repeat the success.

5. *Legislative:* "Here's what we are going to do . . ." In the right kind of environment, the meeting participants and others affected will have had a chance to express their opinions before the conclusions were reached.

6. *Brainstorming:* When there are no obvious answers to a problem, a no-holds-barred discussion where there are no bad ideas or dumb suggestions could be appropriate. An open-ended question like "How do we double sales?" or "How do we deal with our backlog and too-long lead times?" is thrown out for any and all suggestions.

7. *Training:* These meetings are for the purpose of instructing your salespeople on a new product line, a new program, a new application, or for retraining. By using meetings for training you get to use techniques that are not suitable for one-on-one coaching, and you get the involvement and contributions from the group. Naturally, some training should be a part of every meeting.

Some consultants like to distinguish between "process-oriented" and "mission-oriented" meetings. This is unnecessary. *All* meetings should have a mission even if it is sharing information (Type 3 above) and all should aim at developing action steps. Meetings that do not include these necessary elements deserve the put-down that this kind of activity sometimes gets from time-conscious managers.

Even a one-day sales meeting may contain two or three or even all seven of the above elements. The main purpose, however, should be thought through before the agenda is outlined. Each item on the agenda should be included and the meeting should be conducted with a sharp eye on only one of the above reasons at a time. Brainstorming and legislating, for example, are by definition mutually exclusive reasons or objectives. Let's look now at some guidelines that will work for all types of meetings.

WHAT TO DO TO MAKE YOUR MEETING TIME- AND COST-EFFECTIVE

1. All meetings should have an agenda distributed at least two days ahead of time for short meetings and two weeks ahead of time for long national meetings.

2. *Issues* and *not personalities* are the only fair game for discussion during a meeting. Say "this" happened, and these were the business consequences; not "you" did this, or "you" really messed this up.

3. Meetings should be conducted on a "same team" basis and all meeting participants should share this feeling.

4. Minutes per se are optional unless there are legal reasons for keeping them or legal consequences of not doing so. More important are *action steps*—what will be *done* as a result of the meeting discussion:
    — What is to be done?
    — Who will do it?
    — When it will be done? (Break up large projects into smaller subprojects with their own milestone dates.)

5. Set a beginning and ending time for the meeting and stick to it. If you make it clear that 8:00 A.M. means 8:00 A.M. and not 8:05, you'll get more attention to everything else you cover. Not starting on time punishes those people whom you least want to hurt or inconvenience—the ones who got there when they should have. To ensure promptness, one sales manager I know has *his* boss on hand between 7:45 and 7:59 to welcome meeting participants.

    Stopping at the announced ending time will earn you points with other time-conscious salespeople or executives. Besides, you can accomplish just as many important things in a two-hour meeting as you can in a four-hour meeting. You'll also get more participation and support if your invitees know that they will be able to get back to their desks on time and finish the work they consider to be important.

    Consider stand-up, ten-minute meetings for communication or other reasons that don't really need the time and involvement of a long sit-down session if you really want to use meeting time effectively. You might use this technique for all those small special interest group meetings that seem to be necessary at sales meetings—the freight problem in the west, if you are an eastern manufacturer, the import situation in the south, etc.

With these reasons and general rules in mind, let's go on to a meeting planning checklist to be sure you have thought of everything to ensure the meeting's success.

11 THINGS TO DO BEFORE THE MEETING TO MAKE IT MORE PROFITABLE

1. Determine your purpose. What do you want to accomplish at the meeting? Review the list above to decide on the kind of meeting it will be and spell out in one or two sentences what will happen if your meeting is successful and you have achieved all your objectives. Consider the following examples:
   — We identified and addressed or removed all the obstacles that are getting in the way of doubling our sales in the next two years.
   — Our people now completely understand how the new product works, can demonstrate its main features, can turn these features into customer benefits, and know the kinds of markets that represent the best opportunities to sell the product.
   — Our people now completely understand the new pricing policy and terms and the reasons for it.
   — Our salespeople now understand and have the ability to effectively implement the new co-op advertising and other programs.
   — Our regional managers and I now agree on the way we will go about handling our staffing requirements within budget for the next year.
   — The engineering department and our salespeople are now in agreement on the direction for new product development efforts in the monitor area.
   — We worked out a list of twenty-three ways we can increase sales on our old product line and six of them can be implemented within 30 days.

2. Decide on your participants—those who will contribute and those who should hear the contributions. One of the easiest ways to waste time during meetings is not to have the people there who make the decisions on the matters being discussed. (To save *their* time, you should decide ahead of time if they really need to be involved in the entire meeting or if they can be brought in at the summary stage.)

   Another time-waster is not having the people who will implement the decisions in attendance. Instead of creating an action step at the meeting, you'll have to start all over again with the discussion of reasons why. One of the best ways to motivate people to do something is to have them understand the reasons why the course of action is necessary and appropriate. Having them attend decision-making meetings is a good way to provide this background and make them feel as though they were a part of the final decision. They just might even be able to make a contribution.

Still another good time-waster is not inviting the people who can provide the necessary technical information. You should prevent the situations that start with "Well, does Andrew think this new circuit layout will work?" or "What did Kris in accounting have to say about getting copies of the invoices out to the salespeople?" Include Kris and Andrew in the appropriate parts of the meeting so that they can answer questions or reservations on the spot.

3. Prepare the agenda in a logical step-by-step format so that one element flows into the next in a systematic manner. You don't, for example, want to talk about a brand new compensation program without presenting the quotas that the program depends on. You also don't want to present new quotas before laying out a marketing plan to show your salespeople how they are going to meet them. This is discussed further below under the heading, "How to Construct a Winning Agenda."

4. Pick an appropriate location. If you are meeting with your regional managers, your office or a central hotel meeting room should work well. If several home office people are involved, a conference room far enough away from your office to keep interruptions to a minimum should work. Three- or four-day national sales meetings need a lot more thinking, which is discussed below under the heading, "Checklist For Choosing a Site."

5. Determine what visual aid equipment—easels with pads, slide projectors, video equipment, or overhead projectors—you and your other participants will need. Ask the participants ahead of time and have sources for these items lined up in the case of last-minute surprises.

I once made a lot of points with the president of our division who had decided at the last minute to show up with a video tape after assuring me he was only going to "make a few off-the-cuff remarks." I picked up the phone and said, "Kevin, I *will* need the VCR we discussed earlier." It was there in three minutes.

Another good way to make points is to pull a replacement out of your briefcase when a projector bulb burns out.

6. Determine how much time you will need to accomplish your objective, then add 20 percent more time. It's safer to assume that at least one agenda item will take longer than you expected. If it doesn't, you get points for finishing the meeting earlier than scheduled.

7. Get a tentative agenda out to all participants two or more weeks ahead of time with a suggested date and an alternate. Ask them to confirm the suggested date or the alternate right away. Ask them to suggest any other related topics for the agenda.

8. Determine your needs in terms of coffee or lunch even for a two- or three-hour meeting. You want to control the meeting, so you don't want people wandering off to meet those needs or wants. And providing coffee or soft drinks on your tab is a nice touch to get the meeting off on the right foot.

9. Schedule the conference room or off-site meeting place right away or as soon as enough participants have confirmed acceptability of the meeting date. You don't want last-minute surprises or to look unprofessional with last-minute changes.

10. Send a reminder note out a day or two before a short meeting with the final agenda. (The national meeting will have a multi-mailing buildup, so the final notice could be a "We're looking forward to seeing you" note.) The press of day-to-day activities could give rise to "Oh, I thought the meeting was *next* week." The reminder also serves notice that you consider the meeting important for all participants.

11. Think about your follow-through, post-meeting activity before the meeting. How will you communicate the action steps assigned or the decisions reached to the participants and others who should know? You may be able to put your notes together during the meeting or assign someone else to do this in a way that will enable you to get the follow-through job done more quickly.

EIGHT PARTICIPANTS WHO CAN MAKE YOUR MEETINGS MORE SUCCESSFUL

Working from the problem or opportunity that suggested a meeting in the first place, to the purpose of the meeting, to the agenda you will use, should give you a pretty good idea of the people you will want to invite to the meeting. Sometimes, however, it's a good idea to include some not-so-obvious people for communication, persuasion, or motivation purposes, budget permitting, of course. Here are some of the people who might help you reach your sales and career objectives:

1. *Your inside customer service or administrative people.* These people talk to your salespeople or customers on the phone all the time. Besides the recognition and motivational aspects of including them, you just might find that communication improves and that they have a better idea of the sales force's problems and that the salespeople better understand the internal problems.

2. *Your warehouse manager.* I attended a luncheon where the president of a medical instruments company was speaking about the importance of marketing. He said that he wanted to talk about the most important marketing person in the company. The vice president of marketing buttoned his coat and got ready to stand up, be recognized, and take a bow.

   Then the president said, "It's the person in the warehouse who makes the final check to be sure the product is the right one and there are no obvious flaws in the equipment being packed." Including the warehouse manager should guarantee more communication and attention to your needs and more understanding of the reasons for sending out perfect shipments.

3. *Your director of manufacturing.* You may fight all year long about the trade-offs necessarily involved in balancing customer service requirements and efficient manufacturing scheduling. A sales meeting, especially if the manufacturing director spends most of his winters in Buffalo and your meeting is in La Jolla, is a good way to get on the same team.

   Treating the manufacturing director as an important cog, getting across the idea that the salespeople really are interested in company profits, and having him discuss the manufacturing problems with the salespeople face-to-face will get you points and improve communication.

4. *Your director of engineering.* This makes sense for the same reasons as including the manufacturing director. You get another advantage, however. Many engineering departments are developing products isolated from the real world in which the products are sold. Including the engineering director may help ensure that engineering will design what the market wants and not what they want to design.

5. *Your controller.* The reaction I usually get to this suggestion is "What? You want this bean-counter to see first hand the amount of money we're spending?" Yes, I do. More to the point, I want him to see how effectively it's being spent and what really gets accomplished at these sessions, so I have him on my side when I present the budget for the next meeting.

   If you have clearly thought through the purpose of the meeting and the most efficient way to accomplish it, you should have nothing to be afraid of in inviting an accounting representative. If you are spending the company's money unwisely, you should stop, or you'll deserve to have this practice exposed.

   I've usually found that accounting people come to sales meetings prepared for a vacation from all the war stories they've heard and are amazed at how much work really does get done. They look at sales expenses in a different light after that.

6. *A production line person.* Again, we're promoting communication. The inclusion could be a reward for performance in the factory. You can be

sure that it will have the attention of most production people who will be eagerly awaiting the line person's return to find out what it was really all about.

You will be points ahead when the production people learn from their representative that salespeople are not happy-go-lucky, money-wasting, two-headed monsters. You just might also get a few good selling ideas from the person who puts your product together.

7. *A customer or two.* This could also be an award for purchases or performance. What better way to cement your relationship with a key customer than to recognize him in this way? You'll get from-the-horse's-mouth ideas that have to work (at least with this customer) because they are his ideas.

You might consider finding alternate activities for the customer, like golf or tours during confidential or sensitive sessions, or confining the participation to a new product or program introduction that will be announced publicly in the near future.

8. *A representative from the press.* If you are introducing a significant new product, that's news. If you are discussing programs, an editor could have some objective ideas about what will work. Obviously, you don't want to have the person present if and when you are discussing something you wouldn't want to see printed in next month's trade magazine.

Have a publicity release prepared in advance and, to be fair and ensure the most complete coverage in all trade publications, send it out to the other publications at about the same time you hand it to the editor who is attending your meeting.

I once held a four-day combination national sales meeting and new product introduction at Ponte Vedra, Florida. Because we didn't have a big advertising budget we invited 35 key dealers from whom we felt we could get a commitment to buy our introductory promotional period production.

The main topic was "How can manufacturers work most effectively with dealers on new product introductions?" Naturally, we had a good case history to work with in the new product we were introducing. I invited the editor of the leading trade publication in our industry to attend the soiree and offered an exclusive on the story if he would guarantee coverage in the magazine. He refused to provide the guarantee, but suggested that we would get the coverage if we were really doing what we said we were doing.

We did and he did. We wound up with a *seven-page feature* article, complete with several pictures in the leading trade publication. Our sister division, which was introducing a similar product at the same time, couldn't match that exposure with an advertising and promotional expenditure of several times the cost of the meeting.

Getting the dealers in attendance this kind of publicity certainly helped our position with them and the industry as a whole and put more focus on the new product introduction efforts. Pulling off this kind of public relations coup didn't do my career any harm either.

There are probably other examples you can think of to provide rewards, improve communication, increase exposure, and use new sources of ideas. It could be expensive, but balance the cost against alternative ways of providing the same result in so short a time before you make a final decision.

If nothing else gets accomplished, inviting your Cleveland warehouse manager to a sales meeting in Scottsdale in March has to get your needs and requests more attention. Having 30 or 40 salespeople beat up on him for three or four days about deliveries (in a diplomatic way, of course) also has to help make this function more responsive to sales needs.

HOW PICKING THE RIGHT SITE CAN HELP YOU ACHIEVE YOUR MEETING GOALS

Before even beginning the site-selection process, you have to decide the kind of meeting you are going to have. There are generally three types of sales meetings, whether we are talking about regional meetings or full-blown national annual get-togethers. Determining the kind of meeting you want to have will get you half-way to site selection. Here are the types:

1. *Working meetings:* These are appropriate for start-up efforts where a product line's marketability or profitability is not yet determined. This is no time for play, so the meeting site and facilities and even timing (hold it over a weekend?) should be dictated by considerations of efficiency.

2. *Award trips:* This is the other extreme. These meetings could be held for the sales force (possibly including spouses—usually a very good idea, if not a must) or for the sales force members who are over quota and the top customers or distributors based on previously determined contest criteria.

3. *Reward/working meetings:* This is a combination of the two. You may have some real work to get done like introducing your marketing program for the coming year or new products, but if you feel your people have done a good job during the past year, a half-work, half-play meeting could be in order.

Award trips, properly handled for large groups, usually require the services of a professional meeting planner, so we won't go into detail on this kind of meeting. If you have a small group and don't have to be overly elaborate, most of the suggestions for "reward" meetings will apply.

We are also going to assume that you have followed the steps outlined in this book and your people deserve a reward in addition to the other reasons for the meeting, so we will discuss this type of meeting in some detail. However, you may, indeed, be involved in a start-up venture, so we'll also cover the working meeting that is appropriate in this situation.

GUIDELINES FOR SELECTING THE RIGHT SITE
FOR A SUCCESSFUL REWARD MEETING

A resort location is almost a must and, for most of us, going to a warm place in the winter is still more of a treat than sloshing around in St. Paul's snow in January or sweating in Sarasota in August. If your company is on a calendar-year basis, a February or March meeting would be an ideal way to banish the winter blues. You should have a pretty good idea if you will qualify for a reward by the eighth or ninth month of the year, so have enough time to plan final details of the trip (three to six months ahead of time and compute the final standings of your people).

Some companies I know hold their national sales meetings the first week of May. This is when a lot of resorts in the Southwest and Southeast change their rates so bargains can be had. It's still cold enough this time of year for most of the country, so you haven't lost the advantage of having your people get a spring, if not winter, tan to show off.

At the risk of offending some parts of the country, here is a representative listing of locations I've found effective for reward meetings. The purpose is to show the kinds of choices that are available rather than hawk the particular locations. They are all relatively easy to get to, have adequate meeting facilities, and offer appropriate recreational activities:

- *Biloxi, Mississippi area.* Yes, Biloxi—a sleeper and refreshing change of pace from the conventional resort areas with the ability to accommodate you, and February is off-season in many hotels. It could well be the one place your salespeople haven't been.
- *Hilton Head Island, South Carolina.* It was probably a better deal before everyone else discovered it and it's not the easiest place to get to, but you can hardly go wrong with this location. A lot of new facilities have made it an even better meeting place.
- *La Jolla (near San Diego).* The advantages of Coronado Island in a more laid-back setting with beautiful views. All the facilities and recreational activities you could want, a short hop north from the San Diego airport.
- *Las Vegas, Nevada.* Besides the obvious entertainment and gambling attractions, recreational activities abound and meeting facilities are excellent. Move away from the strip a couple of hundred yards and you'll find a peaceful, almost Carefree (Arizona), setting.

- *Marco Island, Florida.* The charm of Florida's west coast in an off-the-beaten-path setting that is only a little more difficult to get to than Florida's major cities. Good tennis, golf, dining, and shelling.

- *Miami, Florida area.* You have a choice of the metropolitan area, the beach, or a laid-back setting on one of the Keys. Just about any sport you want including jai-alai. The choices are so many I sometimes think the Miami Chamber of Commerce invented sales meetings.

- *San Antonio, Texas.* Another sleeper that has more than just the Alamo and Riverwalk. A suitable place to look at if you want someplace different, and about twenty minutes from the airport on a bad day.

- *Scottsdale, Arizona.* About a half-hour from the Phoenix airport with golf, tennis, horseback riding, and even sailing. Several hotels with excellent meeting facilities. Be careful about the month of February, however—it can be cold and rainy.

Again, these are not specific recommendations for the above areas, and note that there are many other fine resort facilities in other parts of the country. We've also talked about locations with several facilities to match your needs and budget, so we've left out single facility locations like Tarpon Springs, Florida and Woodlands, Texas. The list is intended to show the variety of options available. Now let's look at a step-by-step list of things to do to select the location:

17 POINTS TO CONSIDER WHEN CHOOSING THE SITE THAT HAS WHAT YOU NEED

1. On a blank map of the United States, place a dot or a pin at the locations of all the people who will be attending the meeting.

2. Determine the geographical center for these people and look for concentrations. Include your home office people who will attend. If many of your people tend to be in the northeastern area, the southeast may prove to be a lot more economical than the southwest. Air fare could represent up to one-half of your total expenditure for the meeting.

3. Pick three general areas for consideration close to where you have the most pins or dots. If you are in the central or western part of the country and a lot of your people are in the west, you might consider Las Vegas, Palm Springs, and Scottsdale, for example, to keep the air fare costs as low as possible.

4. Pick three hotel facilities in each location and get their addresses and the name of the meeting director so that your request for a proposal can be mailed to a person. A publication like *Meeting News* (Gralla Publications, 1515 Broadway, New York, NY 10036) can be helpful.

Their January annual directory issue can at least help you pin down a beginning list.

Ask for a floor plan layout of the facility, including meeting rooms, to study before your actual visit to the site. Work out your own meeting layout in one or more of the most suitable-looking meeting rooms so you can visualize how it would work.

5. From your agenda, make a list of the number of people who will be attending each function next to the list of those functions. Since you don't know yet who will be playing golf or tennis, assume that everyone will be doing something so you can gauge the availability of recreational facilities when you make your premeeting facility scouting visit.

The hotels on Waikiki, for example, all advertise tennis but, unlike Maui, for example, you'll be hard-pressed to find the courts and will find it even more difficult to organize a tournament if you have a lot of racquet swingers. Other possible meeting sites may advertise golf but you'll find that you have to arrange transportation for your divot-makers.

Recreational costs will be a minor part of the total cost compared to air fare, rooms, and meals, to say nothing of the time cost in having your people out of the field. Your purpose in including an estimate of the number of people likely to want to take advantage of an activity you offer is mostly to find out if the location can accommodate the number.

6. Prepare a form like the one shown in Figure 11.1 and send it to the nine locations you have selected, addressed to the meeting director whose name you have obtained. This will give you a standard to deal with and make reviewing proposals a lot easier.

To repeat, most of your costs will be for air transportation, rooms, and meals, but the other items are included in Figure 11.1 in case you have to figure your budget very precisely. Some hotels will have a low room rate and nickel-and-dime you for any extra services and charge separately for meeting rooms. Others will have higher room rates but throw in coffee, meeting rooms, and even a free suite for use as an entertainment center.

If you are having one or more cocktail parties, check out this cost carefully since it can blow your budget to the moon. Do they charge by the bottle or the drink? Do you own the bottle when it's opened or do they estimate? What do canapes cost?

7. Evaluate the total costs for each location and have your travel agent figure air transportation from the origin cities. Consider the discount arrangements available since you'll be planning well enough ahead of time to take advantage of this saving. By planning over a year ahead you may be able to nail down this year's cost for next year's meeting.

SALES MEETING CHECKLIST FORM

COMPANY _____ MEETING DATES _____

COST

Number of people attending _____

Number of sleeping rooms required _____

Main meeting room for _____ days from _____ AM to _____ PM

   with seating for _____ people.

Other meeting rooms:

   _____ days from _____ AM to _____ PM for _____ people

   _____ days from _____ AM to _____ PM for _____ people

   _____ days from _____ AM to _____ PM for _____ people

Meeting room equipment:

   VCR player for _____ days   Sound reinforcement

   VCR recorder for _____ days   equipment for _____ days

   OH projector for _____ days   Slide projector for _____ days

Breakfast for _____ people for _____ days

   Sit down _____ Buffet _____ Private room: Yes _____ No _____

Luncheon for _____ people for _____ days

   Sit down _____ Buffet _____ Private room: Yes _____ No _____

Dinner for _____ people for _____ days

   Sit down _____ Buffet _____ Private room: Yes _____ No _____

Coffee and danish for _____ mornings for _____ people.

Coffee and soft drinks for _____ mornings for _____ people.

Airport transportation for _____ people.

Other _____

Figure 11.1

8. Add the costs together and narrow your choices down to no more than three. Get some more information from people who have used the facilities and make a stop at all three if possible as part of your regular travel schedule. You should get at least your room, and probably dinner, free.

9. Visit the sites. This is a must. Meeting rooms and even sleeping rooms sometimes have a way of looking fantastic in brochures. When visiting the sites, find out if varying the chosen time by a few days in either direction will get you a better deal. You could have chosen meeting dates that are just before or after the season breaks or at the same time as a big convention that eats up room space.

10. About a week before traveling to the site, send yourself a letter marked "Hold for arrival (date)" to see how it gets handled.

11. When you get there spend a few minutes walking around the facility observing the level of service and general attitude of the employees toward guests before you announce yourself. Check to see if room service trays have been cleared. Look for towels or bedding in the halls. Ask the housekeeping people a question to see how helpful they are. A good facility keeps on top of these little details.

    Go to the house phone and ask the front desk for information about something like the next limo to the airport or if a meeting room for twelve is available. Check the activities board to see how easy it is to find a meeting place. Call the front desk or ask a service person where the meeting is to see how aware they will be of *your* meeting should you choose this site.

    When you check into your room, call and leave a message for yourself and see how soon you get it and how accurate it was. Call from the house phone and ask what room you are in. The operator should know that you are indeed there, but should also offer to connect you to the room or take a message but should not give out your room number without specific permission to do this. Female sales managers tell me that this is particularly important to them. "Who needs someone knocking on your door at 2:00 in the morning?" they ask.) You can always give your room number to the people you want to have it.

12. If there is more than one type of sleeping room, make sure that all your people will get the same kind of room. You may be put up in a spacious VIP room during your visit with no guarantee that your people won't get closets. Identify the types of rooms and make sure that they are specified in the agreement.

13. When checking out the meeting room(s) you have at least tentatively chosen, visualize your meeting layout, probably a U-shaped arrangement with a lectern in the center or top of the U. Check for the possibility of noise or other interference from adjoining meeting rooms.

How close are the restroom facilities? How close are the phones? In a vertical facility, are there long queues in the elevator lobby?

14. Check out the emergency exits and other fire safety precautions and facilities. Check the security arrangements if you are in a metropolitan or other area where this may be important. You don't want to be morally or legally responsible for harm to your people in the event of a fire or other catastrophe.

15. Bring along a checklist of all the above items and rate the facilities from one to ten to help in your evaluation. Before you leave, however, discuss your ratings with the meeting director. You'll get more attention because of your organization and thoroughness if you decide to use this site and may just find that you misunderstood something or there were unusual circumstances.

16. Ask the meeting director for any other suggestions on how to save money or make the meeting more effective and enjoyable. Ask what seemed to work particularly well with other meetings.

    I once had a meeting director suggest an outdoor, private barbecue with a country and western band instead of the usual dinner with strings. It turned out to be a high point of the meeting. I found out only later that it was the first time they had done this and wanted to see how it would work. This may suggest that you also should ask questions about the experience the facility has in doing what you want done.

17. Remember that the service level is *the* most important thing that will make or break your meeting and checking the place out in this way will give you a good indication of how well *your* meeting will be served and save you a lot of headaches later on.

As we have suggested in several other sections of this book, rehearsing on paper well ahead of time is the best way to make any event successful. Allow plenty of time for planning and doing it right, document your objectives, and make your moves in accordance with your plan.

HOW TO PLAN RECREATION FOR THE GREATEST MOTIVATIONAL IMPACT

Following the checklist outlined above and the agenda suggested below should ensure that the business part of your sales meeting goes well. But, if you really are rewarding your people, you also want to pay attention to the recreational aspects of the meeting. In terms of scheduling, you have two basic choices:

1. Finish the business portion of the meeting in two days (and perhaps nights) of intensive sessions and then go on to the recreational activities.

2. Schedule morning meetings for business and leave the afternoons free for recreation and/or informal meetings among your sales force and the home office people.

The latter alternative usually works best. I know one sales manager who followed the former because he felt that everyone would be happier and better able to relax if they got the business out of the way first. He and his people worked day and night for two days to get through the agenda. The weather was sunny and beautiful and the salespeople couldn't have been paying maximum attention knowing what it was like outside. It was cloudy the third day and rained the fourth.

Where there is a great deal of work to be done in a limited time and you have your people at a resort location, you might consider working in the morning, playing in the afternoon, and scheduling some after-dinner business activities. Be careful, of course, about the kind of after-dinner activities you schedule. Your people won't be as fresh at 9:00 P.M. as they were at 9:00 A.M. One sales manager I know let his people *vote* on the schedule. It's certainly one good way to keep dissension to a minimum. An alternative is to schedule a full day of meetings the first day and then go on a half-work, half-play schedule.

Since a reward meeting should have a lot of rewarding elements, it's probably best to work in the morning, play (informal conferences) in the afternoon, and schedule things like award ceremonies or state-of-the-company talks for evenings. Your morning agenda items should be intensive and this format gives your people the chance to digest what happened and to compare reactions among themselves in a nonpressured setting.

I've held sales meetings where a foursome couldn't wait to finish the eighteenth hole to get back and discuss the great idea they had developed somewhere on the back nine. I've seen salespeople who didn't seem that interested in the morning spend all afternoon by the pool debating some of the points made during the morning sessions.

If your group is typical, most people will be playing tennis or golf, although in some areas a deep-sea fishing trip may be appropriate. Since special arrangements specific to the site would have to be made for this, or for horseback riding or sailing, we'll discuss some pointers on golf and tennis.

TEN WAYS TO KEEP THE GOLFERS HAPPY—AND MOTIVATED

The first step is in the selection of the site itself. While the golf course isn't the most important consideration in selecting a sales meeting site, you don't want to have to bus your people over to a public course. On the other hand, unless you have a lot of scratch golfers, you don't want a monster golf course that devours balls and frustrates the people you are trying to motivate.

You can do some of the planning even before your site selection trip. The first thing the facility golf pro will ask is, "How many people will be playing?". If golf is important to the meeting, find out ahead of time. You might appoint a golf chairperson either from the field or the home office. Here is a checklist of things to remember:

1. Make sure you pin down the number of golfers and the days they will be playing. Some people prefer to mix it up—golf one day and tennis the next.

2. Think about the nongolfers who don't play tennis. Maybe they would like to be involved even if it means attending a clinic given by the facility pro or taking a lesson or two.

3. Check out the weather conditions where you will be going—if it's unbearably hot in the afternoon, your golfers and tennis players may prefer to play in the morning and work in the afternoon.

4. Remember that it usually takes between four and five hours to play eighteen holes of golf. Be sure the schedule will accommodate this or plan on only nine holes each day.

5. Try to get a shotgun start if you have more than three or four foursomes. This means that each foursome starts on a different hole and winds up at about the same time. This will avoid multiple tee-off time problems and help ensure that you finish in under five hours.

6. Plan an alternate activity for the golfers if there is any chance it might rain. (Some diehards will, of course, still want to play.)

7. In setting up the foursomes, consider your objectives for the meeting:
   You might want to make sure a home office person is included in each foursome and pick the right ones—like the biggest complainer about shipping being matched with the warehouse manager.
   Do you want people from different parts of the country to get to know each other better? Make sure you or your chairperson pick the foursomes with this in mind. It's tough for a group to spend four or five hours together on the course and not get to know one another better.

8. Have the golf pro set up a handicapped system that will be fair to players who don't have an established handicap as well as those who do and that will give the duffers a chance at "low net."

9. Set up a series of awards with trophies and/or plaques as prizes. This could be tokens or valuable objects determined by your budget. Depending on how seriously your group takes their golf, there could be serious awards, humorous awards, or a combination of both. Serious awards would include:
   — Low gross (least number of strokes before handicap).
   — Low net (least number of strokes after the handicap).
   — Closest to the pin (usually on a par three hole).
   — Longest drive (usually on a par five hole).
   — Special prize for an eagle (two under par on a hole) or the greatest number of birdies (one under par on a hole).

Humorous awards (which should not be disclosed ahead of time) would include:

— High gross and/or high net.

— Shortest drive (If shotgun starts are not used, this would be used at the most visible tee.)

— Greatest number of balls used.

— Highest number of strokes on any one hole (no capping off at ten).

— Most putts taken on any one green.

— Best sunburn award.

Both types of awards have their purpose. The serious awards recognize the serious competitors the way they like to be. The humorous awards provide a feeling of camaraderie among the group and provide a nice reminder of the meeting for the "winner."

10. Remember that the most important reason, besides the recreational aspects of providing golf, is to *get people together* in the right kind of setting. This means careful attention to all the details to make sure the experience is a good one, and judicious selection of the foursomes who will play together.

12 WAYS TO TURN YOUR TENNIS PLAYERS INTO "ACES"

In the last decade or so the number of tennis players in many groups has exceeded the number of golfers. It seems to some to be better exercise and certainly requires much less time. Tennis also fits a busy meeting schedule better—you can adjourn the meeting at 3:00 to 4:00 P.M. and still get in some good tennis. Planning ahead to make sure courts will be available and attention to detail are, however, as necessary as planning a golf outing or tournament.

Your planning should start on your site selection trip with a meeting with the tennis pro. Be prepared to have an idea of how many people will be playing for how long and what their skill levels are. If tennis is important to your group, knock off a few points on your evaluation tally if the courts are not on the premises of the facility.

As with golf, you might appoint a tennis chairperson from the field or home office to handle the details once you get to the meeting site, and the ahead-of-time matters like determining awards and appropriate prizes. Here is a checklist of things for your tennis chairperson to take care of:

1. Determine ahead of time whether the tennis is for fun or serious competition or both. Since your group will probably include different skill levels, plan for both. Your "A" players will need to have their skills recognized in tough competition and your "C" players could get easily turned off if you were to base all the formal tennis on elimination tournaments.

2. Consider arranging with the pro for lessons for those nonplayers who have always wanted to hold a racquet in their hands and hear the thwack of the ball. You might even arrange a clinic with or without video tape for all your tennis players.

3. Work out a round-robin format with the pro so that everyone gets to play and gets better acquainted with everyone else.

4. At the same time, plan a semifinals and finals match for either the winners of the round-robin or for those who are clearly acknowledged as the contenders for the championship prize. Give the hackers their round-robin prizes and recognition, but give the "A-class" players a chance to compete for a different "champion" prize.

5. Check out weather conditions. Golfers can still play in 90-degree heat, but the 100-degree-plus temperatures at court level that this will cause could give you problems. Consider holding the recreation in the morning and the business sessions in the afternoon.

6. Make sure that your court time is clearly blocked out to accommodate your group and reserve some extra time for those players who want to set their own matches. I've seen avid players who didn't get to face each other in round-robin matches get up at 5:30 a.m. the next day to hold their own tournaments.

7. Check out the availability of the closest indoor courts just in case the clouds decide to open up. The tennis chairperson at one sales meeting became an instant hero when she pulled up outside the lobby in a bus to transport the disgruntled tennis players to a nearby indoor court. We couldn't get quite as many courts at the indoor facility, but the afternoon was saved. The players arranged to get her a special award because she had been as meticulous about her "Plan B" alternative as she was about her "Plan A."

8. Consider having someone videotape the play. Besides being instructional (especially if you can arrange to get copies of the tape to the individual players) some neat editing could produce a very funny feature for your sports award night. Most facilities can put you in touch with a local video house who can shoot in the afternoon and have an edited tape ready for you in time for the after-dinner program.

9. Save the competition for the finals matches among your top "A" players and make the "tournament" fun. You might handicap your known top players in the round-robin by having them play every defensive (where they don't serve) game with their other hand or, in Bobby Riggs fashion, put a chair on their side of the court.

10. As with your golf outing, set up a series of awards with trophies and/or plaques to the extent you can afford them. Combine the serious with the humorous. Serious awards could include:

— Round-robin tournament winner—singles and doubles if you are doing both.

— Round-robin tournament second place—singles and doubles if appropriate.

— "Pro" tournament winner and second place.

Humorous awards would include:

— Longest ball hit. Unlike some golf shots, the object is not to hit the ball far, but accurately.

— The most unusual serve or form displayed.

— The best (most unusual) tennis outfit.

— The nicest legs—women's *and* men's categories.

— The most double faults.

— The best sunburn award.

11. Because you will have meeting attendees who prefer to spend their recreational time watching rather than participating in the activities, allow for spectator tables to be set up, especially for the "A" player tournament action.

12. Remember, as in the golf section, that your most important objective is to *get people together* in a setting that is conducive to becoming better acquainted and participating in a shared experience. *Don't* leave people on their own to play—make sure the activity is organized to achieve *your* meeting objectives.

TAKING MEASURES TO HANDLE
THE "OTHER" RECREATIONAL ACTIVITY

For some sales meeting participants the favorite nonsession activity will be elbow-bending. Unfortunately, there is a history of some sales meetings which have encouraged this. It used to be that part of the measure of success of some sales meetings was the number of bottles of alcohol consumed. A great deal has changed in the last decade or so, but it's still an area that deserves attention and control. You want to send your people home with a message and not a hangover. If this could be, or has been, a problem with your group, you should find the following guidelines helpful:

1. As part of the ground rules for your meeting, tell your people that cocktail parties (and perhaps wine with dinner) are a part of the program but that their other bar bills are their own to be paid for in cash and not charged to the room or master account.

2. Also as part of the ground rules, express your policy against any driving when the possible driver has had more than the acceptable limit. If your people are likely to go off the facility premises, encourage a "one-sober-person-per-group" policy. Doing this won't ensure that you will have no problems, but you will have planted a warning that will be helpful to your people and may save you a potentially costly legal situation if there is a problem with any group that gets stopped or involved in an accident.

3. Limit your "open bar" activities to specific times. If you schedule a cocktail party for 6:30 P.M. to 7:30 P.M., instruct the bartenders not to serve anyone until 6:30, give a "last call" signal at 7:15, close up promptly at 7:30, and allow no bottles to be taken from the bar.

4. Have plenty of alternative beverages at your cocktail parties, such as mineral water, soft drinks, and fruit juices. Always have a variety of different wines more easily available than hard liquor. Have extra ice, soda, and mixers scattered around the cocktail party area so that people can freshen up their drinks without having to add more alcohol.

5. Don't have waiters or waitresses circling around offering drinks or carrying trays of champagne.

6. Have plenty of hors d'oeuvres on hand. Consider opening your hors d'oeuvres tables before your bar opens. Pretend a delay in setting up the bar if you think you may have a problem with your group.

7. Set an example for your group. I know one sales manager who, as a policy, doesn't take a drink until the sales meeting is over. He doesn't disapprove of other people drinking, but explains that he has a lot of things to do that are inconsistent with drinking.

8. Consider having a wine-tasting party instead of the usual cocktail party. I did this at one sales meeting and got the restaurant sommelier to give a brief talk on the wines to be served at the beginning of the hour. He was so delighted to have the chance to share his expertise that he refused to be compensated, and most of the group felt that it was the most interesting cocktail party they had ever attended.

9. If you are not the senior company official at the meeting, explain to the person who is, what you are doing and see if he will also go along. If you are the senior person, see if you can get your regional managers to help set an example. You are not discouraging drinking—only trying to keep it under control for the benefit of everyone attending. You can all get together after the meeting and let your hair down if you want—as long as you are not driving.

10. Remember that your company may be held responsible if a member of your group gets drunk and is hurt. This may be unfair, but companies have paid millions of dollars in liability insurance or settlement of lawsuits for this very reason. Your meeting facility will be interested in

reducing any liability they may have, so this aspect of your meeting may be one of the things to put on the agenda to discuss with the appropriate person at the facility.

HOW TO CONSTRUCT A WINNING AGENDA

The particular things to be covered at your meeting will vary according to your needs and situation. There are, however, some agenda items that should be included in every sales meeting in the order indicated:

1. An "Obstacles Session" to discuss everything that is getting in the way of doubling sales.
2. A review of the past year, perhaps with a separate awards ceremony luncheon or dinner.
3. Presentation of your marketing program(s) for the coming year with objectives and quota assignments.
4. An "Opportunities Session" to discuss how to build on the marketing program and implement it in every salesperson's territory.

The specific implementation of the above items will depend on your company culture, practice, past history material to be covered, and current situation. Here are some suggestions that will apply to each, including the reason for the insistence on the above chronological order:

HOW TO REMOVE THE ROADBLOCKS
TO SUCCESSFUL MEETINGS

Most of the reasons your salespeople aren't as effective as they should be relate less to their innate ability or work habits than to the real or imagined obstacles they perceive. I've found few salespeople who don't have a long list of "if-onlies" ("If only I had . . .," "If only I didn't have to . . .," "If only they would or would not . . .")

They are coming to your sales meeting with these thoughts in their heads, sometimes armed with all kinds of examples of how the company is getting in their way whether they express these thoughts or not. You won't get far talking about your new program and all the good things it will do if the salespeople are stewing about literature stockouts, excessively long lead times, or getting invoice copies two months after the sale.

Address this and get it out of the way starting as soon as 15 minutes after your sales meeting begins. The gripes and complaints, whether they are legitimate or not, are in *their* heads and you won't be able to get any new positive information across until you flush out the old negative perceptions. Here's how this session could work:

1. Announce the ground rules—you are going to list every obstacle that is getting in the way of doubling sales (no time period specified) no matter who has control over the area, without getting into a lot of examples or censoring any contribution to the list.

    With a group of more than ten, it's a good idea to break up into two or more subgroups so that everyone is compelled to participate and so that no one theme, person, or group dominates the entire exercise.

2. Commit to addressing, if not resolving, every obstacle listed and promise a report to all participants on the obstacles and a follow-up report every 30 days until every item has been covered.

3. Allow two hours on the agenda for the process. It usually won't take this long. Your salespeople will probably run out of things to list much faster than they thought and will sit back and look at their lists asking "Is that all that was bothering me?"

    I've found a natural relationship between the size of the group and number of items listed that is fairly consistent. Groups of 10 to 20 will come up with about 20 to 30 items. Groups of 20 to 30 will come up with 40 to 50 items. Larger groups seldom can find more than 60.

4. Stop the subgroup meetings when you see them start to slow or when the people start to repeat themselves or get into specific examples of things they have already listed. Call the groups together and get a report from each subgroup or task force. List the items on an easel and tape the pages on the wall. Group similar items under one statement as appropriate.

5. When you have all reports, have the group vote on the five (seven or ten) obstacles that are most important to them or are the biggest hindrances to doubling sales. Give each member five (seven or ten) votes and record the number of votes on the easel pad sheets.

6. Have someone take down the list in order of the number of votes each item got, and repeat your commitment to address, if not resolve, every one and report on the progress ever 30 days. You may find that you'll solve many of the items before the sales meeting adjourns. Include this in your first report.

7. Take your regional (district) managers to a separate area and hold your own meeting, checking back from time to time on the progress of the main meeting. Plan on reporting your conclusions last.

By handling the perceptions in this way, you've done several things that will make your sales meeting and marketing program for the year more successful:

1. You've cleared the air and gotten rid of the gripes that might have interfered with your positive presentations.

2. You've told your sales force that their perceptions about difficulties really are important and that you want to deal with them.

3. You have a clear-cut mandate to go back to the home office and present the consensus of the sales force. It's no longer you alone who feels that an issue is a problem that is getting in the way of success.

4. As you address and resolve the obstacles, you've knocked the support out from under the excuses for being below quota. You've called their bluff.

5. You have a firm, objective platform from which to direct your efforts for improvement; this is particularly important if you are new to the position. You'll be able to point to specific accomplishments, item by item.

With this out of the way and competently dealt with, and with everyone heaving a huge sigh, you are now ready to go on to a more objective review of the past year.

USING THE PAST YEAR'S ACCOMPLISHMENTS TO PAVE THE WAY FOR THIS YEAR'S SUCCESSES

There are three areas that should be included in this review although you can add as many elements as you like:

1. Performance against quota—by salesperson. I know many sales managers who are squeamish about this because they feel it puts down those on the bottom. This should not be a problem if quotas were fairly set. If they were not, you'll change the method and can announce this to the group if there are any gross inequities.

2. Awards for performance whether given in the meeting or at a separate session. Awards might include:
   — First and second place for the quarter just past.
   — First place, second place, and third place for the year most recently concluded.
   — Other significant contributions such as pioneering work on a new product line that was shared with all other salespeople.
   — Significant contribution awards to home office people who helped make the overall sales quota (perhaps including your boss, if appropriate).

Your award hierarchy might look like this:
   — Special, functional "trophy" for the salesperson of the year such as a clock or desk set with an engraved plate clearly spelling out the reason for the award.
   — 8" x 10" plaque for first place for the quarter, second place for the year and for significant contributions by others.
   — 5" x 7" plaque for second place for the quarter and third place for the year.

Be careful about handing out too many awards. I know one sales manager who was trying so hard to be popular that he handed out an award that had previously been pretty exclusive to everyone over quota—two-thirds of the sales force that year. It may have made him better liked, but demeaned the award for past recipients and for the salespeople at the very top of the list.

HOW TO PRESENT THE MARKETING PROGRAM

The content of this part of the sales meeting will vary considerably from company to company and even product line by product line. The important thing is that it be based on what your customers and sales people have said they wanted and that it be *sold*, however indirectly and subtly to the salespeople. One of the best ways to do this, of course, is to point out the elements that the salespeople themselves have contributed to. Here are some elements that most programs will have in common:

1. An overall theme that will be the rallying cry for the year and a goal to be reached.
2. Specific programs by time period—program of the quarter, for example. A year is a long time to keep up enthusiasm for a single program. If it really is a single effort, break it up into quarters.
3. Specific objectives to be reached that will tie into the overall quotas and compensation program.
4. All of the broadcast, space, direct mail, collateral material, and other support media that will be used to enhance the salespeople's efforts. Have specific dates for at least the first quarter.
5. Room and perhaps a budget for other supporting efforts that will be implemented locally or with a particular customer or client group.

The last point leads us to our next session.

RUNNING THE SALES PLANNING SESSION TO UNCOVER OPPORTUNITIES YOU DIDN'T EVEN THINK WERE THERE

This should be one of the last items on the agenda. By now, you and your salespeople will have, at least for now, put past problems in the past, dealt with the reality of the present, and are now ready to build for the future.

Using your marketing program as an outline and planning guide, you could have your sales force break up into subgroups as you did for the obstacles session and charge them all with coming up with as long a list as possible of ideas on how to effectively implement your marketing program. As in the obstacles session, there are no bad ideas or dumb suggestions. Again, split with your regional or district managers and report your ideas last.

You can then call your group back together, list the ideas on the easel pad, tape the sheets to the wall, and have your group vote on the best ideas. Your commitment should be to consider all contributions carefully, possibly with your product managers, supervisor, advertising and promotion people, and your outside advertising agency. You should then get back to the salespeople with a plan to implement as many of the ideas as possible, or an explanation of why some aren't feasible.

If most of your group decides that skywriting is a great way to promote your new trepanning machine, you had better have a good reason to exclude it from the program. This is admittedly a far-fetched example, but remember that *their* mediocre ideas may work better than most of the brilliant things *you* or your advertising agency come up with.

The opportunities session will bring the group back to the real world of field selling. You've dealt with the obstacles, reviewed the past year, handed out awards, shown the future, and brought the whole thing back down to earth by having your salespeople think about how they are going to implement the plans and programs when they get back to their territories.

TESTED ACTION STEPS TO TAKE, RIGHT AFTER THE MEETING, TO MAINTAIN THE MOMENTUM

You should have a long list of assignments from the obstacles session, the opportunities session, and all the other notes you've made and converted to action steps. This first step is to sort it all out and assign priorities. Since you've been away for a while, it's tempting to jump into the big pile of mail on your desk and catch up on your work (I've found it effective to just stay at the sales meeting site for an extra day and organize all the paperwork. Doing this has saved two days back at the office and enabled me to get the ideas down more easily.)

If you go right back to the office and get involved with other pressing things, the excitement and freshness of the ideas generated at the meeting and the resolve to do something about them will wear off. Grab your dictating machine and make a formal list of action items, especially those that can be assigned to others. Get out directives with due dates to your people and requests to your colleagues. Summarize in two separate formal sales bulletins the obstacles session and the opportunities session.

Make up your own action item list with due dates. You'll want to address the items on the sessions lists that your salespeople voted most important, but look at some of the items that are easily correctable and strike a balance between the perceived importance and ease of resolution. Now, get back to business as usual or, almost as usual—the sales meeting should have had such a significant impact that business as usual won't ever be quite the same *if* you follow up effectively.

IN CLOSING. . .

Sales meetings are different from most other types of meetings in that their content must always be laced with motivation. How well you prepare for, conduct, and follow up on your sales meetings will reflect favorably on your leadership capabilities. In so doing, you can make your meetings both productive and motivational by setting the example.

12

Avoiding the Ten Biggest Money-Losing Mistakes Made at Industry Shows and Conventions

Probably you, like most other sales management veterans, would acknowledge that trade shows are the most competitive of all sales activities. You are competing with as many as several hundred other sellers. You compete for the time of the attendees with association meetings, training sessions, workshops, and panel groups. You also have to convince your prospects that a visit to your booth is worth more than a tour of the local art museum or zoo.

Trade shows can also be the easiest and most cost-effective way to quickly bring your product to the attention of a lot of prospects. Your message may be old hat to you, but most of the people attending trade shows have probably never even talked to one of your salespeople. If you have a new product or new program, you will be able to introduce it in the most concentrated way possible. And you have an audience that came specifically to look for information to make a purchase now or in the future.

Several marketing studies have shown that the cost-per-prospect-contacted is about half that of a personal sales call. The attendees are generally interested in learning something about your product or they wouldn't be there. You get a chance to really tell your story with a multi-dimensional display backed up by skilled salespeople. The studies further suggest that a prospect can often be closed in two calls instead of the usual five required with personal sales calls. The whole selling cycle can be squeezed into a much smaller time frame.

Like sales meetings, however, trade shows can also be big wastes of time and money if not handled properly. Objectives must be thought through, and the show properly positioned as a part of your total sales and marketing effort. Participants from your company have to be properly trained and directed, and the follow-through must be adequate.

HOW TO PICK THE SHOWS THAT WILL TRANSLATE INTO ADDED SALES.

1. Are the purpose and theme of the particular show or exhibit consistent with your overall sales and marketing objectives? Are your product's benefits relevant to the show attendees?

2. Do the show's attendees represent the primary market group you want to reach? Do they really represent the market for your product?

3. Will you be able to measure the benefits and results obtained so you can make the right decision next year on a particular show and pick or reject shows that appeal to similar audiences? "Results" may not necessarily be orders written at the show.

4. Some shows are deliberately intended to be exposure and contact shows rather than selling shows. Associations might risk losing their non-profit status if there is too much order-taking. Determine if the show's purpose fits your order-writing objectives and if you can afford to engage in an expensive activity that won't pay off in immediate sales revenue.

5. Have your customers asked if you are going to be there? Sometimes you can be conspicuous by your absence, which will give rise to rumors that your competitors will be happy to create and spread. This should not, of course, be the main reason for participating. However, you can ask your customers why they feel it is important for you to be there and get some intelligence on your exhibit theme and overall purpose.

6. How much attention do the shows get in your industry trade publications? If the feature articles for months ahead of time herald the upcoming show, you have to conclude that it must be important in your industry.

7. How many of your direct competitors attend? They may be only trying not to be conspicuous by their absence, but it's an important factor to consider. The person who just left the room is sometimes the most likely to be talked about in a less-than-favorable way. Most exposition managers or trade associations publish lists of exhibitors ahead of time

and some provide a directory of those who attended. These lists can help you pin down the attendees and determine if they represent the market you are trying to reach.

8. Can participation be a good training experience for your salespeople? A good way to really take the pulse of the market? A way to launch trial balloons? Or, could they get the same benefits by attending rather than exhibiting at the show?

9. Is your product one whose market you can only define accurately by gauging the interest shown at an activity like a trade show? You could conceivably have a fascinating product which draws a lot of interest and still be unable to close orders. Robots and similar gadgets are always interesting at shows but few people actually buy them.

10. Is your (new) product designed for a horizontal market so that trade shows are the most efficient way to develop a prospect list? Actually, the market research work done before the product was developed should have answered this, but even effective sales managers sometimes get stuck with an unresearched product to sell.

These criteria make sense whether or not you have a new product line to introduce or a new market to approach. Instead of accepting, "Well, we've always gone to this show," use the listing to see if the shows scheduled still make sense in view of your current sales and marketing objectives and if this is really the most cost-effective way to accomplish these objectives. Let's look at some other mistakes that even effective field sales managers make in scheduling, planning, and participating in trade shows and exhibits:

DOLLAR-CONSUMING MISTAKES TO AVOID WITH TRADE SHOWS

1. Assuming that all such activities are a waste of time and money because of past experience with unproductive participation in trade shows (probably ones that were not thoroughly thought through and organized).

2. Making the decision to participate in shows as they come up instead of having an overall exhibit plan derived from the marketing plan wherein shows are just one medium for reaching identified prospect and customer groups.

3. Forgetting, as much marketing literature does, that you will be dealing with customers or people attending the show and not "markets." I've never seen a market that bought anything. Customers or people sign orders and it will be your product benefits addressing their needs that will get you current and future orders.

4. Not having specific objectives for the people who will be manning the booths or supervising other peripheral activities at the show. Not telling your salespeople well ahead of time who will be at the show, what customer benefits you will be featuring, and what you intend to accomplish there.

5. Not having ways to measure the accomplishment of these objectives and not having some kind of reward for their successful accomplishment.

6. Not having firm, but realistic, booth schedules—expecting people to spend all day in the booth and still perform at their peak or, at the other extreme, letting people wander in and out as they see fit.

7. Not having standards of conduct like guidelines on welcoming visitors, recording prospect information, sitting, slouching, smoking, drinking, or eating in the booth when on duty.

8. Not having an overall theme for the exhibit that is consistent with your other marketing messages through your salespeople and other media. Not having a phrase or sentence that acts as a "hook" to tell the show attendees that they should be interested in stopping at your booth and talking to you about your product.

9. Having no organized, planned method for capturing prospect names and other information in a convenient (for the prospect) way. Not using a standard form that ensures that you get all the information you will need for follow-up sales calls.

10. Not having a follow-up mechanism in place for the interest and leads that will be generated before the show starts so that the entire effort can be effectively and efficiently coordinated. Returning from the show exhausted, but with no action plan.

11. Assuming that people will find you if they really want to see you. Not sending out mailings and using other media to give your customers and prospects a good reason to come by your booth.

12. Not qualifying prospects adequately. Spending the same amount of time with each person who comes by the booth, or who can be persuaded to talk with you, instead of saving your best shots for the truly interested prospect who is capable of buying your product.

HOW TO SELECT BOOTH ATTENDANTS WHO CAN MAKE TRADE SHOWS PAY OFF

Now that you've made up your mind that the shows on your list are the right ones to help you accomplish your objectives and you are determined not to make the typical mistakes, you need to cast your production with the following players:

1. The salespeople who are the most experienced and knowledgeable about the product or product line being featured *and* who can provide the most effective demonstrations or explanations. (You may need to offer extra incentives to make these people feel comfortable away from their territories. If they are that good, they could probably make more money by not attending the show, unless they know that a lot of their customers and prospects will be there. Ensure their active participation by selling them on the benefits.)

2. The salespeople who can most benefit from the training experience. Be careful not to confuse this objective and the objective spelled out in item 1. You want to provide training opportunities for your people, but you can't afford to have inexperienced people talking to knowledgeable customers. You also need people who can close (if only for an appointment) quickly and efficiently.

3. The salespeople who really want to be there. Trade shows involve retail selling to strangers instead of comfortable sessions with known accounts. Some salespeople thrive in this kind of atmosphere and some shrivel. Since the booth attendants will be representing the company and developing prospects for everyone, you want people who are motivated to do more than look for their own customers.

4. Your home office people who have to talk with customers on the phone—sales administrators, customer service people, product service people, etc. Make participating in the show a reward for a job well done or a training experience, but distinguish between the objectives.

5. Home office people who have to prepare advertising or service material. Seeing a customer or prospect try to find the way through the literature and answering questions during a demonstration is a good way to ensure that future efforts don't take place in an ivory tower or a vacuum. Their specific booth duties should depend on their capability to present your product or service in a way that is consistent with your objectives.

6. Your engineering or manufacturing directors (or warehouse manager if your business depends heavily on distribution efficiency). Again, this is a good way for them to find out what the real world is like in a concentrated way and make their products more responsive to marketplace needs. Naturally, you'll lend moral support to the expenditure approval, but have them take the cost from their own budgets.

HOW TO PICK THE SHOWS TO SPEND YOUR EXHIBIT DOLLARS ON

It would be possible to spend a lifetime going from show to show, hitting a different show each time. If you concentrated on only those shows that might be applicable to your product line or marketing effort, you might cut this down to ten years.

Associations can report big attendance figures, but you have to be sure that they represent *your* prospects. This could be as little as 5 percent of the attendees in large, general interest shows, such as a home show, computer show, or builders' show to 20 percent in smaller, more focused shows. Here are some ways to narrow down the choices:

1. Get a list of all the shows your company has participated in over the last three years with the direct costs and, if possible, the results expressed as you would now measure results.

2. Get a list of all the shows your company could go to in the next year or two. This information could come from industry associations and publications. If this isn't readily available, the American Society of Association Executives (1575 I Street NW, Washington, D.C. 20005) could steer you in the right direction or you could check the *Encyclopedia of Associations* edited by Denise S. Akey and produced by Dale Research Company. You could also check with the Exhibit Designers & Producers Association (521 Fifth Avenue, New York, NY 10017) or the National Trade Show Exhibitors Association (4300-L Lincoln Avenue, Rolling Meadows, IL 60008).

   World Convention Dates (79 Washington Street, Hempstead, NY 11550) can give you international schedules, and Exhibits Schedule (633 Third Avenue, New York, NY 10017) can give you a pretty complete listing.

3. Compare the two lists and determine the possible universe of shows that you could attend. Then, based on your total marketing and trade show budget, begin paring it down by talking with your salespeople, former sales managers, customers, association executives, trade magazine publishers, and other field sales managers in your industry about their familiarity and experience with these shows.

4. Pick the ones whose objectives most closely match your sales and marketing objectives; whose attendees most resemble your market targets; and whose purpose comes closest to meeting your sales, prospect development, or exposure needs. It's nice to look busy at a trade show, but you want to make sure you are spending your time and money on qualified prospects.

SIX DOLLAR- AND TIME-SAVING STEPS TO TAKE
BEFORE THE SHOW

We're going to assume that you have an advertising department which takes care of all the details of developing, planning, building, shipping, and installing the exhibit. They should also arrange with the exposition manager for carpeting, lights, seating, etc., and handle the mechanics of shipping and set-up. They are the stage managers who arrange for the theatre and the set. Your job then is to produce and direct the effort, starting several months before the show date:

1. Dig out your marketing plan and look for those elements that will lend themselves to trade show exposure, producing prospects or selling. Do you have a new product or line that needs exposure to a lot of people quickly? Do you need to learn more about the actual field applications of the product? Will there be a lot of people there who have never been called upon by your salespeople and don't know your company?

2. Translate your marketing plan theme into a trade show theme and objective. If you want to sell 1,000 CAT scanners this year, your objective for the show could be to develop a prospect list of 2,000 with at least 200 qualified prospects with whom you have made tentative appointments for demonstration after the show.

3. Get out a mailing four or five months ahead of time telling your salespeople about your tentative plans and get their suggestions. Explain how the trade show efforts are tied into the overall plan for the year. (This assumes that you've thought this through. If you haven't, you could be wasting money on shows.)

4. If you haven't seen it, review the display by uncrating it or reviewing pictures. Do the graphics match your current theme? Are there the kinds of product display opportunities that you need for *this* year's marketing effort? Is the traffic pattern conducive to your intentions at the show? Is there enough room for the people you intend to have man the booth?

5. Does it take full advantage of the multi-dimensional show-and-tell opportunities a trade show offers? This is especially important if you have a product that won't fit in a salesperson's sample case. Remember that your prospects are coming to the show to see a product or an application that will solve their problems, not to admire elaborate, award-winning graphics.

    Your prospects are spending the money to come to the show to get new ideas and see new products sooner than they would filter down through your sales organization. Booth design is too often like advertisements that win awards for the advertising agency, but don't ask for the order and don't sell anything.

6. Poll some of your key customers and prospects to find out what *they* would like to find out or be shown. Besides helping you put the exhibit plans together, this may help you discover some new prospects or product opportunities you didn't know existed.

    I did this one time and found many customers asking for more information and demonstrations for a product line we didn't even make. Talk about discovering new opportunities—we went right to work to make sure this was included in our new product plans and eventually wound up adding it to our line on an OEM (original equipment manufacturer) basis.

Even if you don't get any new information or good ideas with this effort, you will have shown your salespeople and your customers that you really care about their thoughts and opinions. Armed with this information, you can now go to work setting your detailed show objectives and changing your booth layout if necessary. Here are some examples of the kinds of things you may want to include on your list:

CHECKLIST OF SHOW OBJECTIVES THAT WILL HELP YOU REACH YOUR SALES GOALS

1. Write orders at the show totaling at least $100,000, including $50,000 worth of spring special sales and $20,000 worth of advance orders on our new product. But remember, some shows are deliberately planned to discourage active order-writing.

2. Enhance our image as a quality, service-responsive organization, and not as a cheap and dirty supplier. Clear up any misconceptions that may exist.

3. Introduce a new or proposed new product and get as much prospect/customer reaction to any minor design changes needed before formal introduction.

4. Determine where our product should be positioned and who the really important buying influence is. Does the safety director or the human resources director, for example, make the final decision on this kind of product? Are there other buying influences?

5. Get some definite feedback on the reasons the product we introduced last fall isn't moving as well as we thought it would by now. Ask booth visitors a specific and direct question.

6. Give customers and prospects the opportunity to ask technical questions and, through this process, get the answers we need. Use this information to develop or revise instruction manuals, service manuals, and collateral material or brochures.

7. Find out from customers and prospects about new applications that can be incorporated in our collateral material and referred to our new product development committee, developed into feature articles for the trade press, or used as case histories.

8. Recruit a sales force of company people, a network of independent manufacturers' representatives, a group of dealers, or a number of distributors. Improve our communications with our existing groups.

9. Get a handle on what is happening in the marketplace and what our competitors are up to. Look for chinks in their armor that we can take advantage of.

10. Develop a mailing list of qualified prospects for a future marketing effort.
11. Become closer to our industry trade association by showing support through exhibiting in the show.

If you would like additional information on what is going on in the trade show business as a whole, contact the Trade Show Bureau, New Canaan, CT (203-966-7133).

You may find prospects in surprising places. I was involved in a trade show for office products. A toy buyer showed up at our booth. She had a great idea of how one of our products, with some different packaging, could be appropriate for her market. We attended the Toy Fair in New York the following February and wound up with a successful product in a market we hadn't even thought of previously.

In evaluating trade show audiences, try to separate those shows that attract "lookers" from those that attract buyers who need your product and have the money and ability to spend it on your product. Even if you don't attend the show, getting the mailing list of attendees could give you a good head start on a prospect list.

HOW TO BEHAVE AT THE BOOTH
TO BRING PROSPECTS YOUR WAY

If you've attended even one trade show, you've seen the mistakes the exhibitors make which indicate the absence of someone competent in charge and the lack of planning and organization:

1. The booth people are earnestly talking to each other and you get the impression that asking a question would be an interruption of their real purpose for being there.
2. The booth people are sitting down, reading magazines or product literature and you hesitate to interrupt their concentration.
3. Two booth attendants are smoking cigars and you can't stand cigar smoke.
4. The lone attendant looks exhausted and you'd like to see her go back to the hotel for a nap rather than tax her with your questions or order.
5. You ask if the word processor being shown will automatically word-wrap or right-hand justify and this complicated question throws the booth person into a tizzy since the "technical person" just left.
6. The booth attendant is talking on the phone, long distance, so you don't want to take him away from a phone call that is obviously more important than you.
7. You ask for information or a demonstration as the mailing promised, but all the booth attendant wants you to do is sign an order for the special

being offered. Or, you get a perfunctory run-through since you are not the attendant's customer.

8. When you ask to be put on the mailing list or have the local representative call you for an appointment, the booth attendant whips out a used cocktail napkin and promises you that the information will promptly get to the right person.

9. The booth is too crowded or looks too empty. Think about how many times you have driven by a restaurant and decided not to stop because there were too few or too many cars parked outside?

Let's look at some winning techniques you can use to avoid mistakes:

1. Get out a written sales bulletin at least six weeks before the show to salespeople and others who will attend and those who will not, explaining your purpose and spelling out the guidelines as discussed below.

2. Get out a mailing to your customers and prospects at least a month before the show telling them that you will be there, what you will be featuring, where you will be (booth number if you have it), and what hotel you will be staying at. Send a copy of this mailing to your salespeople with the bulletin suggested in item 1 above and tell them who it is going to and when.

   Give your prospects a specific and powerful reason to come to your booth. Being as specific as possible about the reason or product you will be featuring will get you the most qualified prospects, for whom your booth should be a must, and ensure that you get a minimum of souvenir collectors. You could use a draw, from a new product demonstration to a free sample or even a free T-shirt, depending on your product line and target audience.

   If you are involved in a start-up venture with a brand new product, get a list of association members or those who attended the last show. If even this isn't possible, rent a mailing list of your likely prospects and get the show mailing out to them. Among the sources you might use for this are:

   American Businesses Lists, P.O. Box 27347, Omaha, NE 68127

   Compilers Plus, Inc., 2 Penn Place, Pelham Manor, NY 10803

   Concord Reference Books, Inc., Subsidiary of Whitney Communications Corporation, 850 Third Avenue, New York, NY 10022

   U.S. Business Directories, 5707 South 86th Circle, Omaha, NE 68127

   If these tentative prospects don't attend the show, you will still have awakened some interest in your new product and plans and given it some credibility. Enhance the mailing and your ability to follow through with a reply card that will put the prospects on your mailing list for further information. Include a "Please have your salesperson call me for an appointment about my _____ application." and a "My need is _____ (immediate, soon, future) sections on the reply card.

3. Hold a meeting with everyone who will be representing your company at the show the day before the show opens or the day it opens, if there is time, and make the guidelines even clearer. Rehearse situations. Role play. Try to find flaws in your plans or methods of presenting the product and discuss ways to eliminate them. Discuss the kind of people who will be attending and what is likely to turn them on. Review the procedures for collecting prospect information and making appointments for the field salespeople.

4. Have a firm schedule for booth duty that is written and posted. Break the schedule up into shifts of no more than two to four hours depending on the type of show and the people you have available. Appoint a captain or leader for every booth shift and make sure that every team includes at least one technically expert person if your product or presentation is a complicated one, and possibly an administrative back-up person.

    A four-person team might include a sales pro, a technical person, a sales trainee, and a receptionist and information recorder. Rehearse their roles with them ahead of time and make sure they understand and respect each other's position. Assign specific people to specific duties like filling out prospect cards, making appointments for the field salespeople, making sure the booth is neat and clean with ashtrays emptied, and making sure there is an adequate supply of literature.

    Allow your people to trade off times, but not days. The idea is to keep booth attendants at their peak efficiency and about three to four hours is the maximum time for most people. Don't let your people trade shifts so that they'll get a whole day off in exchange for working a whole day. This defeats your purpose.

    I once had two district managers come up with what they thought was a fantastic idea. They proposed to arrange their booth schedules so that each manager had a full day off to tour San Francisco in exchange for working a full day at the booth. This wasn't the idea of the schedule, so I nixed it. They would both have been exhausted by the last half of their shifts and not doing me or the company any good.

    On the other hand, it made sense that people from Nashville and Baltimore would want to spend time in San Francisco, so I made them a deal—hit the objectives for their shifts and they could have the day on me *after* the show and I would explain, if necessary, to their spouses that this was part of the show deal. One made it and one didn't. One stayed over (on me) and the other on his own tab, but in the winner's hotel room.

5. Have a nearby suite where your people can gather or rest when they are temporarily off duty or when the show is over for the day. Use it for quiet meetings away from the exhibit floor, but have your people schedule the meetings with a coordinator so you don't have two competitors in the room at the same time.

   Remember that the decision-makers you will invite to the suite can get a free drink at 200 other suites, so have something to show them besides a bar. Have a more elaborate product display or a video tape that is shown only to the privileged few.

   Use the suite for post-mortems on the day with your people and to prepare for the next morning meeting. Whether you have invited customers or prospects to "drop up and see us anytime" or have a planned party, schedule people for suite duty and have ground rules for this important part of the show activity schedule.

6. Have at least a half-hour meeting before the show opens the following day to review the ground rules again, deal with any situations that occurred the previous day, and share any sales techniques that seemed to work well. Use the time to announce the results of the previous day's "contest" and compliment the people who performed particularly well. You might have a coffee and doughnut session at the suite for those who didn't get up in time for breakfast.

7. Invite your independent manufacturers' representatives to all functions that your company salespeople will attend. Invite them, but don't demand they attend these functions unless you are paying for them to be at the show and you both have a clear understanding of their duties ahead of time.

   (See Chapter 16 and the subheadings, "3. Local or Regional Shows and Exhibits" and "4. National Conventions.") Remember that your IMRs have their own agenda and their own set of priorities.

8. Set rules of conduct—no sitting unless talking with a customer or prospect, no smoking when a customer or prospect is present, no eating or drinking in the booth, no talking on the phone if a visitor is waiting, and dropping conversations with colleagues if a visitor is even approaching the booth.

9. Tell your people what you expect from them in quantitative terms—so many dollars in orders written, so many complete demonstrations held, so many qualified prospect names recorded, etc. Keep track of the performance and announce the standings at your evening or morning meetings.

10. Make it a contest with a prize for the person doing the best job on these expectations as long as it doesn't get in the way of the overall objectives. You don't, for example, want to give a prize for most orders written and have booth attendants ignore people who may not want to place an order that day.

PROSPECT FOLLOW-THROUGH FORM

Show or Other Activity _____

Name _____ Title _____

Company _____

Address _____

City _____ State _____ Zip _____

Phone _____ Alternate _____

Type of Business _____

_____

Area(s) of Product Interest _____

_____

Specific Applications _____

_____

_____

Add to Mailing List _____ Have Salesperson Call _____

Send More Information On _____

Comments _____

_____

_____

Information Taken By _____

White copy—Salesperson   Pink copy—Regional Manager
               Canary copy—Advertising Department

Figure 12.1

11. To get everyone working as a team, provide a modest reward (dinner for two on you in the person's home territory) if the group meets the overall objectives. Or, set individual deals that make sense to the people participating (see paragraph 4 above). Or do both.

12. Have a simple but effective way to capture prospect information. Use a preprinted form like that shown in Figure 12.1 to get all the information. Use a two- or three-part form so the salesperson can get a copy and the prospect can be added to the mailing list.

13. Caution your people about late night merry-making since you expect them to be at their best during their booth duty, suite duty, or information-gathering times, but make sure you have also allowed the opportunity for them to have fun.

    After four or five days at a trade show and convention your people will probably want to head for the airport as quickly as they can. You might plan a group dinner in a private or semi-private dining area the night *before* the show closes. You all have responsibilities to entertain customers, but there is no reason not to reserve one evening as *your* night to relax, let your hair down, and regroup for the next day and the follow-through back at the office or in the territory.

14. Work out the final details of your follow-through effort which will have been refined based on what you learned at the show. Have a meeting with the salespeople there on how they are going to follow up in their territories to get their ideas and share them in a sales bulletin to all salespeople which is to be prepared before you leave town.

    After being at a convention all week or at least several days, the last thing you want to do is spend another day in the same hotel room or suite. You'll find, however, that doing so will pay off in efficiency and peace of mind during the next two weeks. It may even make sense to your family.

15. Carefully track your follow-up efforts and the results you get. Develop a cost-per-prospect contact and a cost-per-sold order so that you can weigh trade show costs and results against cost and results from other media. See if the general rule that you can close in an average of two calls instead of five holds true for you.

HOW TO MAXIMIZE THE BENEFITS
OF YOUR BOOTH ATTENDANT'S EFFORTS

Assuming you are the top-ranked person assigned to "work" the show, you are in charge. This doesn't mean that you spend every hour the show is open at the booth. In fact, this would be a waste of your time and an indication that you aren't doing the job that only you, as the person in charge, can do. Let's look at some of these nonbooth responsibilities you have or should have at trade shows:

1. Setting the overall objectives for the show and the standards that will be observed by all participants.

2. Conducting the post-mortem sessions each day after the show and holding the pre-show morning meetings. Congratulating and complimenting the people who won the contests or otherwise did excellent jobs.

3. Being available for key customer meetings or entertainment (or a combination of both as in a dinner meeting) arranged by your district or regional managers.

4. Negotiating with other vendors at the show for products you could market on an OEM (original equipment manufacturer) basis or for joint marketing efforts.

5. Being the company spokesperson at association meetings or other activities, possibly including duty as a panel member in a discussion group or as a speaker.

6. Spending enough time at the booth and at other booths on the show floor to get a feel for what is happening and how to relate this to marketing plan implementation.

I know a president of a company who feels (or at least used to feel) that he should be on duty at the booth every hour the show was open. He had a back problem, so he wound up exhausted and irritable by mid-afternoon and not in shape to do his real job—those things identified in paragraphs 1 through 5 above. Other people can effectively man the booth under your direction. You have more important responsibilities at the trade show.

IN CLOSING. . .

A lot of questions are raised about dress at a trade show. Depending on the show, many of your prospects will come casually dressed. There are few reasons, however, why all your male attendees should not be attired in ties and coats, or possibly company blazers.

The blazer has a lot going for it. It makes for an easily enforceable dress standard and it makes it easy for a prospect to identify the booth personnel. It also provides company identification when your people are roaming the floor or getting a cup of coffee.

In their efforts to come up with a "theme," exhibitors will dress their people up in pirate costumes, sailor suits, police uniforms, or cowboy outfits. That's fine for the kid shows, but your prospects come to a trade show to get information they can use to make money in their business, and dressing up as though you were putting on a musical comedy detracts from your objectives and theirs.

Sales literature is another question. I used to feel that we should have enough literature on hand to give people anything they wanted to carry away from the booth. Then, after one show had closed, I was walking down the hotel corridor at the time the housekeeping people were cleaning up the rooms.

Something familiar was sticking out of one of the trash containers—one of our brochures. Checking further, I found many more. On the next floor, I found that all the trash containers were loaded with left-behind literature—materials that had cost $1 to $5 a copy to produce.

From then on, we had enough literature available at the booth to give copies to people who requested it, but made it a point to offer to send material later.

13

How to Get Your Major Account — And Make Your Career

As a regional manager, you could spend from 30 percent to 60 percent of your time on sales administrative duties, formal training programs, and in-the-field coaching of your district managers. As a national field sales manager, you could spend 50 percent to 80 percent of your time on all the field and office activities we've covered so far.

The balance of your time should be spent with key accounts, with or without your district or regional managers:

- You are the only field sales manager (in your area) your salespeople have.
- You are their only direct leader.
- You may have particular expertise that others on the sales force or even in the company do not.
- Unless you have a strong product management or brand management group, you are the logical person to coordinate the activities of your peers in engineering and manufacturing.

For these reasons, there are some chores that you have to be involved in actively and some that only you can handle.

You must be careful in performing your field sales role to confine your activities to only those things that you, and you alone, are needed for. Otherwise, you'll find that your entire field sales force would just love to delegate their responsibilities to you. They would be delighted to get themselves off the hook and get you on it.

Let's look at some of the kinds of customers and situations where your involvement is necessary and appropriate.

12 PROVEN TECHNIQUES FOR IDENTIFYING AND PROFITING FROM KEY ACCOUNTS

1. National wholesalers or distributors. These customers sell into several territories and need the attention of the national coordinator. If you don't have a wholesale sales manager, this person is you.

    In many cases, your job will be to sell the national headquarters on giving you and your people a "hunting license," and your people will have to sell the customer's branch managers.

    Some companies give the job of covering a national distributor headquartered in Chicago to the Chicago salesperson, manufacturers' rep, or the midwest regional manager. Don't do this. You would be insulting the customer, depreciating his importance to you, and not getting the national scope results you need.

2. When you are involved in a pyramid sale. This happens when you are getting a new product off the ground or getting an existing product into a new industry. If you can sell the first customer and show a successful application, you can open up the rest of the industry to your product, account by account.

    This first sale has national implications, so it should be personally directed by you. You will be dealing at a higher level than if it were an already existing product or concept for your customer and it will be up to you to direct the repetition of the success in other territories with other prospects. You should also be the one to coordinate the efforts of the home office team that will be involved with technical support.

3. When you are testing a new product or market and it's not a whole new application—just a new one for you. Again, the success of the test will have national implications, so it's too important to be left in the hands of the local salesperson.

4. When there is a long (one- to two-year) selling cycle. If you are selling incentive programs, for example, that will have a long-term impact on the prospect, you will want to actively manage the project and orchestrate the close. Here are some of the steps toward the final close you will want to monitor, even though your local salespeople will carry out the details:

    a. The salesperson will get all the information he can about the prospect, the market environment the prospect operates in, and the company's requirements. You might provide the salesperson with a checklist of things to cover and include based on past projects and presentations.

b. Arouse the prospect's interest in your proposition at the highest level. A new company-wide computer system, for example, might involve the president, chairman, and even the board of directors of the prospect company. After some initial preparatory work, you might even want to get your company president involved in the first meeting with the prospect company's president.

When you get the presidents together, leave them alone for a period of time while you work with your local salesperson to pursue some detail of the project. I've found that presidents usually enjoy talking with other presidents with whom they might be doing business.

They both have lonely jobs and often enjoy commiserating with each other or discussing large issues that your salespeople wouldn't understand. Fostering this kind of relationship will put you many points ahead in conducting the survey and closing the sale and won't do your career any harm either. It's one of the few ways you can legitimately end-run your boss and get close to the head of your company.

c. You present the benefits to the prospect company, explain your unique qualifications to meet the prospect's needs, and close the meeting by getting permission to make a study.

d. You will want to supervise the study, even though your local people and some people from your home office will do the actual work.

e. You develop the final proposal and presentation. This may be a one-meeting close or it may take place over a series of meetings. You will orchestrate the close that will probably involve the presidents of both companies.

5. Other situations where a team effort is involved to develop the situation or close it. With small accounts or small potential sales, it may be fine to have your home office peer work with your local salesperson. When the stakes are larger, or you are asking for a special favor, your involvement is necessary to make sure that sales still controls the account and the situation, and for political reasons.

I've seen instances where the technical person has taken over the meeting with a prospect to the detriment of the sale. What is the poor local salesperson to do with the big engineering director from the home office? He can't risk alienating one of your peers even if mistakes are being made. Your involvement keeps sales in control of the situation and the account.

On the other hand, being involved together in the field on a project with a customer or prospect can be an excellent and unique opportunity to cement and solidify relationships with managers in other functional areas of the company. You and your people may not see your peers socially, but if you are out of town, it's logical to have dinner or do other things together. You, your peers, and your people may come off this kind of field effort realizing that you all really are pretty nice people and wind up being grateful for having had the opportunity to find this out.

6. Other pivotal sales opportunities. You might be selling a relatively small telephone system to the branch office of a large, national company. If you handle this opportunity properly, you just might parlay it into a national account sale. This is too important to be left to the local person who will still get credit for the sale.

7. When your particular expertise is required. You may, for example, be selling a product to a distributor or mass marketer who wants to pursue television advertising for your product. Your company may have never done this, but *you* have experience with this medium and the complicated considerations that are involved from other companies for whom you have worked.

    It's fair for you to get actively involved in the kind of sales effort that has elements that are over the heads of your local people. However, use it as a training experience for your salespeople so that they can do more of the work next time and grow from the experience.

8. When you are pursuing an idea that is uniquely yours. You may have this crazy idea that one of your industrial products, usually sold in a completely different way and to a completely different market, could, with some modifications, be ideal for the toy market or the giftware market.

    It might be unfair to ask your salespeople to spend time on what might be a wild goose chase that does nothing to contribute to their achievement of quota. And they won't pursue it with anything near the vigor and enthusiasm you will. Naturally, when it works as well as you always knew it would, you'll delegate the follow-through to your people and give them the credit for the successes they achieve. You may even find many of them taking credit for the origination of the idea in the first place.

9. When you are getting into a new market and your salespeople are scared or at least apprehensive. Whether you have experience in this market or not, this will be a good time for you to teach by example. Research the market, talk to other sales managers who sell in this market and do your other homework so you'll be prepared to look good and be able to show your salespeople how easy and nonscary it really is.

10. When there is a limited market for your product. You may have a computer-controlled process for synthetic rubber plants and know from

your research that there are only 100 such operations in the country. Since each of these prospects is very important, you may want to be involved in every sale even if you have your salespeople do all of the legwork on the detail projects involved in pulling it off. In these types of situations, you should follow a process similar to that described in item 4.

11. Where there is a unique problem with an important account that, because your communication process is so good, has been brought to your attention. Finding out that your salesperson has been thrown out and told never to come back is a reliable indication that there may be a problem. It could be a major misunderstanding, a personality conflict, or your salesperson may have just left the purchasing agent's daughter at the altar.

Even if you feel that the problem will go away after a few days, you'll get points for yourself, your company, and your salesperson if you treat it as an important issue and get on the phone right away to tell your customer that his well-being and feelings are important to you. You may also be the only one who can mediate in this kind of situation. Offering to fly out to the customer's location "tomorrow" will make an impact although you will seldom have to go to this extreme.

If your salesperson is just enforcing company policy, you obviously have to stand behind the person and the decision made. You can, however, as an objective manager, get the customer to focus on the issue and try to resolve it on the basis of the issue rather than killing the messenger.

You have the advantage of some time elapsing since the blow-up, and some perceived objectivity because you haven't been involved in all the details because of your position as the big wheel from the home office. Handling it well will let your sales force know that they do, indeed, have a leader at the helm.

Your job, if it really is a matter of enforcing company policy as opposed to your salesperson's having humiliated a customer in some way, like overtly flirting with her husband at a cocktail party, or returning to the hotel with his seventeen-year-old daughter at 6:00 A.M. at a local trade show, is to find a way for both parties to save face and pave the way for a productive future relationship with the customer.

I once had a situation occur when the district manager, quite properly, refused to accept the return of a piece of equipment without a restocking and refurbishing charge. It had obviously been abused by the dealer's customer. This dealer was important to us and his customer was important to him.

After some sympathetic listening and negotiating, I made a deal with the customer (our dealer wouldn't let my district manager within 100 miles of his customer) to accept the charge in exchange for a payment for a "testimonial" on our equipment—every other piece of equipment that was installed was working well. We didn't make a cash payment—that would have been too obvious. Instead, we gave the dealer's customer three months worth of free supplies for the equipment.

Naturally, the district manager personally communicated the settlement we had with our dealer's customer and, at my insistence, took credit for it. So here's what happened:

a. Our dealer's customer was happy. She knew she was wrong but was looking for a face-saving way out of the predicament. We gave it to her. She could go to her boss and talk about how she had agreed to a small charge but had wangled a bigger amount out of us in supplies value.

b. Our dealer was happy. He knew he was wrong, but had to put up a show for his customer. We also gave him, with his customer, a lot of credit for solving the problem.

c. Our district manager was back in the good graces of our dealer. He, after all, had solved the problem as far as anyone was concerned.

d. We had a nice testimonial letter to use in our advertising and collateral material and a dealer customer whom we had hooked on our supplies for the equipment which the customer had not, until then, been buying from us.

As every customer service manager worth his salt knows, a serious problem is nothing more than a cloud with a fantastic opportunity as its lining. They welcome these kinds of situations as should effective field sales managers. Paraphrasing John Gardiner, in his book, *Self-Renewal*: "We are faced with a number of great opportunities brilliantly disguised as insoluble problems."

As an effective field sales manager, you might even look for these kinds of opportunities and work on your techniques to solve them well. Situations like the ones described above are the stuff legends are made of. You may not particularly want to be legendary, but these kinds of legends *can* add to your perceived effectiveness as a leader.

12. When, by the very amount of the actual or potential business, the account is an "AA" account. (This means an even more important account than the "A" accounts described in Chapter 4.)

If you have 1,000 accounts and you have 200 who account for 70 percent to 80 percent of your business, you probably have something like five to ten accounts that deserve the "AA" rating and, therefore, your personal attention. This doesn't mean that you get in the way of your salespeople, who are charged with the ultimate responsibility for getting sales from these accounts, or that you take over any of the actual account responsibility.

Your role is that of a "supernumerary," adding to rather than replacing anything your salespeople do and making the accounts feel as important as they really are.

This can sometimes get a bit sticky. Your customer knows very well how important he is and knows that he merits your attention. At the same time, however, you have to find a diplomatic way to ensure that most routine matters go through your district manager. You also have to make it clear that, whatever your involvement or contact with the customer, your district manager is responsible for the sales volume and whatever else happens. Here are some things you can do to make sure you tread this tightrope warily:

a. Sit down with your district and regional managers and, together, work out the ground rules. You can't accept their telling you to keep your hands off—they will handle everything. The account is just too important to do this and the account deserves home office attention. Instead, make lists of the kinds of things you will be involved in and the kinds of things you will leave to them.

b. Make it clear that whatever supernumerary or home office role you play, *they* are responsible for the account and that you will communicate with them on everything you intend to do and will even take direction from them on issues that should be local issues.

c. Meet with the customer, tell him that he is important and that *you* want to be involved in the most effective way. Involve your district and regional managers in this discussion.

No matter what kinds of games you may have to play as a field sales manager, there is no substitute for an open and honest face-to-face discussion of the issues with the objective of both parties walking away from the table as winners. Suggest to the customer however, that there are some things that the district or regional managers can accomplish more quickly and more easily than you can. Have the customer suggest specific things he will go to the district and regional managers for. Find out if there is anything else the customer needs or wants from you, the home office, or the district and regional managers.

d. Work out your own list of things you will be in touch with the customer on—new pricing policies, new freight policies, etc., and have your district and regional managers agree on the parameters.

e. Consider having these "AA" customers as the nucleus of a "Customer Advisory Council." If you have nine or ten, you could have one-third of them serve each year with other members drawn from your other customers.

f. Entertain them—at trade shows and when you are in town for another purpose. Naturally, there will be occasions when your district or regional managers should make the arrangements. Remember from Chapter 12 that one of your most important roles at trade shows is engaging in this kind of activity.

As you can see, there are all kinds of ways to increase sales through your involvement with your key accounts without getting in the way of your district and regional managers and without taking them off the hook for results with these customers. Because it's natural for your people to want to delegate their responsibility to you, given half a chance, you have to watch this carefully.

In the next section, we'll discuss how you achieve a balance by looking at some things you should *not* be involved in.

HOW TO AVOID TIME-WASTING SITUATIONS WITH MAJOR ACCOUNTS

1. When your involvement is requested by a district or regional manager who clearly wants to delegate some responsibilities to you. Explain again what you intend your role to be and make it clear that the district and regional managers have primary responsibility for what happens with the account. You are just a (presumably) useful supernumerary.

    If they ask you to get involved in a credit hold situation, tell them to work it out with the credit department and get back to you only if there doesn't seem to be any resolution. If they ask you to supervise a service activity, tell them to work it out with the engineering or service department. If they want you to do a routine product demonstration or hold a normal sales meeting, remind them that this is part of their job responsibility. If they try to get off the hook in presenting a price increase or more stringent freight terms policy, tell them that they are responsible for selling the customer on all company policies.

2. When the customer is calling you for special favors. This is a tough one. You always have to say, "Yes, but . . ." instead of "No" and make sure that you can give the same to any other customer on a pro-rata basis that you are giving to a major account. (The Federal Trade Commission has some pretty specific things to say about this.)

    For example, if a big dealer or distributor customer wants you to pay for an advertisement, you can say that you would be happy to if he will commit to a purchase of so many dollars of your product. You can then turn around and offer other customers the same percentage deal on the product line, assuming, of course, that this fits your overall marketing program and that you have reserved a part of your budget for things like this.

3. When the customer or his people are calling you for routine stuff as checking on a shipment date or to place an order. You don't want to do anything to imply that their order or shipment isn't important, but it

doesn't make sense for you to get involved with this. Tell the customer that you will get back to him and then have your customer service person do it, telling the customer that she is returning your phone call and making good on your promise to get back.

Suggestion: When the customer calls, such as for some product information, say "You know, something just came in in the last couple of days on a new application that might be just what you're looking for. I haven't had a chance to go through this, but Joe (your district manager) is thoroughly familiar with this. Let me check it out and *one of us* will get back to you."

Naturally, Joe gets back to the customer with all the right information that you said you didn't have, whether you did or not. After a few such calls, the customer just might get the idea that it would make more sense to call Joe in the first place.

Your job now, as supernumerary, is to make a courtesy call back to the customer and ask if she got all the information from Joe that she wanted. You've given the customer the deserved attention, but kept your district manager in the loop so that, maybe next time, the customer will call Joe direct on things that don't really require your attention.

At the same time, you can't forget that a part of your job is to deliberately *coddle* important customers so they feel like important customers and will remain important customers. Make them feel that you're doing the best job you can to get them what they want and never make them feel that they are being sloughed off. Use your time, however limited, to give them the kinds of things they want and need that only *you* are capable of providing. It may take a while, but if you are consistent, you just might get the message across to the benefit of all concerned.

STRATEGIES AND TECHNIQUES FOR MAXIMIZING THE PROFITABILITY OF TIME SPENT WITH MAJOR ACCOUNTS

You have the same kind of balancing act here that you have with most of your other activities and responsibilities—a full-time job in the field with the major accounts and a full-time job in the office doing the kinds of things to provide the support to them that is part of your responsibility. You need to be effective at both. Here are some of the ways you could manage to get 75 percent of each of these jobs done:

1. Set up your own A, B, C stratification scheme similar to that suggested in Chapter 4 of this book. Not all your key accounts are of equal importance, so you have the same kind of problem addressed in that chapter that your salespeople have.

2. Weave in your key account *prospects* as well. Just as it's important for your salespeople to spend 20 or so percent of their time prospecting, it's necessary that you do this also.

3. Set a definite schedule for keeping in touch with these major accounts—every two weeks for some, every month for others, etc., and stick to the schedule.

4. Remember that you have at least three tools available for "keeping in touch"—letters, phone calls, and personal visits. With the capability and flexibility of today's computer and word processing equipment, you could easily write one letter to all your key customers and individually tailor it to each.

5. At trade shows, conventions, and other industry get-togethers, start way ahead of time with the A accounts from the select group to make your plans to meet with them. If one of your C accounts is booked solid for the period of the event, it's no great loss and you will have gotten credit for asking. But you want to make sure you get together with as many of your A accounts as you can.

6. Consider inviting two noncompeting customers on the same night or for the same luncheon meeting, especially if they are from widely different parts of the country or different kinds of companies within your industry and wouldn't normally have had the chance to meet each other. They should enjoy and appreciate the opportunity and remember you kindly for having brought them together. You will also have at least doubled your effectiveness in time spent with both.

7. Keep a profile sheet on your key customers' particular interests and make it a point to save material that you run across that they may find interesting. If a customer is thinking about going to a combined CAD/CAM (computer-aided design/computer-aided manufacturing) system and you see an article in an airline magazine discussing the subject, send it off to the customer with a personal "thought you would be interested" note.

   If you know that your customer is a tennis nut and you see an article on a new material being used for tennis racquets, mail it out. The material may not even relate to anything you are selling, but this personal attention is appreciated and you will have made it even clearer that your interest in the customer is in helping to solve problems. Send a copy to your district and regional managers so they know what you're up to and will get the idea that they, too, can do this kind of thing to their advantage with their customers.

8. To be effective, keep your selling activities subtle and low-key, especially if your regional manager or district manager has quota responsibility for the account. Your role is not to sell directly, but to do things like discussing pertinent industry events and trends, philosophizing about their meaning and significance for the customer, and being helpful because you have a wider scope of exposure than your customer usually does.

You could bring to the customer and interpret copies of industry studies. This should help to set you apart from all the other people calling on the customer. You could bring along copies or excerpts from some work your market research people have done that relates to the customer's problems. *Your* job is to sell by providing solutions while your district and regional managers write the orders.

9. In the beginning of your involvement with an account, lavish a lot of time and attention with personal calls, weekly follow-up phone calls with information you promised to provide when you were there, and letters confirming in writing what you promised.

   Then, you can let a couple of months go by before you have to see the person again. With the right kind of attention up front, the customer will get the impression at the start that you're "always" right there. Doing it right may cause the customer whom you feel you may have neglected to ask "So soon?" when you call for an appointment. It will seem that you were just there for a personal call last week.

10. Continue to check your activities and involvement to be sure that you are doing the things that only you can do. It's easy to get enlisted for things your district managers can do and should do.

IN CLOSING...

Given the precious little time left from other tasks, your time for key accounts has to be spent on the right accounts at the right time. Devoting time in any other way is wasteful and, at times, counterproductive.

14

A Profit-Wise
Guide to Using
Distribution Channels

For most products, different channels of distribution are more appropriate than others at different stages of the life cycle. Often, the field sales manager is the person who must recognize the arrival of the product or product line at these stages and implement or recommend changes in the distribution strategy.

There are some exceptions, of course, to the product line process or progress. A new brand of toothpaste will probably not be sold directly to the end user, tube by tube, and wholesalers will not stock jumbo jets for resale to the end user by retailers.

On the other hand, in the late 70s and even early 80s few people foresaw that computers would be sold by distributors, dealers, and even mass marketers. But all this product was doing was following a natural evolution that happens with many products.

HOW TO APPLY THE RIGHT SALES-PRODUCING APPROACH TO A PRODUCT OR PRODUCT LINE

As has been the case with computers, there are four stages in the evolutionary process for most products.

THE FOUR STAGES OF SELLING

1. Direct sale by company salespeople where personal selling effort is the main way the message is carried to potential end users.

2. Sale through specialized, "franchised" or "protected territory" dealers where the selling effort is channeled through these dealers; they are given a lot of support by the manufacturer and carry a good deal of the weight of the advertising and selling effort.

3. Sale through open line dealers and, possibly, wholesalers or distributors who carry literally thousands of similar or dissimilar products. They can't afford the advertising effort for a particular product line, so a lot of the marketing effort falls back to the manufacturer, at least in terms of "umbrella" support which will be discussed further below.

4. Sale through mass marketers where there is no outside selling, but *advertising* which induces the customer to come in to buy the product. In most cases this advertising is provided or supported by the manufacturer in the form of "co-op advertising" programs.

Figure 14.1 illustrates this phenomenon in the form of a pyramid since the potential users grow larger in number as the product proceeds through the life cycle from the top of the pyramid to the bottom.

The Direct Selling Stage

When a new product is developed that differs substantially from anything that preceded it, it often requires direct, one-on-one selling by a specially trained company sales force. They are selling a *concept* as opposed to a product. It also requires a lot of advertising and other support from the manufacturer.

Consider the first calculator sold. It took more than an advertisement in the newspaper to convince the accountant that this several-hundred-dollar whirring machine with all its wheels, buttons, and springs would replace his two-cent pencil. The concept had to be sold by knowledgeable direct salespeople, and skilled service back-up capability had to be provided by the manufacturer of the machine.

The Specialized or "Franchised" Dealer Selling Stage

Later, as the concept becomes accepted and, perhaps, the product simplified, there is a broader group of potential customers. The manufacturer can choose to try to reach these prospects with a direct sales force, but it's expensive. The price of the product usually comes down as the demand increases, and margins, in absolute dollar terms, shrink. It becomes less economical to sell the product through salespeople who have only this item in their bags to offer to customers. It also becomes more appropriate to shift the burden of advertising and service support to the dealer group.

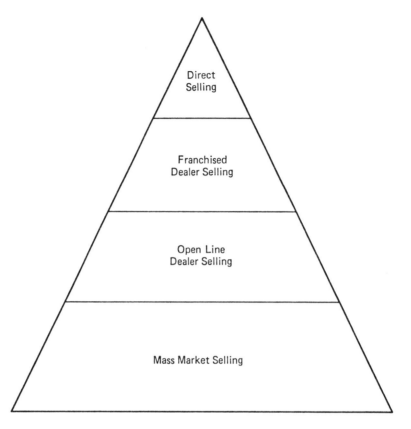

Figure 14.1

It wasn't long after their introduction before calculators were being sold by office machines dealers. They could spread the cost of the sales call over a line of products and had developed the capability to service other kinds of office machines. They also had a reputation in their business areas and a following among prospects developed with other machines products. So, "indirect distribution" appeared in the sale of calculators through these specialized dealers.

The Open Line Dealer Selling Stage

As the concept of the product becomes more widely established, the scariness of the novelty goes out of it. Potential customers have more familiarity with it and increase the demand by going from one company that is using the product to another that has not yet started to. The base has broadened, the technical skills required to sell it become less, and it becomes just one more product to be added to the repertory of nonspecialized or open line dealers.

In the case of the calculator, the dealer who sold pencils and paper clips or even office furniture began to get calls for the product from his customer base. It was, after all, another product used in the office. The open line office products dealer salesperson with a wide range of products called on the potential customer a lot more often than a specialized salesperson could and had already developed a relationship with the customer, so the customer base broadened even further. Service problems became minimized through technical improvements so anyone with a little skill could "sell" the calculator.

The substitution of electronic components for electromechanical wheels and levers reduced the service problems and dropped the price even further. The calculator became a product that a broad base of people were asking for and the smart office products salespeople began to learn enough about it to answer questions and write up orders from their existing customers.

The Mass Marketing Stage

At some point, many products become so inexpensively priced or develop such a broad appeal and acceptance that creatively selling the concept or even the product is almost unnecessary. The important thing at this stage is that the product be as widely and easily available as possible.

Advertisements announcing the availability of the product and inviting end users to come in to try and to buy the product replace product knowledge-based selling effort. Service demands are lower, factory-supplied service capability becomes streamlined, and sometimes the price of the product is so low that it is easier to replace the product than fix it. (Try to find an appliance repair shop that can fix your toaster for less than it would cost to buy a new one with more features.)

Obviously, this happened to the calculator some time ago. Within five years of the introduction of the four-function, electronic, hand-held calculator for about $400, drug stores alone were selling more calculators than the entire office machines industry combined. Some savants are predicting the day (if it isn't already here) when a calculator, already smaller than a pack of cigarettes, will cost less.

SELLING FOR MAXIMUM PROFIT THROUGHOUT THE PRODUCT LIFE CYCLE

Besides the calculator, we've seen the computer go through the same life cycle stages from direct selling, through the specialized and open line dealer selling stages, to mass market distribution. It may be only a matter of time before you drop in to your local drug or convenience store to pick up an extra computer terminal for the bedroom.

This suggests that any effective sales planning strategy must take the distribution channel into account as an important tactical element. It suggests that continuing to operate in the channel you are now using or used last year may not be appropriate for tomorrow's selling environment. Further, selecting the right distribution channel requires that you correctly identify your product's life cycle stage.

There are two other reasons why this determination requires very careful deliberation:

1. There is usually no turning back from a decision to go to the next step down on the pyramid any more than you can rewrite history. Every manufacturer I know who has wearied of the different kinds of problems involved in selling through an indirect channel and has reverted to direct selling has gone back to the indirect channel and its problems with lack of control and other issues or has gone out of business.

2. There is no holding back the tide that inexorably sweeps products through the pyramid shown in Figure 14.1. If you don't respond to what is happening in the marketplace, your competitors will.

The ideal situation, of course, is to have sales forces active in all four channels. This way, a new product can be introduced at the top of the pyramid and work its way down as prices fall, demand increases, marketplace realities dictate this, and competition begins to make inroads in your marketplace through these other channels.

It is essential, however, that this be recognized as a firm and consistent company philosophy. If it is not, the established sales force will be reluctant to let go of a product line even if it has clearly overstayed its welcome at any particular stage of the product life cycle.

In order to be able to let products flow down to the next step on the pyramid, there have to be new products added at the top so the importance of any distribution channel sales force increases rather than diminishes. There needs to be a transition period when a product is handed off from one distribution channel to another, but when two sales forces claim the same product line, at least for a limited period of time, conflict has to result that does no one but your competitors any good. This kind of conflict usually arises because the direct sales force, for example, is getting no new products.

To enable you to perform your own "appropriateness of the distribution channel(s)" audit, we'll look at these channels, their advantages, disadvantages, and cost. We'll discuss when they make sense and what you have to do to work in them.

For the purpose of our discussion, the terms "distributor" and "wholesaler" are interchangeable. They refer to a business that buys from manufacturers and resells to "dealers" or "retailers." The dealers and retailers sell to the end user. (The term "distributor" may be used at times as a generic to apply to all three groups.) Wholesalers and distributors, as we have defined the terms, *may* sometimes sell to end users and are then called "dual distributors." Dealers usually refer to dual distributors with contempt.

WHAT TO DO TO MAKE THE MOST OUT OF YOUR DIRECT SELLING CAMPAIGN

If you have a direct sales force that sells to the end user without any intermediaries, there may be a good reason for it. Here are some of the kinds of products and situations when this may make the most sense, at least until the market matures to the point (if it ever does) when indirect distribution may become more appropriate:

1. The product is a highly technical one that usually requires a degree of value added through engineering and skilled field installation to suit the needs of the customer. Wholesalers, dealers, and distributors are more appropriate for a product line that can be offered to their customers without change.

2. The product requires customization to the needs of the particular customer and application situation so that each copy is unique. Waste disposal plants cannot be stocked on the distributor's shelf, but spare parts for the system could be. As one sales manager once put it, "Wholesalers move boxes, they don't sell products."

3. When you are introducing a new product or new concept. Too often a product faces a "Catch-22" situation—the dealer says that he doesn't get any calls for the product and the end user wants to know who is stocking the product locally before making a purchase commitment. In the beginning, you may have to be your own stocking wholesaler and dealer in addition to mounting your own direct selling effort.

4. When there is no established distribution channel for your kind of product. Rather than try to fit it into one of the existing channels where it doesn't belong and will not get the attention it deserves, it could make sense to go direct until an appropriate channel opens up. You could use direct salespeople for high-ticket products and direct response advertising (print or broadcast media) for less expensive ones.

5. Where the selling cycle is unusually long, requiring months of negotiating with the end user. Wholesalers, distributors, and even most dealers live or die through inventory turnover ratios. They are used to getting products in and out quickly in response to a demand that has already been created.

6. When the price of the item or system is so high that it needs a lot of capital to support the product and sale of the item. Selling jumbo jets or million-dollar pieces of earth-moving equipment are two examples.

7. When the stakes are too high to take a chance on not being in direct control of the entire selling process. An office furniture manufacturer, for example, may usually support a dealer network that stocks, sells, displays, and services the furniture line. When an order for all the

furnishings for a 26-story building are at stake, however, the ball game may change. The manufacturer may handle all the negotiations and arrangements and pay the dealer a finder's fee for the lead and a service fee for installation.

8. Where you feel you need control over the selling and installation process and want the end user's loyalty directed to you instead of the dealer. You could be pioneering a laser-based machine tool and want to keep the efforts confidential and work with end users directly in the final engineering stages. The right dealers could, of course, still be partners in this effort by finding and following through with potential users including their own customer base.

9. When it would be too easy for a dealer to take advantage of your development efforts and switch the end user to a less expensive product because the alternate manufacturer doesn't have your development costs. If you were developing applications for a new, insulated wall covering, for example, and working on site with builders, it might be tempting for your dealer to let you do the work and switch the sale or future sales to the "lowest of three" bidders. You could work out an office design for your carpeting product and see the job go to a carpet mill who doesn't have expensive designers on the payroll.

10. When you are convinced, really convinced, that you can do the job better, less expensively, and more effectively with a direct selling effort than going through an indirect channel. It could be that your three competitors who dominate the industry have all the direct channels locked up so you have no choice but to use direct selling as a flanking maneuver. If you're that good, you may even find dealers knocking on your door when the product is established.

   Evolving from a direct selling effort to an indirect one can be a natural and healthful move. Be careful, however, about changing from an indirect to a direct selling method. As the good people from the Wholesale Stationers' Association of Des Plaines, Illinois put it, "You can replace the wholesaler, but you can't replace the function."

   Someone has to do the job and someone has to absorb the costs. It is only logical that the wholesalers, distributors, and dealers who have survived in their respective marketplaces have learned how to handle this distribution specialty efficiently and effectively—unless you have one of the unusual situations outlined in this section.

   You may find that it makes a good deal of sense to field a special sales force to solicit orders and turn them over to your indirect distribution channel. There is no right or wrong in this area except that doing it on an unplanned basis is wrong and working out a plan to effect your sales method properly is right.

HOW TO MAKE INDIRECT DISTRIBUTION GENERATE PROFITS

As a national supplier of goods or services, you primary business is creating these products and selling them in the most effective way. You may not necessarily be a distribution expert or have the ability to develop the local, point-of-sale resources necessary to effectively reach your end users. Here are some situations where it makes sense to rely on the expertise of the local indirect distribution channel members:

1. You have a single product line. If you are selling copier paper or toner, you could have a successful direct telemarketing selling effort. (See Chapter 17.) Or you may be dismissed as a boiler-room operation "paper pirate" and classed with those who use questionable techniques to peddle shoddy goods.

   Your best strategy could be to hook up with the dealers who sell copy machines. Most copy machines *are* sold by office machines dealers and the copy machine manufacturers must have had a good reason for choosing this route rather than going direct.

2. Your product is part of a system that is put together locally and sold by dealers. To continue with the copy machine example, your business could be making copier stands. Since most of your possible end users would be buying the stands with the machines, machines dealers could make sense. If you are selling a computer monitor stand, furniture dealers are an appropriate distribution outlet.

3. Your product needs to be displayed and it's too expensive to develop your own showrooms all over the country. If you are selling expensive glass cocktail tables, your customers will usually want to see them locally, preferably in a suitable setting, before making the decision to buy.

4. If you are selling a "commodity" item. (It could be argued quite properly that there is really no such thing as a pure commodity since you can add value to the most ordinary products. For our purposes, we'll suggest that there are some products that lend themselves to identification as a commodity more than others.) These items, for example, wood pencils and wire paper clips or screws and nails, will be bought based on availability rather than for unique features.

5. Your product needs to be near other products you don't manufacture in order to be bought. You probably wouldn't think about buying toggle bolts in anything but a hardware section of a mass merchandiser, hardware store, or lumber yard. File folder fasteners need to be sold in the same place file folders are sold.

6. Your product needs the exposure that the distribution channel provides. If you decide you want a desk stapler, for example, your

administrative assistant will go to the office products purchasing agent with the request or purchase requisition. The PA will pull one or more office products catalogs from the shelf, open it to the stapler page and ask you to select one. The stapler is then ordered from the local *indirect* dealer or distributor.

Except perhaps for national accounts or very large local accounts, you can't afford to sell a stapler direct no matter how good it is. You won't be able to build a demand for your stapler that can compete with the catalog listing and local availability. Office products wholesalers publish most of the catalogs used in the country and imprint them for local dealers. How far do you think you will get with your stapler if you don't sell through these wholesalers?

7. When fast shipment is required. Most local garages do not stock all the parts they need to service your automobile. They may have points, plugs, hoses, and fan belts, but most of the time they go to their local auto parts dealer *after* they have diagnosed the problem to pick up the parts they need to solve the problem.

    The part has to be locally available, not through a direct selling operation that stocks only a limited line. This is why, in metropolitan areas, the auto parts dealers' market area seldom exceeds a five-to-ten-mile radius and the garage can have the part in an hour or two, if not in a few minutes. How far would you get with even an extensive line if you had to spot an outlet every ten miles or so?

8. When the product or part requires service or the potential buyer perceives that it will, and you are not that well known in all marketplaces. Your end user prospect is a lot more likely to trust the local appliance store to make sure there is post-sale service than an unknown factory a few hundred or a few thousand miles away.

    It's true, of course, that a lot of machines and appliances *are* being serviced by the factory, but the local dealer, by selling the product, has provided the necessary endorsement. The end user is still relying on the local dealer's reputation in taking a chance on your product even if you actually perform any service.

9. When you have an impulse item that lends itself to an add-on sales opportunity. Weed killer, for example, could more easily be sold to the person who has just walked up to the garden center counter with a bag of fertilizer and a carton of grass seed.

10. When you need the credibility of a local business that has been established for many years. You might buy a radio by mail if you recognized and had good feelings about the manufacturer. You might not think twice about ordering a cassette or compact disk from someone you hadn't hear of. However, if you are going to spend several thousand dollars on a stereo system, you would probably rely on a local outlet who had provided this kind of equipment for someone you knew.

If you *are* the local manufacturer, you may decide to go direct in this limited market area or open up a "factory outlet" that could have some advantages as a test market laboratory for you.

PROVEN TECHNIQUES FOR CONTROLLING DISTRIBUTION COSTS TO INCREASE PROFITS

You've seen many of the qualitative reasons for selling your product or service through direct company salespeople and when it may be appropriate to go through an indirect distribution channel. The big missing element in making a final decision is, of course, *cost.* Someone has to pay the dealer, distributor, or wholesaler to perform the function.

But how much? To a large extent, the discount from suggested retail pricing you provide (the way you "pay" these people) will depend on industry practice. If the industry standard is 40 percent off retail to the dealer and 50 percent-10 percent (the same as 40 percent-25 percent or a discount of 55 percent from retail) to the wholesaler, you won't attract many outlets with a discount of 30 percent unless your product or entire value package is so good that you have dealers waiting in line to stock your product or retail your service.

Conversely, if the standard is a 30 percent discount from list and you can afford 50 percent, you would be leaving money on the table if you did what you could afford instead of going with the standard. Use some of the difference to put money in your stockholders' pockets and some to provide even better support to your distributors in order to keep a dominant position in the marketplace. At the same time, you should ask yourself why there is such a big difference:

- Are you really that much more efficient than your competitors and adding that much more value?
- Do you just happen to be in a very profitable industry or are you all ripping off the dealer or end user?
- How long can this last?

Whether or not you can afford the distribution channel, no matter what the conventional discount structure is, will also depend on what it would cost you to perform the functions yourself and what you can afford based on your gross margins. Before even looking at this, make sure you have a handle on what your inventory carrying, shipping, promotional, and branch office costs really are. I've seen operations converted from direct branches with the branch office managers taking over a dealership. They find, all of a sudden, that the country club dues that were necessary when they were representing the company are not necessary and that the conference area they *had* to have as branch managers would do just fine as a typing pool area.

This determination has more options than may be immediately obvious. In many cases, I've advised clients to go the indirect route and raise their prices at the same time. The distribution channel provided enough benefits and provided enough value added to make this move possible.

To put this in better perspective and to help you choose the distribution channel that makes the most sense for you, we'll list some of the functions performed by dealers, wholesalers, and distributors. In addition, we'll assign a value (as a percentage of the suggested retail selling price) to each of these. Not all dealers, distributors, or wholesalers will perform all these functions, so the percentages apply to those who do.

This last move is, admittedly, a bit risky since it will change so much from industry to industry and distributor to distributor. The percentages, then, should be viewed as guidelines to help boost your thinking ahead a little, rather than as rules or standards that will always apply.

INDIRECT DISTRIBUTION CHANNEL FUNCTIONS

Function	Value Added
1. Receiving, storing and shipping merchandise, breaking up such merchandise into smaller lots.	10%
2. Financing the inventory purchases and carrying customer accounts receivable.	5%
3. Maintaining a field sales force, providing catalogs and other promotional tools.	5%
4. Providing a delivery service for which the end user is not charged.	3%
5. Accepting, assembling, providing credit for, and sending back to the manufacturer returns of merchandise unsuitable for use.	2%
6. Assembling merchandise for the end user.	1%
Total	26%

This indicates a total of 26 percent of the selling price for these *value added* components. However, in addition to these items which represent money out-of-pocket for the distributor, there are *costs* involved in providing these services that could add another 10 to 15 percent to the total. Also, a wholesaler providing merchandise to a reseller would not have the same percentage of costs as would, for example, an industrial distributor selling direct to the end user.

It is also not possible to translate the above percentages directly into an appropriate discount to the dealer or distributor. The figures may be appropriate for some industries, but in others the costs will be much lower or much higher and the value added more or less.

There is also the question of discounts given by the distributor. In an industry where 10 percent to 20 percent is routinely given from the suggested retail price to almost any business user, manufacturer discounts have to start at 40 percent to 50 percent in order to give the dealer or distributor anything close to the above numbers and a reasonable profit.

Again, the purpose was not to provide absolute standards, but to suggest the kind of thinking that should be involved in:

1. Comparing indirect distribution costs against direct selling costs, recognizing that you will also have some costs of getting your product to the distributor.
2. Coming up with a list of what your costs would be if you chose to stay with direct company salespeople.
3. Developing a checklist of the kinds of functions performed that you should be looking for in a distributor. Distributors who add value through training sessions for their customers, for example, or who conduct active promotional campaigns obviously add more value for you than those who do not and should logically be entitled to a larger discount to cover their costs of doing this.

WHEN TO ADD THE THIRD DISTRIBUTION STEP
FOR ADDED SALES

It's not unusual in some industries for a product to pass through three or more hands on its way to the end user and we're not talking about pyramid schemes. Where a product needs to be widely and readily available as in the case of office supplies or automotive parts, the retailers or dealers who sell to the end user have found it advantageous to have another middleman consolidate purchases from manufacturers and repackage a bundle of value-added services for them.

Wholesalers in most industries have progressed far beyond the days when the main function was to buy in big quantities and sell in small lots. Part of this bundle of service includes automated ordering systems, inventory control systems, catalogs, store design, and promotional aids.

Your job as an effective field sales manager is to use the above guidelines to determine if and when this third step would be appropriate for you. You'll look at industry practice and balance the extra discounts you'll have to provide against both the costs you would incur to perform the functions and the likelihood that you'll be able to get to the end user with just one step given the extra service wholesalers provide today. (Remember the stapler example.)

There is in many industries a constant tug of war between manufacturers and wholesalers, and in others, a smoothly running partnership between the two. It seems sometimes that manufacturers would like wholesalers to accept merchandise in carload lots, after paying for it in advance, and handle every aspect of getting the product through the dealer channel to the end user without looking to the manufacturer for any additional help or services.

To many manufacturers, wholesalers want the manufacturer to make the product, ship it on a 90-day consignment basis, freight prepaid in whatever quantities are convenient to the wholesaler, create the demand for the product among end users, and solicit orders from the dealers to be turned over to the wholesaler. (In some cases this may come close to being an accurate reading of the wholesalers' expectations.)

As in most marketing situations there is a balance that can be struck. It is suggested that each "partner" concentrate on and be responsible for doing what it can do best. The manufacturer is obviously in the best position to provide market research to develop new products, product modifications, and to suggest new applications. The manufacturer can provide an umbrella of national advertising support and wholesaler salesperson and even dealer salesperson training, from product brochures to elaborate visual aids to actually conducting sales training meetings.

The wholesaler is in the best position to solicit orders from the dealers, publish catalogs containing the products of hundreds of manufacturers, and sponsor promotions for dealers. These promotional activities could include the preparation of newspaper ad mats, in-store banners, store displays, and flyers.

Questions arise when the responsibilities are not clear-cut. If a manufacturer is trying to convince the wholesaler to make a substantial investment in putting the manufacturer's product in stock and back it with promotional activity, the wholesaler looks for "turnover" orders to at least prime the pump. This means that the manufacturer is not only providing an extra discount to the wholesaler, but also has to pay for the effort of selling to the dealer to get the orders.

This issue of turnover orders has probably caused wholesalers' and manufacturers' salespeople more grief and consternation than any other issue. To the wholesaler, it's almost a divine right. To the manufacturer, it suggests paying for something not earned or even deserved.

Who's right? Suggest that it depends on the circumstances. However, at the risk of offending possible future customers or customers of clients, the following guidelines are suggested:

1. In the case of an old established product, it might be fair to suggest that the wholesaler salesperson would normally get the order from the dealer instead of the factory person if he were doing his job and the manufacturer deserves the extra profit on that order because of the extra cost of making the sale.

2. If however, the wholesaler has made a commitment to stock an unknown product (a more substantial investment for most wholesalers than many manufacturers realize) on the strength of the manufacturer's promise to support the wholesaler's efforts, turnover orders gotten by the manufacturer's salesperson could be a legitimate part of that support effort promised.

These guidelines will obviously not satisfy everyone, but could be a good starting point for discussion. The discussion between the parties involved is really the most important issue. If the wholesaler's expectations and the manufacturer's willingness (or lack of willingness) to meet these expectations are discussed honestly and openly up front, the relationship has a much better chance of becoming the mutually beneficial partnership it can and should be.

The wholesaler has survived in the marketplace by doing something useful or he wouldn't be there. The assumption, then, has to be made that the wholesaler's customers perceive that the wholesaler provides some value. If the manufacturer really wants to reach this group of customers and can see that the extra discount saves some costs or provides some value, the role of this third step in the distribution channel has to be carefully and thoroughly explored.

IN CLOSING. . .

Today's marketing and sales "event" is inevitably tomorrow's cliché and the next day's nostalgia. Certainly the Marketing Staff at the home office is responsible for sensing when the emphasis should shift from one stage to the next in a product's life cycle. Yet, as a field sales manager, you cannot afford to be out of touch with these shifts in product "age" and customer response. In fact, you are, as the daily point of contact, the first to know. It can only pay you to be the first to act.

15

Making the Home Office Work for You

HOW TO GET THE HOME OFFICE TO MAXIMIZE THE PROFIT PICTURE IN YOUR SALES AREA

In many ways a sales management career is a make-it-or-lose-it game. If your company or division makes it, you get a lot of the credit for it. If not, you share in the blame. The results may be grossly unfair, but it's the deal you accepted when you took on a sales management responsibility. One way to improve your chances of success is to get along well with the home office and use their resources maximally. "Getting along" does not mean "bootlicking" or doing anything that is inconsistent with your perceived role. It does mean recognizing that the role of these people can assist your efforts. It also means making your objectives clear and letting everyone know that you are receptive to using all the resources available to you. How you accomplish all this depends on your position in your company and your degree of responsibility for "marketing functions."

ALTERNATIVES FOR STRUCTURING THE HOME OFFICE

While there are an almost infinite number of combinations, there are three basic ways the home office sales and marketing areas can be structured:

1. Headed by a vice president of marketing and sales with all of the sales and marketing functions including the regional managers reporting directly to him. (See Figure 15.1.)

2. Headed by a president or executive vice president with a vice president of sales and a separate vice president of sales and marketing reporting to him. The field sales people report to the vice president of sales and the marketing (advertising, market research, sales administration, etc.) people report to the vice president of marketing. The inside sales and/or customer service people may report to either vice president as may the sales administrative people. (See Figure 15.2.)

3. Headed by a president or executive vice president with a vice president of sales and marketing reporting to him. This is different from item 1 in that a field sales manager reports to the vice president of sales and marketing and has no regional management structure between him and the district managers or field salespeople. (See Figure 15.3.)

It would be nice to suggest that the choice of alternative structures always depends on the best way to meet the needs of the company or organization. Nice, but usually not accurate. It depends very often on the personalities of the people involved in the organization, their backgrounds, and their personal needs and orientations.

The structure shown in Figure 15.2 might suggest that the organization has a president or executive vice president who doesn't want to let go of the sales and marketing function. He, perhaps justifiably, wants to keep an active hand in sales and marketing activities, control the important decisions, and balance the staff function (marketing) off against the line function (sales).

It might be because this person came from sales and marketing or that sales and marketing functions of the organization are perceived to be more critical to the company's success than the manufacturing, engineering, and financial areas are. This would be true of a consumer product like soap or socks or an industrial commodity that isn't too technical in nature. The structure, whatever the reasons for it, is not in itself good or bad, but it's important for the field sales manager to understand the structure and the reasons for it as a first step in getting the most from the "home office."

Figure 15.1 and Figure 15.3 suggest that the president or executive vice president has a lot of other things to worry about and is content to leave the balancing of the sales and marketing functions to a single executive. Depending on the nature of the company and its market *and* on the personality of the person, the company's orientation could be weighted in one of two ways:

1. There could be a heavy marketing orientation with the staff people setting goals, policy, and procedures for sales to follow through on.

2. There could be a heavy sales orientation with the sales group deciding what should happen and the marketing people acting in a support role.

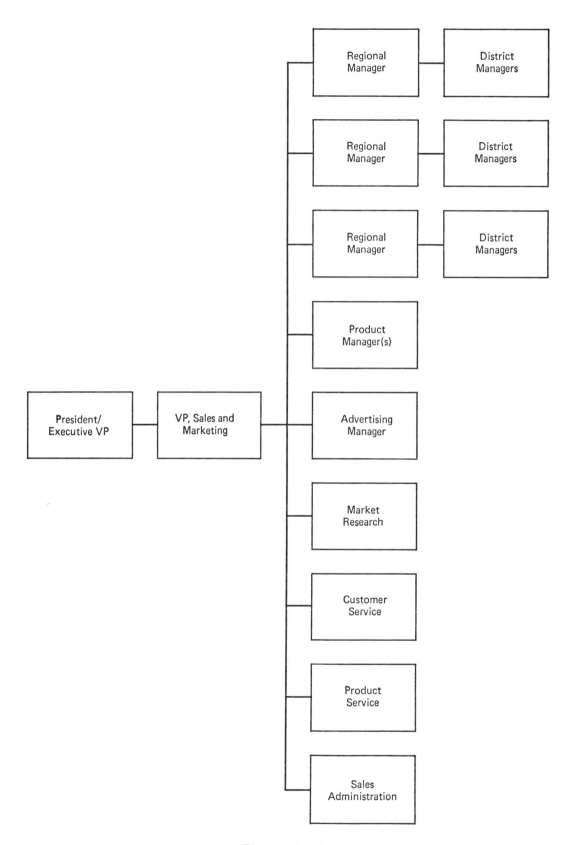

Figure 15.1

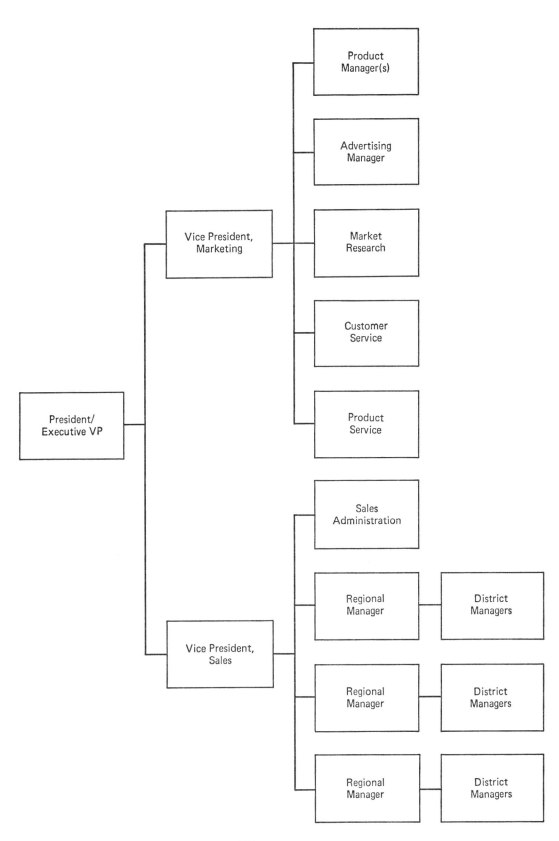

Figure 15-2

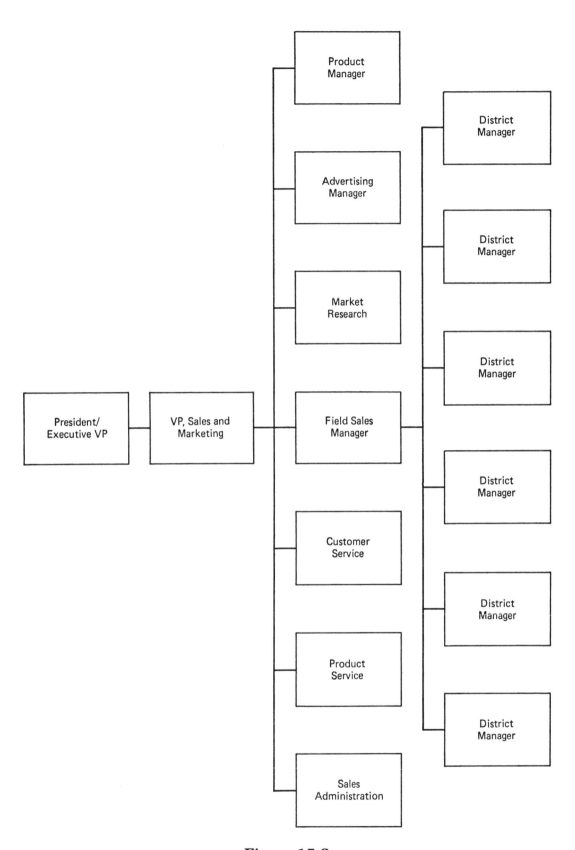

Figure 15.3

This is particularly likely to happen with the structure shown in Figure 15.1 where the regional managers report directly to the top sales and marketing executive on an equal basis as the marketing people.

With the structure shown in Figure 15.3, the field sales manager could carry a good deal more weight than the organizational chart would indicate, especially if the vice president, sales and marketing started as a salesperson and held the field sales manager position. Or, he could be a nondecision-making coordinator of the field district managers, taking direction from the vice president, sales and marketing as established by the other marketing staff members, and from the staff members themselves.

The amount of authority or decision-making power usually depends more on the personality of the individual and how he has met the company objectives assigned than on the organizational chart placement. You hear from conventional management seers that "You have to delegate authority as well as responsibility." Or, "You can delegate authority but you can't delegate responsibility." Both statements are nonsense in the real world. Nobody gives you authority. Authority is *earned* and then it is *taken*.

I've seen a lot of companies where the staff people forgot that their function is to *serve* and *support* the line people who are producing sales. They assumed the function of *ruling* the line people and took the authority whether they had earned it or not. Maybe they got away with this because they had the time. The staff people in these instances could dream up power plays and get away with them because the line people were too busy out in the field generating sales.

This danger exists in all of the three structures discussed. The only solution is to create an atmosphere overflowing with same-team spirit where people are rewarded based on what they contribute to the team effort and overall good of the company. While the leadership for this "culture" has to come from the top, there is much you, as a field sales manager, can do to contribute to it.

For the purposes of this chapter, we're going to assume that you are a vice president, sales, in the structure shown in Figure 15.3 or that you are operating with this kind of structure and aspire to be the vice president. We made this choice since this kind of reporting arrangement involves the most difficult set of circumstances—the "home office" people you need on your team don't report to you, but you have an important decision-making role to play.

Rather than being able to make the trade-offs between sales and marketing objectives or assume that the staff and line people will always agree on what is best for the company, you have to sell your programs to the president or executive vice president. You also have the vice president, marketing there with his own set of objectives and demands on the company's total sales and marketing budget. In response to the need for higher sales, you may want to hire more salespeople, and he may want more space advertising or a market research study. Before we get on to guidelines on handling these issues, let's address a point that might be the subject of some misunderstanding.

SALES AND MARKETING—WHICH IS WHICH?

There are probably as many viewpoints on this as there are products to be sold. General dictionaries offer no help in defining the terms, and business dictionaries don't provide answers that would satisfy either types of people who identify themselves as sales executives or as marketing executives.

There seem to be three ways of looking at this:

1. Sales and marketing really mean the same thing—they are interchangeable terms for the same activity or group of activities. These activities involve identifying customers and selling them.
2. Sales and marketing are two distinct disciplines as indicated by the division within a sales and marketing organization between line people (sales) and staff people (marketing). "Marketing" (if you really have to use the term) consists of all the supporting activities to the "real" job of the sales and marketing department—generating the maximum volume of sales.
3. "Marketing" describes *all* of the business activities involved in getting merchandise and services from the hands of the producers to the hands of the users. It starts with identifying a market, proceeds through the steps involved in reaching the market with the seller's message, and includes the physical distribution and delivery functions. Sales is but one link in the chain, although, for many companies, it is the most important link.

With apologies to those sales executives who feel that they are indeed the whole chain, we're going to opt for the definition in item 3 as the best to deal with most situations in most organizations. This doesn't put down the sales function in the least, but suggests that sales managers who would occupy the top sales/marketing spot in an organization need to know something about:

— *Market Definition:* the first stage in the whole process that defines the product that should be made or service to be offered.
— *Market Reaching:* this includes space, direct mail, broadcast and other media, besides personal sales calls or individual salesperson effort.
— *Distribution:* this includes a knowledge of transportation and warehousing as well as the distribution channels that are the most appropriate for the company and the stage to which the product line has progressed in its life cycle. (See Chapter 14 for a complete discussion of product life cycles.)

With these definitions and distinctions in mind, let's look at some of the "marketing" resources which should be available and the ways the field sales manager should be able to take advantage of them.

CHECKLIST OF THINGS TO EXPECT FROM THE HOME OFFICE

1. A constant, ongoing effort to identify potential markets that match the company's strengths and capabilities. If the market research department is smart, they will use you and your people to help them do this job.

2. A flow of information, through you, about changing conditions in the marketplace that may affect your ability to sell your product or service. If you are selling computer software programs, they should know and tell you which operating systems are becoming the most important. If you are selling machine tools, they should have the latest information on foreign competition and how the foreign exchange rates will affect your ability to be competitive. Again, if they are smart, they will look to you and your people for as much help as they can get.

3. Direction to the engineering, manufacturing, and other departments on the kinds of products, product modifications, packaging, etc., that are needed by the marketplace you have defined. Working with the accounting department, for example, to hammer out solutions to problems with invoicing, credit, collection, or pricing.

   The product managers should be talking with you and your customers to constantly improve your marketplace offering. The service manager should be investigating warranty and other repair work to look for any possible product defects or improvement opportunities. The customer service department should provide information and follow-through for correction by the appropriate departments on customer complaints regarding packaging, labeling, legibility of invoices, timeliness of shipping notices, problems with transportation companies, etc.

4. An effective advertising program that is well-coordinated with your overall sales implementation program and is based on a good deal of input from you, your salespeople, and even your customers, about the kind of support you feel you need and the information your customers feel they should have. While you should work together to put the total program together, you should have a good deal of say about *what* the message to your customers should be and the advertising people (the inside and the outside agency) should mostly determine *how* to get the message across.

5. An effective collateral material program (catalogs, brochures, photographs, ad mats, spec sheets, demos, ad reprints, stuffers, etc.). There should also be a mechanism in place to ensure that salespeople get all that they need, but that a record is kept of usage by sales territory. (As suggested in Chapter 6, which dealt with setting sales budgets for maximum profitability, you may want to charge all collateral material to the individual salesperson's budget.)

6. A comprehensive publicity program starting with press releases and feature articles in the trade press to special efforts like getting a company spokesperson or a company video tape on a national television show. This is one of the most cost-effective activities your advertising and public relations people can engage in.

   There should be opportunities every month in the areas of people, products, and programs to get your company better known through articles in the trade press. Copies of press releases should go to you and your people at the same time they are sent to the trade papers. Reprints of significant articles should be available to you.

7. Support for national or local trade show activities. This support should include:
   — Booth or display design, production and refurbishing when necessary.
   — Arrangements for shipping the booth with the literature, special signs, and product samples you need for the show.
   — Contact with the exposition management for local help needed to set up the booth—carpenters, electricians, etc.
   — Arrangements with the exposition management for other booth material needed—chairs, tables, ashtrays, drapery, etc.
   — Supervision of the booth set-up, dismantling, shipping back, and storage.

8. A customer-responsive customer service department. The customer service personnel should view letters, phone calls, and requests from your customers as the *reason* for their job and not an *interruption* of it. They should view every customer complaint as an opportunity to show just how good your service is and just how important the customer is to you, themselves, and their company.

9. A customer-responsive product service department. They should attempt to settle all warranty (and even out-of-warranty) claims with the overall benefit to the company in mind. Some product service departments seem to think that every such claim is an affront to the integrity of the company and side with the engineering department in coming up with creative ways to prove that it is the customer rather than the product that is at fault.

   Arguing about a $20 part on a $5,000 machine is a very good way to ensure that you sell fewer $5,000 machines. The right kind of customer service and product service people look for these kinds of problems so they can find creative, customer-oriented ways to solve them.

   I was director of marketing for a company that sold a machine for around $1,000 that had a $20 accessory with which there were adjustment problems. Our engineers, assisted by the product service people, began issuing instructions on how to adjust the machine to the accessory (a minimum $50 service call). We put a stop to this, reeducated the product service people, and, until the problem was solved, offered a free exchange with no questions asked. We sold a lot more of those $1,000 machines.

As we pointed out earlier, you can have nineteen successful, problem-free transactions with a customer and then have a problem with the twentieth. You will be measured, positively or negatively, on the twentieth transaction and the other nineteen will be forgotten if you don't handle this problem one well.

10. Assistance to your people in the field when they need it to solve a sticky problem or sell a customer on a different or complicated application for your product. You have to be careful your salespeople aren't just being lazy or lonely and that they don't cry wolf too often.

Handled properly, these field calls can be very impressive to your customer—"Well, that is a very unusual situation. We'll have one of our home office engineering specialists come out and take a look at it." They can also be a good way to get the technical people out on the firing line and involved in the applications of the products they are developing and refining so that the effects of the ivory tower syndrome can be kept to a minimum.

11. Any other reasonable assistance that is needed to create, expand, or maintain sales. "Needed" means balancing the cost in time and expense of providing the assistance against the real benefits to be gained. It also means that you don't ask for home office marketing or other staff assistance for things you and your people should be able to handle yourselves.

CHECKLIST OF THINGS THE HOME OFFICE MAY EXPECT FROM YOU

All of this "same team" effort is a two-way street. Since you *are* all on the same team, you all have a stake in increased sales and profit even though yours is a more direct one. You are on their team just as much as they are on yours. There are some things your colleagues need from you if they are to do their jobs well and if the overall effort on which you will *all* be measured is to be as successful as it can be:

1. A 150 percent commitment to your job. You recall that we have often suggested that a field sales manager has a full-time job in the field and a full-time job in the home office. We suggested further that he has to figure out how to get the most important 75 percent of each of these jobs done.

In most cases you will be the only field sales management person on the executive marketing staff. If you don't do 100 percent to 150 percent of your job, there is no one else to pick up the ball and run with it, so your colleagues are dependent on you to do an effective job in the field.

2. Effective management on your time. (See Chapter 8.) It's very easy in a field sales job to look at that mountain of paperwork on your desk and neglect field responsibilities. It's just as easy for some people to stay too long in the field doing things that could be done by someone else because it's more comfortable.

   It's possible to forget to plan your field trips a month or two in advance so that you wind up making a trip to Atlanta one week and find yourself flying to Orlando a week or two later instead of combining the two trips with, perhaps, a stop in Jacksonville to handle something else.

3. *Leadership* of the field sales force—assisting all the district and regional managers to do the best jobs they are capable of doing. Your home office colleagues can provide information, communication, and company. *You* are the only person who can provide the atmosphere for motivation. (You recall that we suggested earlier you can't motivate people. They have to motivate themselves. You can, however, make sure that everything you do is aimed at providing the right environment to ensure that this happens.)

   I was involved in a situation where the sales manager was clearly not doing his job with the salespeople and reps in the field. Since I had responsibility for several divisions, it took a few weeks before this became obvious since he *was* doing an excellent job in the office. The other home office people tried to fill the leadership gap by spending time with the field people. It didn't work. All they did was listen to complaints about the sales manager. This is important, but is not a substitute for the right kind of leadership that the effective field sales manager must provide.

4. An honest and objective approach to the problems and conflicts that always arise when field sales people and home office marketing people have different ideas on reaching the same objective. Too many sales managers take a "my people can do no wrong" approach and get defensive about what they perceive as criticism. Your job is to sell the field viewpoint to the home office and the home office viewpoint, whether you feel it is right or wrong (if you can't change it), to the field.

5. Communication on issues, events, and circumstances that you and your people see happening in the field with competitors and with customers before they might become obvious to your marketing or other staff people. Sometimes things that don't involve an immediate benefit or solution to a problem for your salespeople get forgotten:
   — If your customers seem to be welcoming a new trade magazine, for example, your advertising people should know about this.
   — If your competition has recently substituted a plastic part for a metal one in a key product, or has made some other significant change, your engineering department should be told.

— If your competitor recently dropped several models from the line or added new models, your product manager should have this information.

— If you hear your customers quoting from a new industry survey, you should make sure your market research department is aware that the study exists.

6. Hard copy market intelligence. Your people are in the best position to obtain copies of competitors' catalogs, price lists, brochures, spec sheets, training manuals, etc. You should create an atmosphere where your people will compete with each other to see who can get the latest information to the home office the fastest. Don't worry about duplicate copies—your market research people will always find a use for them.

   (We're assuming that you have either a market research department or a single person who is responsible for keeping an up-to-date file on your competition. If you don't, you should have, even if you have to have one of your people do it.)

   Reinforce this effort by sending brief "thank you" notes to your people for particularly valuable information. Have the other staff people do the same so the salespeople know that their efforts are recognized and appreciated. Too often, salespeople stop sending information because they don't realize how valuable it is or even if it is being used.

7. Participation in the development and implementation of market research efforts. With the right kind of complete marketing plan, this information really is important and should be looked upon as an important part of the selling effort rather than an interruption of it. Naturally, you'll want to get the results and provide them to your people in a way that really will help their sales efforts.

8. A sales plan. The direction of the field selling effort is too important to be left solely to the staff people who may or may not have field sales experience. It's important that you be involved in the development of the overall plan. Your price of admission to this effort is the commitment to develop a sales implementation plan based on the overall marketing plan. We'll discuss this further in the next section.

HOW TO EARN AND MAINTAIN THE RESPECT AND SUPPORT OF YOUR HOME OFFICE BY SELLING YOUR SALES PLAN

Getting the most from the home office people necessarily requires that you have their respect. The best way to get this, other than your performance in the field, is to show them that you are on their team, speak their language, and share their objectives.

They may not appreciate the subtleties of your leadership approach. They may not know how hard you worked to help your salesperson bring in that big order. They may not value the selling technique that opened up a whole new distribution channel. But, they do understand a written and comprehensive plan. This is where they live.

You got a good head start on this by refining your quota-setting activities through Chapter 3. You got an additional boost in Chapters 6 and 7. These chapters dealt mostly with field activities. Now, let's list some of the elements that should be included in your portion of the home office sales plan:

1. A recap of the total sales-by-product line for the past five years compared to this year's quota. A simple line or bar graph with separate colors or shadings for the various product categories would be helpful here.

   The narrative or text in this section of your plan could express your views of why some product lines are growing faster than others and pave the way for you to get new products or improvements in present ones. A chart like that shown in Figure 15.4 is the simplest way, and works well to give a perspective, particularly if you joined the company just before the big northeast angle.

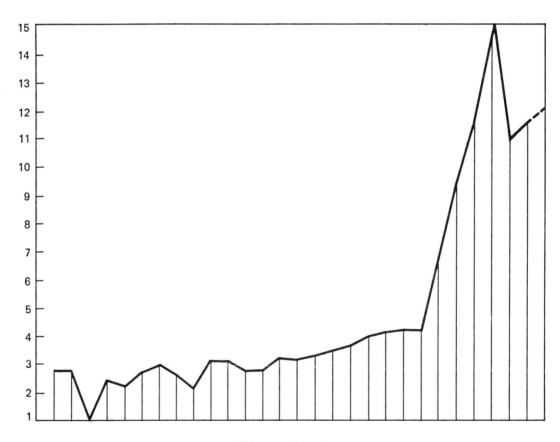

Figure 15.4

2. A recap of total sales by region and/or territory for the past five years compared to the individual quotas for the current year. Depending on the information, you could use graphics to show areas of growth or the lack of growth. The narrative or text could identify geo-economic reasons for this, or honestly identify salespeople with whom you have a performance problem.

3. A breakout of your key customer base by groups. If you are selling a broad-appeal product like computers, you might use major SIC categories. If you are selling medical equipment, you might break out sales to hospitals, clinics, medical practice groups, etc. Or, you might break out sales to hospitals by the number of beds (0 to 100, 100 to 499, 500 and above, etc.). If you are selling office furniture or accessories, you could break out sales by wholesaler, machine distributor, supplies dealer, furniture dealer, mail order and machines dealer categories.

   You might show how a few key customers account for a significant part of your total sales if this is true. You undoubtedly have something close to the 80-20 syndrome at work (20 percent of the number of customers account for 80 percent of your total sales dollars). This could be interesting for your colleagues and could help explain why you are "always" asking for special favors for and attention to certain customers.

   If appropriate, you might show your share of the market in these categories. You may need some help from the marketing staff in putting this together, but the working together has to make for a better team effort and you'll get points for being interested and taking this kind of approach. You may also find some weaknesses in the market intelligence available.

   The narrative or text would express some of the reasons for particularly good penetration or the lack of it with some groups or market areas. This could then pave the way for a plea for more advertising or other effort directed to the market you want to reach. If you are at a disadvantage in being able to discuss this information because it's not available, you at least won't be politically disadvantaged if this is disclosed in a tactful way.

4. Your sales implementation plan for each quarter (or other time period by which you measure specific programs). The overall plan of which this is a part would, of course, have been worked out jointly. This could include:
   — An explanation of the objective expressed in total dollar sales, new orders, new customers signed up, product demonstrations, or whatever measure is appropriate.
   — A step-by-step outline (not complete detail) of the method by which you expect to achieve these objectives. You could describe the

general approach and go on to outline specifics, as how the prospect market will be defined. You could go on to list the steps your salespeople will take to set up initial appointments and then follow through with these prospects.

— An explanation of how you are going to dovetail your efforts with the publicity and advertising efforts that will be undertaken. Explain how you are going to use the leads generated to complete the steps suggested in the paragraph immediately preceding this one.

— A description of the reward/award system you will use to recognize those who do the best job on the programs.

— A description of the measurement standards and procedures you will use to determine the degree of success of the programs. Explain how this will be communicated to the marketing staff for their use in developing future programs.

— A description of your follow-up activities that will ensure that there will be lasting benefits for each program. You might use this as a platform from which to ask for the additional support you need.

— A description of what *your* and your staff's activities will be during the promotional periods. By detailing the part you will play, you will give the other team members a clearer idea (and hopefully more appreciation) for what it is you really do.

5. A breakdown of your sales budget by territory showing the total expenses as a percentage of sales. The narrative would explain the reason for any significant differences in the percentages. If you can get (favorable for you) industry figures on sales expenses as a percentage of sales, use them.

6. A breakdown of your sales budget by category of expense as you expect it. (You remember from Chapter 6 that we suggested providing a specific, affordable, overall *total* budget to each salesperson, district manager, and regional manager, but that you let them spend it, for the most part, in the way they see fit, remaining responsible for attaining quota and staying within the budget.)

   The narrative would detail things like spiffs, dealer promotions, or product demonstrations in a public room. Again, your colleagues should get a better idea of what you do and, ideally, vote to give you a bigger portion of the total sales and marketing budget. (Don't, however, hold your breath on this last point.)

7. An explanation of how you help your people decide where to spend their time. This is the "account stratification" bit as outlined in Chapter 4, "Spending Time Where It Counts—Account Stratification."

   Your narrative or text might include an explanation of how little time your salespeople actually have for face-to-face selling efforts. This may help keep the staff's demands on your sales force's time in

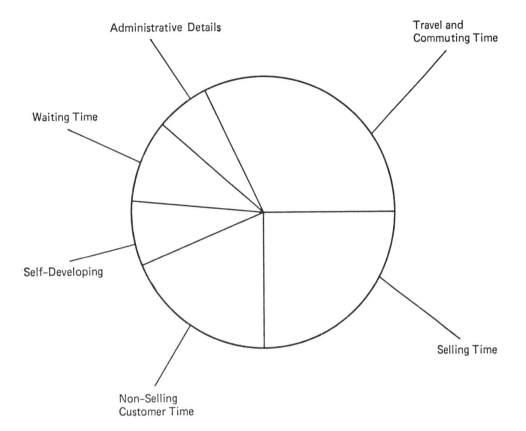

Figure 15.5

perspective and explain why they may not always be enthused about filling out questionnaires. You might show a pie chart graphic like that shown in Figure 15.5 to illustrate the point.

8. Take this step further by showing how you help your salespeople set call frequency patterns. Use an illustration (or a simplified version of it) like Figure 5.4 shown in Chapter 5. Your staff colleagues cannot fail to be impressed by your detailed sense of organization.

   Your narrative and text should explain why it's so important to balance the conflicting objectives of using your salespeoples' time most effectively with staying in touch with your customers. More important, you are demonstrating that you have a handle on this and a method for doing something constructive about it.

9. Describe your compensation plan, even if you feel that everyone on the marketing staff is familiar with it. Show how it helps motivate the entire sales organization to reach and exceed the overall sales and marketing goals. Use bar charts to show the percentage of income that comes from base salary and incentive commission at different percentages of quota levels attained by your salespeople.

10. List the trade show activities unless they are clearly the territory of another member of the marketing staff. Even if they are, you can list them anyway, explaining how this is important to your sales implementation and what you will do to capitalize on the leads and other interest that will be generated.

In some companies, the staff people are always pushing for company people to attend the shows and the salespeople, who have to man the booths, would rather have a head-on collision with a Sherman tank than go to another trade show. In others, the marketing staff (who have obviously never worked a trade show) look on this as fun and games time especially if the show is in a resort location and they think that signing up for a trade show is like putting your name down for a cruise to the Azores.

If your company is in the former category, you might, in your presentation, rank the shows in descending order in terms of their contribution to your sales effort, thereby inviting some cost-conscious soul to suggest that the ones at the bottom of the list be dropped. You will, of course, even if somewhat reluctantly, oblige and make sure you suggest an alternative use for the money so that you grab it before someone else does.

If your company is in the latter category, you might describe all of the hectic activity that takes place, perhaps as a typical 6:00 A.M.-to-1:00 A.M. day. You could talk about the cost per qualified lead generated versus cold calls. You might even pull out of your hat a story about a customer you had never heard of before the trade show who wound up buying hundreds of thousands of dollars worth of your product.

You could talk about effective close rates from the leads generated at trade shows as opposed to other sales activities. (You recall the suggestion that the average trade show lead takes two calls to close versus five for conventional sales activity.) You could talk about the things you got accomplished just by getting together with your people in a group.

If you need more ideas, go back to Chapter 12, "Avoiding the Ten Biggest Money-Losing Mistakes Made at Industry Shows and Conventions." This should provide some ideas to help you justify the participation.

You might also suggest that you could use the support of the most ardent skeptic of trade show participation at the next show because of his special expertise. He might come back from the show with a better appreciation of its value.

Like the accounting people attending sales meetings, as described in Chapter 11, in the section on "Eight Participants Who Can Make Your Meetings More Successful," this skeptic may learn a thing or two. If nothing else happens, you will at least have an extra body on hand who, hopefully, will do more good than harm. Just make sure you assign this person specific duties and responsibilities and have appointments set up.

11. Wrap up your plan report and/or presentation with a statement of your mission. Since organizational objectives, staffs, and the political situations differ so much from company to company, it is difficult to provide specific guidelines. Instead, think about what it is you and your sales force really contribute to the total marketing effort and express it in terms that everyone else will understand, endorse, and agree with. Sure, this could be considered a form of flag-waving, but much of the world *is* political.

You would have to be a 20/200 optometry patient not to see that a good deal of the above is designed specifically to get your message across and win points (and perhaps budget dollars) for your side. So? *You* have to spend a lot of time out in the field making things happen. You're absent from the home office power center. You don't have time to play the self-protection game or other games, so it's fair to use the plan for this purpose.

It's just too easy for field sales managers to lose control of the decision-making process compared with the staff people whose job it is to sit in their offices developing plans and reports. The sales managers wind up not getting the things they need to make their sales plan really effective. They get frustrated because they *know* what is necessary to really make things happen.

This is not to suggest (although some sales managers I've known do have this paranoid feeling) that the staff people are getting together and plotting against you and your objectives every time you make an airline reservation. But you *do* have to take steps to make sure that *your* company-oriented objectives stay in the forefront even when you are out of the office. The plan suggested above is the best way to do this. Professional-looking handouts will keep your message going while you are out of town working to achieve the objectives which have been set.

Now, you are probably making sure that all presentations by you or your salespeople to your customers are professional-looking and well put together in terms of form as well as content. *This* plan, your sales implementation plan, is no less important. Use graphics. Use professional-looking charts. Don't count on hand-produced charts or information scribbled on an easel pad to get your point across to your boss and your marketing staff colleagues any more than you would for a customer. *This is a selling job just as though you were in front of a customer.*

Put your material together in the form of a well-organized hand-out. Use a three-ring binder or proposal cover (depending on the size). Use a proposal cover for up to 20 pages and a one-half inch binder for 20 to 100 pages. Use a one-inch binder for anything larger. ("Larger" is academic. No one will really carefully read anything you put together that has more than 100 pages.)

Something magical happens when you put information in a binder or proposal cover. It assumes a good deal more credibility than if it were distributed in loose or stapled sheets. Some experienced meeting-goers have suggested that it's like William James' "A problem well-defined is half solved." That is, a proposal properly packaged is half-approved. I can find little in my own experience to dispute this.

So, use those binders and proposal covers, but make sure you don't pick the cheap ones to package your plan in. Select the package for your proposal that reflects the quality that it has in the same way you would select a package for your product. Your plan proposal is, after all, one of your most important products.

Better, do the above, but also put together a professional-looking visual presentation just as you would for an important customer. If you think you can get away with it and really do have a good visual presentation, refuse to send out your plan. Say (before the deadline date) that it is not fully developed and that you need the input from the marketing staff before you can complete it. Who can argue with this? It should be perceived by the marketing staff as being very flattering. Instead, set up a meeting to present it to your boss and the entire staff. Save the copies of the plan, complete with reproductions of all the graphics for hand-outs at the meeting.

Use 35mm slides or overhead projection transparencies (which many copy machines can reproduce) for a part of your presentation. If you have comments or testimonials (or even, depending on the circumstances, complaints) from customers on tape, include them. If you don't, consider getting them before the next time you have to make a presentation expressing your and the sales force's viewpoint. Don't be afraid of the show-biz aspects of this. You do it for customers to achieve an objective.

If you have an in-house facility that can help you put all of this together, use it. If you don't, consider going outside to get it produced. You will be able to use all this material for your sales meetings and maybe even for key customer meetings, so the expense is justified.

You may get some help from the marketing staff in putting your plan together. However, they may have their own objectives which don't necessarily match your own. If you are pushing for more money to be spent on co-op advertising and the marketing vice president is convinced that national television advertising is the only way to go, you won't get a lot of help from his staff people. Don't be afraid to go outside for help.

There is still another area where you may want to call upon the services of outside people. You may recognize that you need help with your artwork, graphics, charts, slides, or transparencies for your printed and visual presentation material. Less obvious is the possibility that you may need help putting the elements of your presentation or even your whole plan together.

Don't be afraid to go outside for this, either. Remember that your job is to lead your sales force to meet the sales objectives. Nobody expects you to be a planning expert. Get outside help for this function if you need it. You and your company could be a lot better off if you do.

IN CLOSING. . .

The home office is an important part of your sales team. If the marketing staff reports to you, be sure to include them in all you do. If, more likely, they are part of the home office to which you report, then you have as big a sales job to do with them as you do with your customers. Even if sales is, according to the organization chart, only a link in the marketing chain, don't hesitate to regard and use marketing as a contributor to your success as a sales manager.

16

How to Make Manufacturers' Reps Pay Off at Lower Sales Costs

While, as we know, the acronym "IMR" really stands for independent manufacturers' representatives, it can also stand for "instant marketing resource." Under the right circumstances, IMRs can help you to penetrate a market area faster, more thoroughly, and at less cost than is possible in any other way.

TEN WAYS TO TELL WHEN IMRs MEAN HIDDEN PROFITS FOR YOU

Check "yes" or "no" for the following ten questions to see if IMRs could be a money-making solution for you:

<u>YES</u>   <u>NO</u>

1. I need help in developing a sales solution for a market area in which my company and my salespeople have never been involved.

2. I need hands-on, immediate sales contact experience with my target market group and I don't have that in-house.

YES   NO

3. I need people with a following who don't have to be trained in my industry but who may need some product knowledge training.

4. I need help with the discount terms, packaging, cooperative advertising allowances, and other sales policies for this industry group I have chosen.

5. My sales and marketing people are good, but I need a specialist in the market I have chosen to expand in.

6. I can't afford to staff an organization for a market area and then find out that it wasn't the right area for my company.

7. I need to be able to control costs and make them a true "variable" cost (see Chapter 13) without the fixed cost investment of a fully staffed sales force.

8. The industry I have chosen is a closed group, so I need people who have an immediate entry and who know the movers and shakers personally.

9. I need immediate presence, recognition, and prestige with my target customers.

10. I need time economies. I can't afford to have people traveling all over the country or a territory with just my line.

Each "yes" is worth ten points. If you scored even ten points, IMRs should be, by your own admission, a part of your overall sales program. If you scored 30 or more points, make this a priority. If you scored 50 or more points, drop what you are doing and start looking for IMRs. But, first look at the key advantages and disadvantages of IMRs:

WHY IMRs CAN BE PROFITABLE FOR YOU

1. You need a quality of representation you couldn't afford any other way. Successful IMRs in most industries earn six-figure incomes and have the following and penetration in your marketplace that an affordable company person hasn't yet developed.

2. You want an *immediate* foot in the door. IMRs have contacts that took them many years to build. You have immediate access to this talent and these contacts.

3. You need a quick start—reps who will start running as soon as their feet hit the ground, without the overhead expenses of a branch office.

4. You need sound, experienced advice on your market approach in *this* industry without spending the time on an extensive and expensive market research effort.

5. You need a specialist in a distribution channel or a vertical market area, but can't yet afford your own person to fill this role.

6. You need *immediate* presence in the industry or market area. You can't afford to wait until your own sales force builds this presence.

7. You have limited funds for this market area and can't afford a fixed investment but are willing to pay for results on a percentage-of-sales basis.

8. You need a long-term approach to your sales effort. This is somewhat paradoxical, but remember that the rep is going to be around in the territory for a long time. The company person has less to lose by making quick scores and getting promoted out of the territory.

9. You are new to the industry and need to get quick and practical experience based on what industry customs and practices are. Reps have this information in their heads. Company salespeople could take a lot of time to get to the same level of experience. Even salespeople hired from other companies in the same industry know mostly what *their* companies did. Reps have a much broader overview through representing several lines.

10. You need a piggy-back on a successful line. If you are selling forms feeders, for example, hook up with a rep who has a printer line for immediate penetration. Every industry has this kind of "strategic partnering" opportunity available for a savvy sales manager.

USING THE BOTTOM LINE TO KNOW WHEN HIRING AN IMR IS DOLLAR-WISE

The "bottom line" is the bottom line, that line on the income and expense statement that says "net profit." As we have stressed throughout this book, *profit-oriented* sales management is the name of the game. It's what makes you successful and gets you promoted. Used properly, IMRs are a route to this goal.

With reps, you have no fixed costs and no investment in salaries, travel and entertainment, branch offices, and benefits. The commission paid is based on sales volume—no sales, no commission expense charged to your budget.

Remembering the distinction between fixed and variable costs from Chapter 13, this is a 90 percent "variable" cost. It's not 100 percent variable because there will be some "fixed cost" investment in expenses not related to sales volume, like providing literature and training the reps.

TEN WAYS TO TELL WHEN HIRING AN IMR
DOES *NOT* MAKE SENSE

There are circumstances when IMRs, good as they are at what they do, are just *not* the answer for your sales and profit goals:

1. When the cost would be prohibitive. If, because of your presence in a marketplace you can field a sales force for 3 percent of sales and the going rate for IMRs is 7 percent, work with your own people.

2. When the sales effort demands a lot of product knowledge and training. You will only "own" 20 percent to 30 percent of an IMRs time, and the training investment could be too costly.

3. When immediate response is needed to a customer's problem. Company salespeople can drop what they are doing and rush to the aid of the customer. Reps have other masters and other commitments.

4. When there is a danger of losing company-developed accounts to a competitor. The IMRs "in" with a customer gives him a salable commodity with your competitor, who can afford to offer a better deal since the competitor doesn't have the same investment in customer development that you have.

5. When the up-front heavy manpower demand will diminish after product introduction. You can reassign company people to new positions or new territories when the initial sales push is over. The IMR is going to stay where he is.

6. When the need for field sales involvement fluctuates. If customers can go months without more than superficial attention (heavy equipment sales, for example) and then need a lot of technical help or hand-holding, it's better to use a roving, at-large company staff.

7. When the field sales position is a necessary career step to fill needed home office positions. Your training investment in company people benefits your company throughout their careers as long as they stay with your company. Most reps aren't going to be lured away from their territories to your company.

8. When you need to change course quickly because of a fast-moving marketplace. You could call in ten company territory people for a sales blitz in Chicago, for example. You could assign five people to a special trade show in Des Moines. You can't move reps around that way.

9. When your start-up venture or other special sales push requires superhuman dedication that will be rewarded by management positions down the road, rather than commissions today. Reps aren't interested in "career ladders" as company people usually are.

10. When you are dealing with very confidential material. It's easier to tie a company salesperson to non-disclosure agreements and make effective threats to deter security breaches than to deal with an IMR who has less to lose.

HOW TO RECOGNIZE THE IMR's PRIORITIES

The major disadvantage, not just in the minds of some sales managers, is the lack of control. The fact that you don't have a fixed cost investment in salaries (one of the *advantages*) also means you have less leverage in terms of expectations.

The word "independent" in the term is no accident. Many IMRs started their businesses because they were tired of saluting the home office or field sales manager. As independents, they have their own sets of priorities, which may not coincide with yours or conventional corporate goals. The lack of control then, is, part of the price paid for the advantages and not just a paranoid reaction from an insecure field sales manager.

Before deciding to use this profit tool, think carefully about what this loss of control could mean to your total sales effort and your own peace of mind.

HOW TO RECOGNIZE WHEN A GOOD IMR
CAN BE A PROFIT TOOL FOR YOU

Hiring people for any position is a tough job. It's even tougher with salespeople since so much depends on intangibles and has little to do with education or past experience. Hiring the right reps is even tougher, but let's look at some telltale signs:

1. He's done his homework even before your first meeting, knows what your line is, how you are presently selling, and who your present customers are. This demonstrates at least a fair degree of interest in your company and an organized approach.

2. You are presented with a version of the rep's business plan with an organizational chart, description of the duties of the people employed, the firm's marketing strategy, and its major strengths. This is an indication that the rep has thought through his firm's mission and objectives.

3. The rep has a limited number of lines. This is arbitrary and may vary by industry, but five to seven is usually the right number. He speaks well of these lines and the people managing the companies.

4. The rep is able to speak confidently and knowledgeably about the marketing and sales strategy for these lines without divulging any confidential information.

5. The rep can give you at least five key prospects for your product in his territory and demonstrates some knowledge about how they operate. He goes beyond the name-dropping stage by being able to describe the profile and hot buttons of key buying influences.

6. Other key people in the rep firm are brought to your meeting, or, if this is impractical, at least referred to in the strategy discussion.

7. The rep has a *tentative* plan to market and represent your product line. Too firm a plan means that you are being thrown into a "cookie cutter" mill. No plan indicates either a lack of interest or an inability to think through what is necessary to make your line successful in the territory.

SPOTTING THE IMR WHO IS NOT FOR YOU

This is even more difficult since most reps are skilled at "handling" manufacturers. They probably have had a lot more experience interviewing manufacturers than you have had interviewing reps. Here, however, are some telltale signs:

1. They don't do any of the seven things outlined above. Any rep, however capable, should be expected to fit at least two or three of the above conditions.

2. The rep is vague about the lines carried. This could be an indication of several things:

   a. The rep has 10 or 15 lines (too many to provide adequate representation to anybody) and doesn't want to admit to this.

   b. Some of the so-called lines the rep professes to carry are still in the talking stage with no definite conclusion or arrangement.

   c. The rep is on the outs with one or more of the lines because of poor performance and doesn't want you to do any checking.

   d. He presently has a line competitive with yours and is looking to upgrade without taking the chance of losing the old line. This may or may not be so bad, depending on the industry and circumstances.

   e. The "rep" is really a company salesperson looking for greener grass, and at the moment, has a lot of "prospects" but no real following apart from the company he is now working for.

   f. The rep is ashamed of the "second class" lines the firm has taken on as "fillers" and doesn't want to admit that they have had to stoop to this.

   None of the above reasons are necessarily bad ones if the rep owns up pretty quickly to the reasons and you are satisfied with the reasons why. You may, in fact, have a diamond in the rough on your hands who will be everlastingly grateful to you. Just make sure things are presented honestly. If you have any doubts, thank the rep and go on to your next interview.

3. The usual reasons for distrusting *any* business associate—late for the meeting without a phone call, inappropriately (or under-) dressed, no clear-cut idea of what he is going to say, etc.

4. Bad-mouthing the factories represented. They may, indeed be the fools he says they are, but a rep is a rep and is being paid to present the principals in the best possible light. Would you like him to talk in this way about *you?*

5. Providing indefinite answers to your questions. When you ask about how the rep would sell your line you get vague answers like "Well, we'll have to look into that," "It depends on what we discover when we get out there," or, cleverly, "Well, what do you think?" The rep should be willing to take direction and listen to advice, but should have some clear, if tentative, ideas of what is to be done from day one.

6. The conversation from the rep is "I" instead of "we." Be careful of the one-person firms. They are usually spread too thinly and have no back-ups in the event of their incapacity or desire to pursue other interests.

7. To make a point, the rep gives you inside information about another principal's activities that could be useful to a competitor whether *you* are or not. Would you like him talking to your competitors in this way?

8. You have a bad feeling, but can't pin it down. *Trust* your feelings; they are probably right.

THE EASY WAY TO PICK A WINNER

Picture this scenario: Your prospective rep walks in with one or two of his key people and asks if you have an agenda for the meeting. If not, you can use theirs. The rep proceeds to ask a couple of additional questions proving he has done his homework, but doesn't assume that all of the answers to the sales approach have been uncovered. He consults with the associates on some of the details.

Based on some input from you, the rep makes a couple of notes on a pad to modify the proposed marketing plan he intends to present and then proceeds with an outline of a plan in which the associates participate. They are confident, but questioning and receptive throughout the meeting. They let you do at least 60 percent of the talking. At the end of the meeting, the rep tells you tactfully that he would be *willing* to take on your line and asks you whether you would like to use your agreement form or theirs.

If you find this paragon, sign on the spot. None of your prospects may follow this scenario exactly, but the closer they come to it the more confident you can be that you have a winner.

HOW TO GET A NEW REP SELLING FAST

You have been through the advantages and disadvantages of IMRs and now you know how to spot a good rep from a bad one and perhaps how to pick a real winner. You have hired a manufacturers' rep group. They already know their marketplace or you wouldn't have hired them in the first place. Now you need results. How do you make them effective *fast*?

1. Train them. Don't bring them into the home office for training and indoctrination as you would company people. Get out in the field and work with them empirically on sales calls. Let them learn by watching you work and then work themselves, with your guidance.

2. Make sure you have made your expectations clear from the beginning. Get an agreement on the number of calls to be made, in which market areas by when, and by whom.

3. Develop realistic goals that are agreed to if the rep is not to be asked to show cause why he should keep the line. Start from month one—no six-month "break-in" or training period as you might have for company people.

4. Monitor activities closely in a supportive way. Call the rep at home the evening of the first sales day and discuss problems and opportunities.

5. Make it clear that you are not only available day or night, weekdays or weekends during the initial period, but that you *expect* to be called and consulted.

6. If your product is a technical one and problems could come up that are beyond your ken, make a deal with one of your engineers for the new rep to call.

7. Provide immediate (hopefully positive) feedback on the rep's activities and accomplishments no more than *one month* after the rep is engaged. Make it clear at this time if there are any areas in which you don't feel the rep lived up to the agreements made.

8. If practical, meet with the rep (while making sales calls) six weeks after hiring. Go over every problem and opportunity that has come up. This is not only supportive, but makes it clear that you will indeed be one of the "squeaky wheels" among the principals that the rep represents.

9. In the beginning, give the rep anything reasonable that he says is needed regardless of your policy. Then demand results from this activity. If the rep has a red-hot prospect that would bite if only you had a cooperative advertising policy, for example, make one up—based, of course. on sales volume produced.

10. *Listen, listen, listen!* Besides the fact that you may just learn something new, you will have demonstrated that you recognize the rep's inde-

pendent businessman status and marketing ability. This should provide even more motivation.

11. Be tough on following up on fulfillment of quotas and other promises made—even in the initial stages of the relationship. You may listen to and commiserate on the reasons expectations were not fulfilled, and even do something about it, but this is the right time to make it crystal-clear that you expect agreed-upon expectations to be met.

WHAT TO GIVE A NEW IMR TO GENERATE REVENUE

We have already agreed that we are engaging a rep, not making a career investment in a company salesperson. You still, however, have an obligation to provide the kind of support that will make your rep productive and profitable. Here are some of the things the rep will need:

1. One complete set of *all* catalogs, price lists, documentation, service instructions, and any collateral material for *each* person in the rep's organization. Make a few extra points and increase the efficiency with which this material is used by organizing it and writing a cover letter explaining all the components. Better, get to the rep's territory and hold a sales meeting to do this with the entire staff.

2. A listing of all customers sold in the previous two years with sales totals and a breakout by product line. A listing in descending order of sales volume would be appropriate for the kind of account stratification suggested in Chapter 4.

3. A listing of all prospects in the rep's territory to whom literature has been sent in the last six months from space advertising, direct mail, trade show, or any other leads.

4. Information on competitors that is directly related to the sales task at hand. Don't go overboard on this. Your rep has several other principals sending information. If the material is too bulky, it won't be read.

5. Directly pertinent marketplace information on your line the rep might not already have. Again, pinpoint the material provided to the immediate sales task.

That's it. It's a short list that could easily be expanded in the case of a company salesperson whom you can count on to study nights while making calls during the day. Your rep has other lines and other interests, so you want to be sure to keep the information provided short and to the point.

Save that neat, detailed, and elaborate material you *know* will be invaluable for solving a particular problem or need that the rep raises. Introduce the more sophisticated material in personal meetings or in a follow-up letter after working with the rep in his territory and key it to a specific customer or solution that was discussed.

HOW TO PREVENT YOUR REPS FROM ADVERTISING
FOR YOUR COMPETITION

Should your sales reps sell against competition? In most cases the answer is no! The question of naming and identifying competition in advertising was around a long time before Avis declared war on Hertz, and most sales courses have a section on selling against the competition.

In most cases, the best answer is, "Forget it." Your competition has enough notoriety in the marketplace without your adding to it by emphasizing it with your reps. Instead, arm your reps with facts about competitors, but teach them to sell the advantages and benefits of your product. Here are some of the tools your reps should have in their arsenal of competitive information:

1. A "yes/no" checklist with the features (benefits) for each major product, product line, or service listed on the right-hand side and a column for each competitor with a "yes" or "no" or short quantitative information in each column.

2. A summary of pricing for comparable products (or as comparable as they can be).

3. A summary of other terms and conditions including:
   a. Shipping terms—freight prepaid, prepaid and allowed, or f.o.b. origin (buyer pays the freight).
   b. Service policy—lifetime, 90-day limited warranty available from a local dealer, return to the factory for repair or exchange, etc.
   c. Minimum order—open, minimum charge, $250, minimum for freight prepaid, etc.
   d. Return policy—anything within 30 days, restocking charge, only when inspected and authorized, etc.

4. A brief analysis of the intangibles that will be important to the rep's customers—company image, perception of quality, service follow-up, sales service friendliness, and follow-through, etc.

Arm your reps with information, especially information that demonstrates why your product (service) provides more benefits, but stay away from that defensive mode that compels you to think that you have to "sell against competition." If you're good, you'll be successful emphasizing your benefits. If you're not, you have problems that rep groups can't solve.

Exception: If you are in an industry that is dominated by one giant, you might want to *consider* (but only "consider") some "selling against competition" points. If, for example, IBM is your competitor and was in the market before you, you have no choice but to demonstrate why your product is better than Big Blue's. But get off it quickly and show your reps why your product will do new and better things. Create your own market niche in this situation and teach your reps how to exploit this niche.

You probably bought this book because the publishers told you it would be the most useful in its field. They didn't name specific books that would not be as useful.

17 PROVEN METHODS FOR MOTIVATING YOUR REPS— AND KEEPING THEM MOTIVATED

Most of the usual rules for motivating sales and other professionals apply, but there are some distinctions, especially if the IMR also receives, stocks, and ships the product (but doesn't invoice customers or own the inventory). Here are some special pointers for dealing with reps:

1. Realize that you are dealing with an independent businessman who deserves to be treated as a peer. Your company salespeople will put up with a lot to get that next promotion. The IMR has been there and has chosen the benefits of independence.

2. Set specific quotas, just as you would with company salespeople. Make it clear that you expect these quotas to be met if the reps are to keep the line. You can't hold out the promise of promotion as with company salespeople, but you can insist on performance with the possible loss of the line as your leverage.

   For example, a rep from Chicago once said, "The world isn't going to end if we don't get this product off the ground this month." Well, my world was going to end since I had staked my marketing reputation on meeting the sales forecast numbers. I had to suggest that his performance on the promotion would be an important consideration when the contract came up for renewal.

3. Define objectives, get the reps' participation, explain why some of their ideas cannot be implemented, and work to assist them in getting the work done.

4. Remember that the rep has other lines. If you provide 30 percent of a rep's income, you should get at least 30 percent of his time. Push for more by providing clear-cut objectives, but respect the limitations.

5. Provide as much notice as possible for sales meetings, promotional programs, and your work in the territory. Remember the other masters the rep has.

6. When working with the rep, provide at least a month's notice, define what you expect to accomplish, and get an itinerary from the rep a week before you leave.

   Here's a helpful tip: One sign of a relationship going sour is the rep's resisting your help or presence in the territory. Ask yourself what doesn't he want you to find out?

7. Make sure that your special demands on reps is in proportion to the commission dollars earned on your line. (Actually, if you do the planning and organizing suggested, you'll get more than your share of time since the other manufacturers' sales managers won't be as well organized as you.)

8. Recognize that you are always competing with other manufacturers for the rep's time and not just for customers. Have the best programs and the most productive plans for the use of time and you'll be successful in this competition.

9. Remember that reps are *people*. Praise them when they're good and make your demands clear when their performance is less than adequate.

10. Treat all company sales territories, reps, and company people equally when it comes to participation in training meetings, product knowledge seminars, annual sales meetings, and award trips.

11. Negotiate arrangements with the reps ahead of time in the case of an unusually small rep territory. You could explain the economic reasons for their exclusion from the meeting, or offer to have them attend if they pay their air fare while you pick up the hotel bill.

12. Be especially aware of the need for recognition in the form of trophies, plaques, and the like. Reps don't have the motivation of the prospect of a promotion for doing an outstanding job.

13. Take pictures of award presentations and send them to the rep's home town newspaper as well as the trade press in your industry. An extra couple of thousand commission dollars won't make a big difference in the lifestyle of most IMRs, but seeing their picture in print is very gratifying.

14. Treat reps equally on sales tools, samples, and literature. If your company people don't have samples charged to their sales budgets, the reps shouldn't have to pay for them.

15. Set budgets for what you will spend for these sales tools in each territory, be open-minded about what works, but have reps contribute to extraordinary programs. You want to encourage them, but giving away the store isn't motivation.

     For example, I was director of marketing for a company that produced a $1,000 (retail) product that sold to dealers for $500 to $600. One IMR came up with an original promotional program that included "spiffs" or PMs (promotional money paid for a period of time to the dealers' salespeople for selling the product).

     The deal was $30 per unit with dealer putting up $10 and the rep $10. I was happy to go along with my $10 and made it a standing offer for all territories. The company people had the $10 charged to their local promotional budgets.

16. Use your reps with major accounts just as you would company people. Excluding them would be treating them as second-class people. *Including* them is motivation.

17. If there is any business in the territory for which the rep will not be compensated, discuss, up front, the reasons for this. Naturally, you will not expect the rep to do anything for you with these accounts.

HOW TO NEGOTIATE A PROFITABLE MANUFACTURERS' REP AGREEMENT

IMR agreements range from a handshake to a multi-page document. While your company policy (and your legal department) may dictate the form of the agreement, here are some pointers:

1. Don't rely on the handshake. Too many reps remember well Sam Goldwyn's suggestion that "a verbal agreement isn't worth the paper it's written on."

2. Unless your legal department insists, or there is a good reason to protect your own interests, stay away from the long agreements.

    The longer the contract, the more points you can be called on during the relationship and in the event of termination of the rep.

3. Use a simple "Letter of Agreement" that includes the following terms and provisions:

    a. The exact names of both parties.

    b. The term "nonexclusive." This will be controversial for some reps, but you want the ability to hire specialized reps if you get into a new market or a new product line.

    c. The exact geographic territory. If a state is split, list the counties included, not something like "northern New Jersey."

    d. A brief statement of your expectations.

    e. The provision that the IMR has no authority to create obligations on your behalf or deviate from company policy and pricing, and that the rep will comply with such policies and procedures.

    f. The provision that all orders are subject to acceptance by the home (regional) office.

    g. The product lines covered by the agreement.

    h. The compensation rate(s), when commissions will be paid, and any exceptions.

    i. Your right to change or discontinue products without notice. (Companies have been sued when reps put in a good amount of time selling a product that was dropped from the line.)

    j. A termination clause, "with or without cause" and the amount of time a rep will be paid commissions on sales in the territory after notice of termination.

    k. A statement that neither party will be held responsible for anticipated profits.

    l. A statement that all rights and obligations under the contract cease except those rights specifically granted in the agreement.

    m. Effective date of the arrangement. Make it effective as of the date you confirm receipt of the agreement. Too many problems have arisen when reps hold up contracts or agreement letters, do nothing, and expect to be paid from the original date.

    n. A provision for charge-backs and delinquent accounts. Credits for returns and for accounts not paid in 90 to 120 days should be deducted from the current month's sales volume.

    o. A place for your signature and a place for the signature of the principal of the rep firm. If there is more than one principal, it won't hurt to have all sign the agreement.

4. Have your legal department or outside attorney review the agreement letter, but don't let them add all the "whereases" they would like to. Make it clear that you want the simplest form possible.

5. Send two signed copies of the agreement to the rep and have one signed copy returned to you. Keep one for your files and send copies to your financial (so the reps get paid) and legal departments.

All of this is not as formidable as it may sound. Figure 16.1 shows a fairly simple two-page letter of agreement actually used for a national representation effort. It was even approved by two attorneys although they did object to the simplicity and talked about things like "gray areas."

SAMPLE AGREEMENT

Confirming our conversation and agreement, _____
is appointed as the nonexclusive Bishop Office Products Co. (BOPCO) Manufacturer's Representative (MR) for the following geographic territory:

The MR will use best efforts to promote the sale of BOPCO products as an independent contractor, bearing all expenses incurred in connection with the MR sales effort, and the MR shall have no authority to create any obligations on behalf of BOPCO.

The prices and terms on all orders solicited by the MR shall be those of the current price bulletins and all orders shall be subject to acceptance by the BOPCO Home Office. The MR will comply with the written BOPCO policies and procedures.

As full compensation, the MR will be paid a commission equivalent to 7% on the line of safe products and 10% on the Protect-A-Ball and Old English element. Commission will be paid on net billed sales (excluding sales tax, delivery, and installation charges and after deduction of returns, accounts not paid within 90 days, and cancellations) attributable to orders solicited by the MR and accepted by BOPCO Home Office. Commissions will be payable monthly before the end of the month following the month during which commissions were earned.

BOPCO reserves the right to change product specifications or withdraw or discontinue a product without advance notice.

Either party shall have the right to terminate this Agreement, with or without cause, by giving the other party sixty days advance notice. Neither party shall by reason of termination of this Agreement be liable to the other for compensation, reimbursement, or damages either on account of present or prospective profits on sales or anticipated sales, or on account of expenditures, investments, or commitments made, or for goodwill or on account of any other cause.

All respective rights and obligations will cease upon the effective date of termination except as to preexisting indebtedness or claims or with respect to orders previously accepted by BOPCO and commissions to become due for those accepted orders when billed.

All obligations under this agreement shall cease in the event BOPCO should lose its representation of manufacturers whose products BOPCO will represent.

    Please sign and return to me a copy of this Agreement representing your acceptance of the terms of your appointment as Manufacturer's Representative. This Agreement will become effective as of the date BOPCO confirms receipt of your acceptance or as of any other earlier date specifically stated in our confirmation.

Cordially,

HOWARD S. BISHOP
President

_____
Signature

Figure 16.1

MAKING SURE YOU DON'T LOSE WHEN COMPENSATING IMRs

In most cases you will be paying a straight commission based on sales volume. Both commissions and sales volume will be determined by the contract. But questions always arise. Here are some pointers to keep any possible disputes to a minimum and ensure that you are getting the most for your money:

1. Base your commission rates on what you can afford according to the pro forma income statement you developed (see Chapter 13) and not what the reps feel they should earn. Naturally, you will have researched the standard industry practice and will have determined that you are not out of line with your proposed rate.

2. Have one commission rate for all reps. You may get the argument that the Rocky Mountain territory is more expensive to cover than New York City, but stick to your guns. The New York rep will start talking about the cost of parking and lunches and you could get into endless arguments with other reps if you don't.

3. Explain the reasons for any other variations. That is, you may pay 7 percent on most product lines but can only afford 5 percent on a close margin line. You may want to pay 10 percent on sales to dealers who buy at 40 percent off list, but only 7 percent on sales to wholesalers who buy at 50 percent-10 percent off. Expect complaints from wholesalers with this policy, but explain up front the reasons for doing it.

4. Develop a list of reasons why your line is a particularly attractive one—superb advertising, great training, hassle-free order handling, etc. It is one of your bargaining tools in getting reps to agree to your determined commission rates.

5. Shop for rates and don't accept "industry practice" as gospel. You want the best rep you can afford, but your list of why your line is easier to sell may help you shave a point or two from your rates.

6. Offer a *temporary* incentive for a new product line or new market area. You don't want to get locked into a higher than necessary rate just because the introductory push will be tough, but you want the reps' attention during this critical period. You may even offer 150 percent of the regular rate for the first 60 days to get them off and running quickly.

7. Don't give in on your pricing policies, terms, and conditions for a particular rep. Besides being illegal (unless it is to "meet competition") you'll be swamped with requests for exceptions once the word gets around. Listen, however to constructive suggestions on how the overall policies should be changed.

8. Similarly, be consistent with other goodies like samples, advertising allowances, etc.

9. Talk to other manufacturers' sales managers in your industry and other manufacturers that the IMR presently represents about what they do. You'll be checking with them anyway to verify the rep's statements about his performance and ability.

Here's a tip: You may be able to set different commission rates for different markets—7 percent for the industrial market and 5 percent for the mass market. Don't, however, make different deals in the same market area just to get a desirable rep. You'll be telling all reps that the rate is up for grabs and you'll spend more time negotiating than selling.

WHAT TO PAY FOR—AND NOT PAY FOR

The reason you chose the IMR route was to avoid fixed selling expenses and to pay only according to sales generated. In most cases, however, your expenses cannot be 100 percent variable. There will be some things you will have to pay for regardless of sales volume. Here are some pointers:

1. *Expenses:* The IMR pays for all normal business expenses of running the territory:
   - Office expenses—rent, stationery, supplies, etc.
   - Telephone expenses, including calls to you, although some manufacturers will accept collect calls or allow the use of an "800" number.
   - Travel expenses within the territory.
   - Expenses of visiting the home or regional office unless you called for the trip.
   - Customer or prospect entertainment.
   - Sales meetings with his staff.
   - Association meetings within the territory.
   - General or specific seminars or other education and training activities you didn't ask for.
   - IMR staff compensation, even if the staff members were hired specifically for your line.
   - Insurance or other benefit programs for the rep or his staff members.
   - "Consumer" work if the line is sold mostly through dealers or distributors.

     Obviously, if it serves your purpose or you want a particular project carried out, you can make an exception to any of the above general rules.

2. *Home Office Sales Meetings and Sales Training Meetings:* Here the home or regional office picks up all expenses, at least for one principal of the rep group. Anything beyond that, such as picking up the hotel bill if they pay the air fare for other members of the group who attend, is negotiable.

For example, figure your overall budget for such meetings and divide it by your sales quota. If your quota is $20,000,000 and your budget is $300,000, you can afford 1.5 percent of sales for meeting expense. If the meeting cost is $2,000 per head, you can afford to have one person from a territory doing $133,000 in sales ($2,000 divided by 1.5 percent), two people from a territory doing $267,000, and so on.

This way you are being very fair by relating participation in the meeting to sales volume, which is the name of the game and something all reps should understand.

---

3. *Local or Regional Shows and Exhibits:* This is the rep's responsibility since he will be showing all the lines carried. There are, however, some exceptions where you might want to split or pick up the tab:

   ● The rep isn't planning to attend but it's important for you to have coverage.
   ● Your line is the only one appropriate to be shown.
   ● You are introducing a new product and this is the most cost-effective way to do it.
   ● You have planned such activities as a part of your overall promotional budget.

For example, in one position, it was important to get this kind of exposure and my reps weren't used to attending local tabletop shows. The standing offer was to pay half the cost of the booth space, but I insisted on dominating the display.

In another instance, I funded a special deal (10 percent extra discount, free goods, etc.) and provided samples but no contribution to cost.

In both cases, I underlined the importance of the activity by showing up to help out whenever possible, planning field trips around the shows.

---

4. *National Conventions:* This is the rep's responsibility since he will be there to solidify relationships with several manufacturers, meet customers, and shop for new or additional lines. Again, there are exceptions where you may want to pick up all or part of the cost:

   ● You need help manning the booth other than an occasional stop there.
   ● You have a specific event planned where you want the reps there for your benefit. (See "tip" below, however.)
   ● You are paying for the trip as a reward.

One of the worst things you can do to your IMRs, especially if you are not paying any of the cost, is to schedule a sales meeting before, during, or after the convention. They have their schedules and their objectives, are very busy, and won't be paying full attention.

If there is a need to communicate in a group form, consider holding an "if you would like to come" breakfast meeting. Make it clear in the invitation that this is not a command performance, but an opportunity that can be taken advantage of if it is convenient.

5. *Field Trips:* A necessary and important part of the rep's job is using you are a resource in his territory. It should enhance the rep's status with customers and your presence should help make money for him. A "trip," however, could have three different scenarios with three sets of rules:

   a. You are taking the trip specifically to work with the rep in or near his home base (the rep lives in Fort Worth and you are meeting in Dallas):

      ● The rep provides a car, meets you at the airport and drives you to the hotel and other business appointments.

      ● You pay for your air fare, hotel, meals with the rep, entertainment with customers, and any side trips you make.

   b. You are taking the trip specifically to work with the rep away from his home base, but on one of his regularly scheduled trips in the territory (your Miami rep meeting you in Jacksonville):

      ● The rep pays for his transportation to your meeting place and hotel bill.

      ● You pay for your air fare, hotel, cab fare, meals with the rep, entertainment with customers, and any side trips you make. Unless you are only going to be there for a day and the rep is staying over, you would pay for the car rental.

   c. You ask for a special meeting with the rep whether you call on customers or not away from his home base (you're asking your Miami rep to meet you in Jacksonville because you are attending a convention in Jacksonville):

      ● You pay for all your and his expenses of attending the meeting you called. If the rep decides to stay over, he pays for the hotel, but you still pay for the air fare.

Obviously, exceptions can be made to any of the above general guidelines. If the rep sincerely offers to pick up a lunch tab, for example, accept graciously. You might even offer to supply change for the toll booth.

HOW TO KEEP THE RELATIONSHIP
HEALTHY AND PROFITABLE

Except for the above special rules for independent manufacturers' representatives, almost everything that has been said in this book about managing a field sales force effectively applies to leading IMRs. Just remember these important points:

1. Your reps have other manufacturers to serve and may not be able to jump or turn around on a dime the way your company people can.

2. They are independent businessmen who have *earned* their positions and deserve to be respected as such. In putting up their shingles, they have put themselves on the line in true entrepreneurial fashion. They produce sales or put the house up for sale.

3. They work for money and recognition, not for the prospect of a promotion. Their status with their customers *and peers* is very important to them.

4. Because they have other lines and will be around in their territories for a long time, they have more loyalty to their customers and less to you than do your company people. Their following can work to your advantage, but remember that you have less leverage.

HOW TO TERMINATE THE RELATIONSHIP

Most of the points made in Chapter 10 also apply to IMRs, especially the discussion on the "three-month plan." There are, however, some subtle differences to keep in mind:

1. The average rep has more standing and presence in the industry than the average company salesperson. This puts a high price on making a mistake since it would have a greater impact on *your* standing in the industry.

2. The rep will still be calling on him (your) customers whether he works for you or not. You don't want your customers' lament about how good old Charlie got shafted to get in the way of your sales efforts.

    You hired the rep partly because of his relationship with the customers. Remember that this can work against you in the event of a termination.

3. The rep is an established presence in the territory with, partly thanks to you, a customer following in your product area.

    There is far more danger in this situation than when a company salesperson goes to work for one of your competitors since the competitor will have no fixed investment in a company salesperson.

4. You could get an especially black eye if you replace an effective and producing rep with a company salesperson. In the rep's and the customers' eyes, good old Alice slaved for years to build the territory and then you took it away from her just when it was beginning to pay off.

   If your decision is economically motivated, like being able to field a company person for 4 percent versus 7 percent for the rep, consider discussing a compromise with the rep. And, make sure you have added up *all* the costs of a company salesperson.

IN CLOSING...

The decision on where or whether to use independent manufacturers' reps is yours. IMRs could have a place in your sales organization if:

1. You like the advantages.
2. You can live with the disadvantages.
3. You can handle their peculiarities.
4. You are willing to give up the degree of control that you have over a company sales force.
5. You can manage and lead as suggested in this chapter.

Independent Manufacturers' Representatives could even be your sales organization.

17

Using Telemarketing and Direct Mail to Increase Sales While Cutting Costs

Once the sole province of the "home office," direct mail efforts were either appreciated or complained about by sales managers and salespeople. Printing and mailing costs were too high to justify local efforts, and salespeople resisted any change in their personal customer call habits.

Today, anyone can create a direct mail effort. With the microcomputer, graphics software programs, multicolor copiers, and fast, high-quality commercial copiers, most territory salespersons can do their own desktop publishing. A customer newsletter can be composed on the computer, including fancy graphics and a customized masthead. The printout can be run off on the salesperson's copy machine or by a local copying service which can usually produce while-you-wait copies that look as though they were printed. The resulting piece can be mailed using the list of customers and sales stored in the salesperson's computer database.

At the same time, telemarketing is being accepted more and more as a cost-effective substitute for increasingly expensive personal sales calls, however routine. Most customers, rather than feeling slighted, have realized that conducting business over the phone saves their time as well. In addition, a modem (a modulate/demodulate device that communicates computer data over telephone lines) provides far more speed and efficiency than having a salesperson call on a customer in person and mail an order back to the home office.

The use of telemarketing and direct mail by your salespeople therefore makes sense. Yet for many salespeople, these methods represent radical departures from the way they are used to doing business.

TEN WAYS DIRECT MAIL CAN BOOST SALES REVENUE

In this section we'll discuss the use of direct mail by your field salespeople. We are assuming that your advertising people and others on the marketing staff have, with your participation, worked out the company-wide direct mail programs in an effective way. Here are some of the ways your salespeople can use direct mail effectively:

1. To keep in touch with the D or even C customers and prospects, letting them know the salesperson is interested in their business and informing them of new company products and programs. (See Chapter 4.) In my own businesses, I've had some customers where this was the only medium. We didn't even talk on the telephone.

2. To fill in the communication gaps between sales calls for the A and B accounts. An effective mailing program coupled with the telemarketing effort discussed below will create the impression that the salesperson is "always around." This will allow the salesperson to call less frequently and add to his customer and prospect base.

3. To provide information on a new program quickly and effectively. If a competitor has announced a regional advertising program to support distributors and you are matching the deal, a letter gets the message out much more quickly than the salesperson can make the rounds through the territory.

   If there is a problem with equipment that is unique to a region—plastic parts melting in the Southwest, for example—you want to get the word out fast about your solution or retrofit before your customers become turned off. You get more points by calling their attention to the problem before they have had a chance to recognize it.

4. To introduce new products selectively or with a tailored message for the territory. If you are introducing a new temperature control unit, for example, your message for Miami would be different from what it would be for Minneapolis.

5. To personalize a sales message. You may have spent a bundle on broadcast, space, and direct mail media. A nice complement to this would be for a salesperson who is known and respected in the territory to get out a bulletin saying something like:

   > "I just got back from a sales meeting on this new product. Boy, you wouldn't believe how great this really is. I can't wait to show it to you. If *you* can't wait, call and I'll give you some of the details."

6. To get orders quickly on a limited time special. You may be moving a local or regional warehouse and find you're overstocked on a heavy (in terms of dollars per pound) commodity product.

    You may find that it's less expensive to provide an additional discount and get the product sold before the move. If it's something like common pipe fittings that your customers use all the time anyway, a quick mailing with an order form reply card could do the job faster and better than personal calls or even phone calls.

7. To follow up on the salesperson's sweep through the territory to introduce a new product or program. Naturally, all important calls will be followed up by a personal call or letter. (If it was worth the time and other expense of making the call, it should be worth the time to get the letter out.)

    This letter can be particularly effective since the salesperson can report on the reaction of other customers to the product or program. Uses may have been suggested that the salesperson was unaware of when the swing began and were not in his presentation repertory. The letter will communicate these new ideas and reinforce the initial presentation to all customers and prospects.

8. To get information for the market research, product management, or engineering department. (See the "Checklist For Things That the Home Office May Expect from You" in Chapter 15.) A letter from a salesperson who is known to the customer is a more personal request than a letter from the unknown person in the home office.

    It will give the salesperson more perceived importance if the customers know that he is involved in this kind of effort and the personalization should help the response rate. Cooperating in this way, as suggested in Part II, Chapter 8, won't do your relationship with the home office any harm either.

9. To provide additional prestige with customers for the salesperson, particularly a new or junior salesperson. By developing and regularly mailing a bulletin or newsletter, for example, creates the impression that the regional or district office is, indeed, a professionally-run place. The status of the salesperson who signs the missive has to be enhanced in the customer's eyes.

10. Any other purpose that serves to communicate ideas, programs, or product information to customers, particularly when the message or idea is a localized one. (Talking about how the city of Mobridge saved money on bridge repairs by using your product, a rock salt substitute, would be of little interest to much of the country, but could go over big in the Plains States.)

Perhaps the most important thing to remember is that the field salesperson, no matter how efficient, has only a limited amount of time available. (See Chapter 1.) It may take some time and additional training before your salespeople are comfortable with these new "selling tools" like the computer and copier, but it will be well worth the investment in increased effectiveness.

TEN WAYS TELEMARKETING CAN BRING SALES DOLLARS TO YOU

As in the section on direct mail above, we will assume that any national or regional telemarketing efforts have been studied and perhaps tested by your advertising or other marketing people.

There is either a telemarketing effort of this kind in place already or there is a good reason for not having one. In this section we'll deal with how the salesperson can use this tool to save time, become more effective, and broaden his customer and prospect base.

First, let's put things in perspective by distinguishing between two types of telemarketing:

1. Telephone activity for the purpose of soliciting orders from existing customers, usually on a planned and regular basis—every second Thursday around 10:00 A.M., for example. This arrangement will have been made with the customers ahead of time.

2. Telephone activity which replaces or augments the usual personal sales calls. This may be the result of arrangements made with customers, but is usually initiated unilaterally by the salesperson.

The first activity listed above is really a customer service function performed by the home office or regional office where orders may be collected. We'll concentrate on the second activity since this involves the field salesperson and field sales manager more directly. Here are some of the reasons to use the telephone in this way:

1. To keep in touch with the C and even the B customers, depending on how large the territory is and how many customers are involved. (See Chapter 4.) This doesn't have to be only a "Can I help you with anything today?" call. The salesperson should have a specific purpose in mind for the call—a new product introduction, a new program, a new application idea that will help solve a customer's problem, etc.

2. To fill in the communication gaps between the sales calls for the A and B accounts. As discussed above in the section, "Ten Ways Direct Mail Can Boost Sales Revenue," the salesperson can create the impression that he's "always around" and reduce the call frequency on customers called on the phone between sales calls.

3. To get information to a few key accounts fast. This would be appropriate if you are in a market where prices change quickly and

significant pricing information is critical to the customer's operation. Being a grain broker is an obvious example, but the same thing might hold true for sheet steel, copper tubing, or other fabricated products.

4. To really tailor a new product or new program message, particularly for A accounts. If you have a new computer, computer peripheral, or computer software package, you might want to talk specifically about the application for your customer. You might even have different application areas in different departments of your customers' businesses. There is no way advertising can do this kind of job as effectively as a personal phone message.

5. To create a sense of excitement about news that is so good and of such benefit to the customer that it can't wait for the mail:

> "I just got word from the home office that the new gunnite nozzle has passed all the tests with flying colors and is going into production next week. Would Tuesday or Wednesday next week be more convenient for me to talk with you and your people about this?"

This is particularly important when you suspect that a customer may be about to make a purchase from a competitor. It may not get you the order, but it should buy you some time to make your pitch.

6. To follow up on leads generated from trade shows, advertising, and other sources. Your salespeople may not have been at the show and talked with the prospect and have no way to gauge the quality of a "bingo card" lead. The first step in the follow-through process is to qualify the lead to see if the prospect is a student, a literature collector, a lonely person, or a serious buyer.

   I've seen too many sales managers exhort their salespeople to follow up every lead without telling them that the lead should be qualified over the phone before a personal call is made. The salesperson makes ten calls and finds nine literature collectors and begins to doubt the company's support program and, perhaps, the wisdom, if not the sanity, of the sales manager who had this bright idea.

7. To set up appointments throughout the territory for a particularly important series of sales calls. This could be for a new product or new program introduction. Even if it is not regular practice to call ahead for appointments, the phone call should stress the importance of the personal call. The salesperson might, as above, use this to suggest that other buying influences or users besides the person usually called upon be present.

8. To develop leads for new product areas from existing customers. During a personal sales call, because time is so valuable, the salesperson may not have time to discuss all the products the company has. A phone

call between personal calls can discuss those product areas that the buying influence may not have been aware of. This is especially important for new or junior salespeople. The message of the call could be something like: "Based on our last discussion, I had an idea about how our networking system might work in your area."

9. To develop leads from new customers. This usually turns salespeople off because it's too reminiscent of the boiler room pitches we all get at home and at the office. The way around this is to position the telemarketing effort as a natural and logical part of the whole sales job.

   All salespeople should be spending at least 20 percent of their time developing prospects into customers. They should agree that the telephone is certainly a lot easier and more pleasant way than knocking on doors. Most salespeople resist using this tool because they think they are imposing on the prospect or because they are not really sure what they should say. (This will be discussed later in this chapter, in the section, "How to Prepare a Telemarketing Guide."

10. Any other situation where a personal message is important and appropriate to a selling purpose. Any other situation where the telephone can substitute for a personal sales call or enhance the value of the personal call.

STRATEGIES AND TECHNIQUES FOR COMBINING DIRECT MAIL AND TELEMARKETING TO MAXIMIZE SALES POTENTIAL

"Synergism" is what happens when the combined result of two or more activities produces a result that is greater than the sum of the individual activities. This is exactly what happens when direct mail and telemarketing tools are used together effectively.

I've had client after client tell me that they had "tried" a direct mail campaign or had "started" (and quickly abandoned) a telemarketing effort because "it just didn't work" or "it didn't produce anywhere near enough results to justify the cost." They convinced themselves that, while these might be good marketing tools for someone else, their businesses were somehow "different."

The problem, of course, was that they were doing isolated "things" instead of plugging elements into a well-thought-out and well-coordinated program. A mailing seemed like a good idea so they sent out 2,000 copies. With what purpose and to accomplish what objective? A friend had some success with a telemarketing effort, so they assigned one of the ladies in the office to get on the phone. To do what?

A thorough discussion on an effective, well-coordinated program would take at least another book, but here are some guidelines on how to work out a practical program at the salesperson (district manager) level to get the synergistic benefits of a combined direct mail and telemarketing program:

1. Start right after the sales meeting (see Chapter 4) or other program kick-off to introduce the concept of using direct mail and telemarketing tools. Make this a part of your first discussion with your regional and/or district managers and provide them with guidelines for explaining the concept and purpose to their salespeople. Make sure you know exactly what you want to accomplish with these tools so that the efforts will be well-integrated with your overall marketing and sales program.

2. Explain the use of direct mail and telemarketing as *solutions* to a sales and time management problem and not as an added chore. If possible, tie the use of these tools into a "Program of the Quarter" or other special effort to show how time will be saved and effectiveness increased.

   For example, if a new product introduction is planned and the requirement is for all A and B customers (see Chapter 4) to be contacted, show how direct mail will accomplish the desired results with C and D customers. Show how a telephone effort could be used with remote B customers who can't be reached within the introductory period, as well as with C customers. Demonstrate how both tools can be used to organize sales calls and enhance their effectiveness.

3. Make sure you have a complete customer/prospect list captured in a usable and duplicatable form (stored in a computer file, on a computer disk, or on pressure-sensitive mailing label sheets). Make sure the list is stratified and organized by B, C and D customers and prospects. (For a discussion on integrating prospects into your customer list by importance, see the section on "How to Weight Your Prospects by How Much They Can Contribute to Sales Revenue" in Chapter 4.)

4. Determine how often the customers, by strata (A, B, C, D), will receive the mailings and phone calls. You may decide to make personal calls on the A customers every month with a phone call in between and a bulletin mailed every month. Your B customers may get called on every two or three months with two phone calls in between and a bulletin every month or two.

   Your C customers may get called on only when there is a special presentation asked for, or in the case of a distributor, for a sales training meeting with a phone call every six weeks and a bulletin every three months. (See the section "How to Set Hour-and Dollar-Saving Call Frequency Patterns" in Chapter 5.) Lay out the mailings, phone calls, and personal visits on a master schedule plan with plenty of room left for problems or opportunities that may come up.

5. "Batch" the prospects. If your salespeople have 100 prospects and feel they can handle phone calls, follow-up mailings, and personal visits to those most interested in your product or service for 25 each month, you have four batches with which to work.

Now, your salespeople are ready to begin the coordinated direct mail/telemarketing effort.

STEP-BY-STEP TECHNIQUES FOR PUTTING THE MAIL AND TELEPHONE TO WORK FOR YOU

In this section we'll discuss specific steps to implement your combined, integrated, and synergistic direct mail and telemarketing effort. This is a substitute for the unorganized, simply "doing things" approach that characterizes so many efforts.

1. Qualify your mailing list so you know that the person to whom the mailing or telephone call is directed is still there and is the person to whom you really should be talking. You can do this over the phone by asking straight questions and perhaps get some points by explaining your purpose.

2. Prepare your first mailing to the 100 prospects. It should include:

   - A cover letter which could introduce your company and the salesperson to the prospect. It should include a specific customer benefit and be written from the viewpoint of "Here's what we can do for you" rather than "Here's who we are." If you are selling fire-resistant files, for example, you might offer to perform a records protection survey for the prospect. You would start with the danger of fires to businesses, offer the benefit (the *free* survey), and close the letter by telling the prospect why *you* are in the best position to perform the survey effectively.

   - A flyer or other piece of literature to add color and interest to the mailing and that ties in with the benefit or solution to a problem promised in the cover letter.

   - A reply card (an often-overlooked must) that should include, besides the usual name, address, and phone number information, check-off blocks for the following requests:

     "Please have your salesperson call me about . . ."

     "I need more information on . . ."

     "Please keep me on your mailing list for additional information."

     "Please take me off your mailing list."

     "You should also send your mailing to _____"

     Using a stamp, especially a commemorative stamp, on the reply card instead of the usual business reply indicia can generate more interest and get more replies.

3. Mail your first mailing to Batch #1. Monday is usually a good mailing day because the letter will arrive Tuesday, Wednesday or Thursday—after the Monday crunch and before the TGIF syndrome.

4. Wait about a week and then call all the prospects in Batch #1. (You can be qualifying Batch #2, in the meantime.) Ask the prospects if they

received the mailing and qualify them further. Make sure they really do have a need for your product or service, that they can do enough volume to justify your keeping them on your prospect list, and that the person to whom the mailing and phone call is directed is at least one of the real buying influences.

If any of the people you call say they didn't receive the mailing or don't remember it, send them another with a personal note as a part of Batch #2 and include them in Batch #2 from now on to keep your batches orderly and straight.

If you want to see them, offer an incentive if you can make an appointment. It could be something like the *free* records protection survey mentioned above or a special report on the prospect's industry that your market research people have recently prepared. With the first mailing you may get only one or two appointments, but you've just begun.

5. Prepare mailing #2. The format will be the same with a different solution to a prospect's problem, perhaps a case history on how another prospect was able to use your product or service to solve a problem, and a different piece of literature.

6. Month 2: Mail out 25 pieces of mailing #1 to the next batch (Batch #2.) Mail 25 pieces of mailing #2 to Batch #1.

7. Wait about a week after this mailing. (Use the time to qualify Batch #3 and to follow through on appointments with Batch #1 people whom you have decided you want to see.) Call the first 25 prospects from Batch #1 as outlined in paragraph 4, and the second 25 from Batch #2. Remind the prospects from Batch #2 of your previous phone call and refer to something specific you discussed so you will be implanted in their minds.

   You'll know exactly how to reference your previous conversation from your Account Profile and Call Sheet. (For a reminder about this, see the section, "How to Effectively Manage the Paperwork," in Chapter 2, Figures 2.1, 2.2, and 2.3.

8. Prepare mailing #3 as indicated in paragraph 5, for mailing #2. Qualify your next batch (Batch #3 and follow through on your appointments from Batch #1 and Batch #2.

9. Month 3: Mail out 25 of mailing #1 to your next batch (Batch #3). Mail 25 mailing #2s to Batch #2 and 25 of mailing #3 to Batch #1.

10. Follow up with a phone call to all 75. This takes less time than you might think unless you get some really heavy questions. And what's wrong with that? It's a pretty good indication that you're close to turning a prospect into a customer. If the activity gets too heavy (there are 100 to follow up on next month, as we continue the pattern) you can always split the batches into smaller pieces.

11. Month 4: Continue the pattern. Mail 25 of mailing #1 to Batch #4, 25 of mailing #2 to Batch #3, 25 of mailing #3 to Batch #2, and 25 of mailing #4 (which you will have prepared) to Batch #1. Follow the other steps as outlined above.

12. Month 5: Continue the pattern. By now you will probably have a Batch #5 from the new prospects you have added during the past four months.

13. Month 6: Continue the pattern. You have no new batches, but you can make mailing #6 to Batch #1, mailing #5 to Batch #2, etc. You should have so many new customers and qualified prospects that a good deal of your direct mail and telemarketing effort will be spent in follow-through. Don't let the new prospect effort abort, however. You will always lose customers, and fantastic prospects have a way of turning cold when the time comes to sign an order.

Four batches were chosen as the basis for the coordinated direct mail/telemarketing effort so the same activity usually takes place at about the same time of the month. If you split the batches, consider going to eight for the same reason. Along the way you'll be adding prospects. You could integrate them into one of the batches or, better, set up a new batch so you can start with mailing #1 and keep everything else in its proper sequence.

Drop from your list only those prospects who are clearly not interested in you, your company, your product, or your service. (Hanging up when you mention your name is a fairly reliable indication of lack of interest.) There may also be some prospects that you will want to keep on your mailing list but will call only every three months. Keep them in the batches for your mailings and code them accordingly on your Account Profile and Call Sheet.

By following through on this effort in the planned, orderly, and consistent basis outlined above, you should double or triple your results for time expended. *But*, don't assume that the first mailing will bring you a 100 percent return. Most prospects probably won't even begin to realize that you exist until the third or fourth mailing unless you get very lucky or are particularly effective in your telephone and personal call follow-through. Consistency and persistence are the keys to making this pay off. Plan on a six-to twelve-month effort, revising as you go, before you make a firm determination on the program's effectiveness.

HOW TO PREPARE A TELEMARKETING GUIDE

The above outline has been well tested and found to be a good strategy to combine direct mail and telemarketing efforts. The telephone follow-up has, in some cases, increased the effectiveness of programs from three to ten times over direct mail alone. However, you can't leave your salespeople on their own. They may still be used to the conventional personal call sales effort and think of the telephone as a tool to get information or take orders rather than as a substitute for a personal call.

They need the kind of boost they will get from a suggested guide whether they follow it to the letter or not.

The guidelines in this section will apply to the telephone follow-up of the direct mail letters outlined in the previous section. They should also be helpful for any other kind of effort where a lot of people have to be contacted within a short period of time with the same basic message or request, such as getting appointments for a new product that has just recently been introduced in a market area which is new to you, your salespeople, and your company.

We've deliberately used the term "guide" to avoid the negative connotation of the word "script" which seems to turn salespeople off. You could call your suggested plan for telephone calls a "calling guide" or even an "appointment-making guide." Whatever you call it, the purpose is to make a directed call with specific information, in a specific way, revising the guide as you go along so that you wind up, after a few calls, with the best guide (script) possible.

Your salespeople will use the telephone and perhaps these guidelines to make all kinds of calls. They could be following up on leads, requests for information, referrals or previous contacts at a trade show, or other contacts. Those are the easy ones. For the purposes of these guidelines, we'll take on a tough assignment. We'll assume that you have a new product (a computer software program for electrical contractor job-cost control) and that you want to get appointments with all the electrical contractors in each salesperson's territory who do more than one million dollars in gross annual revenue. They don't know you, your salespeople, your company, or your product.

Let's look at some guidelines for preparing an effective "appointment-making guide" under these circumstances:

1. Work out the first draft yourself, but first decide just what it is you want your salespeople to accomplish with the telephone call:

   - Are your salespeople trying to get an appointment with all prospects?
   - Are they trying to qualify the prospect so they know that they want to see the prospect personally?
   - Do you want them to do both?

     You could get an appointment with a contractor who just bought a computer with a job-cost control program that is working fine, but what good would that do? Think about the positive end result you want to have had happen by the time your salesperson hangs up the phone.

2. Think about your audience—the buying influences your salespeople will be calling. Your guide should read and sound different for an executive of a Fortune 500 company than from a guide for a small business owner. Think about the perception of your company and your product in the minds of the person called. How much explanation of who you are will be necessary?

You will, of course, have obtained an industrial or association guide and eliminated those electrical contractors who do less than one million dollars a year. You will also know whether your salespeople are talking to the owner of a ten-person operation or the Management Information Systems Director of a two hundred-person operation.

3. Think about what you really have to offer in terms of customer benefits or solutions to problems the prospect may have. Boil the guide down to its simplest and most concise form.

4. Anticipate the reasons why the prospect, however well-qualified your salesperson thinks he may be, may resist making an appointment. Could the contractor be afraid of the idea of a computer? If so, you might want to emphasize the problem-solving elements of the job-cost control program and avoid the terms "computer" and "software." Is the contractor likely to have a computer already? If not, you might want to be armed with information on how this can be easily accomplished.

5. Write out your guide. Be sure to include open-ended questions so that there is plenty of room for prospect participation. This is no different from any other kind of selling—your salespeople should listen more than they talk.

6. Tape-record your guide and listen to it. Have your colleagues listen to it. Does it sound like something that is being read? If so, change it to make it more natural. Does it sound too formal? If so, change it to make it less stilted.

7. Test it before you take it out to the field. Call ten or twenty electrical contractors in your local area and try out the pitch, perhaps revising after the first five. By calling twenty people, you'll get about 50 percent of the objections you are likely to get in calling one thousand.

8. Keep track of the "yeses" and "nos" you get to make sure you (or your salespeople) are not getting stale in using the guide. Revise your guide constantly as you find "hot buttons" that seem to turn on prospects. (One good idea I've seen effective telemarketers use is to put a mirror in front of the telephone. Sometimes the person calling doesn't realize how he is coming across to the prospect. The facial expression could be a good tip-off and a good way to keep the presentation on track.)

9. In writing the guide, forget the chummy "How are you today?" or, "How is the weather in Punxsutawney today?" Unless you know him personally, your prospect knows you don't really care and you could sound like a boiler-room smoothie with this approach. Instead, introduce yourself and your company. Then go right to the purpose of your call:

> "Hello, this is Dan Lightman from SBH Software. The reason I am calling you today is because our company, SBH Software, has just

produced a job-cost control system for electrical contractors. We've found so far, *in companies like yours*, that it reduces posting time by 60 percent and gives you a weekly profitability report on jobs in progress as well as closed jobs. Could you tell me something about your present job-cost control system?"

Notice that we got right to the point, promised a benefit and a solution in almost the first breath, and asked an open-ended question that is also a means of qualifying the prospect. We used our company name twice to make sure the prospect got it. We also used an indirect third-party referral by talking about "companies like yours" to demonstrate the possibility of our package being useful to this prospect.

10. Take the guide out to one territory for further testing and introduction. Obviously, the territory chosen will be the one where you are likely to meet with the best initial success, so you will have a story to tell to the other regional or district managers. Introduce the guide and its use as a time-saving, effectiveness-increasing part of your marketing and sales implementation program. Go through the steps above with your people.

    If you meet any reluctance to use a planned guide, remind your people that the most convincing and realistic actors or actresses are speaking lines memorized from a script. Let your people make minor changes in the guide to make it sound more natural (for them) as long as you agree with the changes and the basic integrity of the guide is preserved. Have them make further minor revisions as they find obstacles or hot buttons with *their* prospects.

11. One final point—most of the telemarketing experts I've met and books I've read will tell you not to talk with secretaries or receptionists if you can't get through to the person you want to talk with. Nonsense! If the prospect is not in (or not in for *you*) when you call, leave your name, your company name, and the purpose of your call:

    "Our company has just introduced a job-cost control system for electrical contractors that is saving time and money for companies like yours. I know Mr. Harkins will be interested in hearing more about it and perhaps seeing a demonstration."

You are not sitting in a telephone "boiler room" peddling valuable land 60 miles west of Fort Lauderdale. You are offering to take some of your valuable time to provide useful information on a time-saving and effectiveness-increasing tool for the prospect's business. You are offering to provide a real solution to a real problem.

    Sell the secretaries or receptionists. Don't ignore them or treat them as mere telephone-answerers or message-carriers. In some companies, the secretary may be the one who will make or substantially influence the final decision. Also, you will be much more likely to be put through the next time you call if the secretary can walk into your prospect's office with the message: "This sounds interesting. I think you should talk with this person." I've had cases where, in conducting tests for clients, the "receptionist" turned out to be the administrative assistant to the president and set up an appointment on the spot.

IN CLOSING. . .

Telemarketing and direct mail can benefit your sales effort in two ways: They can reduce expenses by lowering the cost of routine client calls, and they can enhance sales if used together in the proper way.

Appendix A

Setting Regional Quotas

This appendix presents a realistic situation in which quotas have to be assigned and our "what" and "how" checklists are applied. If you happen to be a Midwestern regional manager, the examples will have a great deal of meaning. If you are not, follow the logic of the example to see how any territory and quota can be set up in as equitable a way as possible. Here is the scenario:

1. The territory is the Midwest, in this case defined as comprising the states of Illinois, Wisconsin, Minnesota, North Dakota, South Dakota, Ohio, Indiana, and Michigan.
   Note: Logical questions at this point might include: Why not Iowa? Why the Dakotas? If you're going to downstate Illinois, why not Missouri or at least St. Louis? These are all good questions, but we have to start with some assumptions, so we have decided that the territory defined above is the "Midwest." (Actually, it's a pretty logical grouping considering travel and area demographics with Chicago or suburban Cook County as headquarters.)

2. You have been given five district managers to work with and it is your job to decide how to divide up the territory.

3. The territory used to be handled by an Eastern Regional Manager based in Philadelphia and you have to decide on a Midwest Regional Headquarters location.

4. Your quota for the region has been tentatively assigned as $5,000,000 for the next year and your territory did $4,416,000 last year. (Don't take the term "tentative" too seriously. This is management lingo for "We want you to look at this and then give us your 100 percent agreement on what we have already decided to do.")

LAYING OUT TERRITORY GEOGRAPHICALLY

Before we begin to work with the numbers, let's take the first step first—how to assign relatively balanced quotas to your district managers considering business potential, size of the territory, and travel considerations. We'll take it step by step:

1. You have eight states in your territory and the one with the most business potential (Illinois) is worth about 30 times the one with the least potential (North or South Dakota—a toss-up).

   Your first step, then, is to look for some logical territorial groupings. Ohio, for example, might stand on its own as might Michigan. The Dakotas won't contribute much business, and could be combined with Minnesota as could Wisconsin.

   Illinois might stand on its own, but then Indiana becomes a question—it certainly couldn't support a full person while Cook County, Illinois, alone is worth almost twice as much as the entire state of Indiana.

   This guessing game could go on and on, but is intended as an example of the kind of thinking process you should employ. Let's put some quantitative numbers on our rough assumptions.

2. We'll assume we're in the office products business. This means that to get some solid information on territory potential (one of the first guidelines we decided to look at) we can go to the National Office Products Association. NOPA publishes a very useful index called "NOPA County Buying Patterns for Office Products."

   This index happens to be an excellent way of measuring office products sales potential. It is based on the clerical population of a county, expressed as a percentage of the country as a whole, averaged against the sales of office products in a county, again expressed as a percentage of the county as a whole.

   Since everyone uses office products and since office products usage is a pretty good measure of economic activity in an area, it could also be useful as a business index for other industries.

   We use it as an example of using an independent index to weigh against actual last-year performance in order to set fair quotas. (Other industries and other industry trade associations have similarly useful indices.)

Page 2 of NOPA County Buying Patterns for Office Products (see Figure A.1) summarizes "State Buying Patterns for Office Products." Let's pull out the percentage of the country that *our* states represent:

Illinois	6.0229%
Indiana	1.9176
Michigan	3.4223
Minnesota	1.9795
Ohio	4.3030
North Dakota	.2050
South Dakota	.2046
Wisconsin	1.7762
Total	19.8311%

A couple of notes before we proceed:

1. Your total comes to 19.8311% of the country, or about one-fifth. This might be useful information to have in negotiating with the home office about your total sales quota.

2. It's probably not necessary to take these percentages out to the fourth decimal place. It might, however, impress your district managers and be helpful in convincing them how precise you are about quotas.

    Let's use this information to work out our territory divisions. First, to make the numbers more useful, we will express each state in terms of the percent of our territory so we add up to 100%:

Illinois	30.38%
Indiana	9.68
Michigan	17.27
Minnesota	9.98
Ohio	21.71
North Dakota	1.03
South Dakota	1.03
Wisconsin	8.92
Total	100.00%

Again, the extra decimals are probably not necessary, but let's use precise numbers as long as we have them. There will be plenty of room for subjectivity later.

3. Now that we have some numbers to work with, let's take a crack at the territories. Ideally, since we have five people, it would be great to assign 20 percent of the total territorial potential to each person. The first pass might look like this:

STATE	1983
Alabama	1.2821
Alaska	.1928
Arizona	1.0602
Arkansas	.7126
California	11.5754
Colorado	1.5920
Connecticut	1.6531
Delaware	.3401
District of Columbia	.7417
Florida	4.4161
Georgia	2.1593
Hawaii	.4647
Idaho	.3368
Illinois	6.0229
Indiana	1.9176
Iowa	1.1702
Kansas	.9709
Kentucky	1.1764
Louisiana	1.6300
Maine	.3011
Maryland	1.9515
Massachusetts	3.1124
Michigan	3.4223
Minnesota	1.9795
Mississippi	.7208
Missouri	2.2539
Montana	.2670
Nebraska	.6778
Nevada	.3046
New Hampshire	.3890
New Jersey	3.2550
New Mexico	.4334
New York	10.5071
North Carolina	2.2818
North Dakota	.2050
Ohio	4.3030
Oklahoma	1.1395
Oregon	1.1024
Pennsylvania	5.1576
Rhode Island	.4372
South Carolina	1.0578
South Dakota	.2046
Tennessee	1.7644
Texas	6.5679
Utah	.5471
Vermont	.2078
Virginia	2.0169
Washington	1.6888
West Virginia	.4063
Wisconsin	1.7762
Wyoming	.1454
United States	100.0000
Standard Metropolitan Statistical Areas	85.5183

Figure A.1
State Buying Patterns for Office Products

Territory	Area	% Total Midwest (#4)
A	Ohio	21.71%
B	Michigan	17.27
C	Illinois	30.38
D	Indiana	9.68
E	Minnesota, North Dakota, South Dakota, Wisconsin	20.96
	Total	100.00%

Well, territories A and E look pretty good and B might even pass, but we have some revisions to make. Let's look at a map and our "NOPA County Buying Patterns for Office Products" listing by state and individual counties within the states (Figure A.2 is a composite listing from the publication) and see what we can do:

1. Looking at Ohio, we see that Toledo (Lucas County) is closer to Detroit than to Columbus or Cincinnati. While it would mean missing out on the hot spots in Tiffin, Findlay, or Bowling Green (Ohio, not Kentucky), it may make sense to assign Lucas County to the Michigan territory since Toledo is an easy straight shot down Route 75 from Detroit or down Route 23 from Ann Arbor.

2. We tentatively identified Illinois as a territory, but Illinois is really two states—Cook County (where Chicago is located) and "downstate." So, let's consider Cook County as a complete territory. But, Rockford (Winnebago County) is a lot closer to Chicago than Springfield or even Peoria. Let's add Winnebago County to Cook and throw in the in-between counties of Boone, McHenry, and Lake.

   Note: This amount of attention to detail really is important. It establishes equitable territories and, more important, lets your district managers know that you know what you're doing.

3. Lake County (Gary, Indiana) is so close to Chicago that it's almost the South Side. Let's add that to the Cook County territory in addition to the Rockford area.

4. Territory E looks pretty good, so let's leave this alone for a while. It may look tempting to add Milwaukee to territory C (Cook County plus) since your territory E district manager will probably set up shop in Minneapolis, but, as discussed below, geography isn't the only consideration in determining territory alignment.

5. It looks as though we've solved the "Indiana problem" by default—we have "downstate Illinois and Indiana (except for Lake County) left over. Let's call them "territory D." (There is a Lake County, Indiana and a Lake County, Illinois. Don't get them confused.) Here's what your territory looks like: (Figure A.3)

ILLINOIS	% of U.S.
Adams	.0341
Alexander	.0034
Bond	.0042
Boone	.0109
Brown	.0014
Bureau	.0108
Calhoun	.0008
Carroll	.0041
Cass	.0040
Champaign	.0592
Christian	.0101
Clark	.0043
Clay	.0035
Clinton	.0074
Coles	.0180
Cook	3.6637
Crawford	.0059
Cumberland	.0029
De Kalb	.0226
De Witt	.0048
Douglas	.0059
Du Page	.3556
Edgar	.0058
Edwards	.0027
Effingham	.0131
Fayette	.0044
Ford	.0054
Franklin	.0087
Fulton	.0111
Gallatin	.0018
Greene	.0028
Grundy	.0097
Hamilton	.0015
Hancock	.0047
Hardin	.0009
Henderson	.0009
Henry	.0131
Iroquois	.0089
Jackson	.0180
Jasper	.0026
Jefferson	.0151
Jersey	.0037
Jo Daviess	.0049
Johnson	.0010
Kane	.1338
Kankakee	.0382
Kendall	.0064
Knox	.0235
Lake	.1639
La Salle	.0403
Lawrence	.0052
Lee	.0114
Livingston	.0120
Logan	.0108
McDonough	.0091
McHenry	.0430
McLean	.0758
Macon	.0647
Macoupin	.0122
Madison	.0880
Marion	.0178
Marshall	.0028
Mason	.0030
Massac	.0031
Menard	.0018
Mercer	.0024
Monroe	.0033
Montgomery	.0103
Morgan	.0158
Moultrie	.0033
Ogle	.0123
Peoria	.1243
Perry	.0069
Piatt	.0050
Pike	.0037
Pope	.0004
Pulaski	.0022
Putnam	.0022
Randolph	.0114
Richland	.0056
Rock Island	.0818
St. Clair	.0763
Saline	.0104
Sangamon	.0974
Schuyler	.0013
Scott	.0009
Shelby	.0036
Stark	.0012
Stephenson	.0244
Tazewell	.0473
Union	.0034
Vermilion	.0358
Wabash	.0057
Warren	.0060
Washington	.0031
Wayne	.0054
White	.0047

	% of U.S.
Whiteside	.0212
Will	.0899
Williamson	.0154
Winnebago	.1268
Woodford	.0066
ILLINOIS—TOTAL	6.0229

INDIANA	% of U.S.
Adams	.0054
Allen	.1686
Bartholomew	.0233
Benton	.0015
Blackford	.0034
Boone	.0072
Brown	.0007
Carroll	.0025
Cass	.0090
Clark	.0212
Clay	.0030
Clinton	.0051
Crawford	.0007
Daviess	.0044
Dearborn	.0074
Decatur	.0036
De Kalb	.0060
Delaware	.0352
Dubois	.0100
Elkhart	.0611
Fayette	.0062
Floyd	.0128
Fountain	.0032
Franklin	.0026
Fulton	.0035
Gibson	.0081
Grant	.0214
Greene	.0029
Hamilton	.0218
Hancock	.0069
Harrison	.0028
Hendricks	.0077
Henry	.0089
Howard	.0274
Huntington	.0126
Jackson	.0073
Jasper	.0031
Jay	.0036
Jefferson	.0058
Jennings	.0028
Johnson	.0184
Knox	.0113
Kosciusko	.0176
Lagrange	.0057
Lake	.1899
La Porte	.0302
Lawrence	.0062
Madison	.0365
Marion	.5411
Marshall	.0105
Martin	.0012
Miami	.0058
Monroe	.0255
Montgomery	.0085
Morgan	.0052
Newton	.0019
Noble	.0063
Ohio	.0004
Orange	.0036
Owen	.0011
Parke	.0016
Perry	.0036
Pike	.0016
Porter	.0358
Posey	.0039
Pulaski	.0016
Putnam	.0082
Randolph	.0045
Ripley	.0039
Rush	.0032
St. Joseph	.1212
Scott	.0029
Shelby	.0078
Spencer	.0024
Starke	.0023
Steuben	.0043
Sullivan	.0024
Switzerland	.0007
Tippecanoe	.0463
Tipton	.0027
Union	.0007
Vanderburgh	.0829
Vermillion	.0024
Vigo	.0382
Wabash	.0083
Warren	.0008
Warrick	.0048
Washington	.0027
Wayne	.0251

Figure A.2

Wells	.0036
White	.0049
Whitley	.0047
INDIANA—TOTAL	1.9176

MICHIGAN	% of U.S.
Alcona	.0006
Alger	.0016
Allegan	.0153
Alpena	.0084
Antrim	.0025
Arenac	.0020
Baraga	.0013
Barry	.0058
Bay	.0324
Benzie	.0018
Berrien	.0634
Branch	.0079
Calhoun	.0604
Cass	.0077
Charlevoix	.0045
Cheboygan	.0043
Chippewa	.0050
Clare	.0035
Clinton	.0077
Crawford	.0018
Delta	.0090
Dickinson	.0084
Eaton	.0251
Emmet	.0084
Genesee	.1486
Gladwin	.0021
Gogebic	.0042
Grand Travers	.0252
Gratiot	.0092
Hillsdale	.0088
Houghton	.0075
Huron	.0065
Ingham	.1158
Ionia	.0078
Iosco	.0042
Iron	.0025
Isabella	.0092
Jackson	.0529
Kalamazoo	.0961
Kalkaska	.0013
Kent	.2224
Keweenaw	.0002
Lake	.0006
Lapeer	.0088
Leelanau	.0018
Lenawee	.0254
Livingston	.0175
Luce	.0009
Mackinac	.0014
Macomb	.2356
Manistee	.0043
Marquette	.0173
Mason	.0053
Mecosta	.0047
Menominee	.0049
Midland	.0297
Missaukee	.0013
Monroe	.0265
Montcalm	.0098
Montmorency	.0012
Muskegon	.0494
Newaygo	.0056
Oakland	.5804
Oceana	.0021
Ogemaw	.0021
Ontonagon	.0019
Osceola	.0026
Oscoda	.0008
Otsego	.0046
Ottawa	.0430
Presque Isle	.0018
Roscommon	.0025
Saginaw	.0817
St. Clair	.0285
St. Joseph	.0124
Sanilac	.0065
Schoolcraft	.0012
Shiawassee	.0137
Tuscola	.0070
Van Buren	.0125
Washtenaw	.1164
Wayne	1.0286
Wexford	.0067
MICHIGAN—TOTAL	3.4223

MINNESOTA	% of U.S.
Aitkin	.0026
Anoka	.0478
Becker	.0066

	% of U.S.
Beltrami	.0073
Benton	.0073
Big Stone	.0018
Blue Earth	.0263
Brown	.0119
Carlton	.0074
Carver	.0099
Cass	.0037
Chippewa	.0050
Chisago	.0053
Clay	.0158
Clearwater	.0013
Cook	.0012
Cottonwood	.0047
Crow Wing	.0118
Dakota	.0684
Dodge	.0024
Douglas	.0090
Faribault	.0058
Fillmore	.0058
Freeborn	.0130
Goodhue	.0120
Grant	.0018
Hennepin	.8333
Houston	.0037
Hubbard	.0024
Isanti	.0042
Itasca	.0073
Jackson	.0031
Kanabec	.0030
Kandiyohi	.0127
Kittson	.0013
Koochiching	.0038
Lac Qui Parle	.0029
Lake	.0031
Lake of the Woods	.0010
Le Sueur	.0061
Lincoln	.0012
Lyon	.0091
McLeod	.0110
Mahnomen	.0006
Marshall	.0022
Martin	.0073
Meeker	.0050
Mille Lacs	.0047
Morrison	.0051
Mower	.0130
Murray	.0033
Nicollet	.0087
Nobles	.0079
Norman	.0019
Olmsted	.0569
Otter Tail	.0138
Pennington	.0063
Pine	.0030
Pipestone	.0028
Polk	.0116
Pope	.0025
Ramsey	.3443
Red Lake	.0013
Redwood	.0052
Renville	.0053
Rice	.0194
Rock	.0031
Roseau	.0032
St. Louis	.0706
Scott	.0080
Sherburne	.0061
Sibley	.0040
Stearns	.0414
Steele	.0164
Stevens	.0031
Swift	.0029
Todd	.0044
Traverse	.0011
Wabasha	.0047
Wadena	.0037
Waseca	.0059
Washington	.0275
Watonwan	.0037
Wilkin	.0021
Winona	.0191
Wright	.0082
Yellow Medicine	.0031
MINNESOTA—TOTAL	1.9795

NORTH DAKOTA	% of U.S.
Adams	.0009
Barnes	.0025
Benson	.0009
Billings	.0001
Bottineau	.0021
Bowman	.0013
Burke	.0005
Burleigh	.0223
Cass	.0508
Cavalier	.0015

Figure A.2 Continued

Dickey	.0018	Mercer	.0125
Divide	.0008	Miami	.0242
Dunn	.0007	Monroe	.0025
Eddy	.0009	Montgomery	.3000
Emmons	.0009	Morgan	.0018
Foster	.0015	Morrow	.0018
Golden Valley	.0007	Muskingum	.0200
Grand Forks	.0215	Noble	.0010
Grant	.0006	Ottawa	.0069
Griggs	.0009	Paulding	.0021
Hettinger	.0009	Perry	.0032
Kidder	.0006	Pickaway	.0068
Le Moure	.0012	Pike	.0029
Logan	.0007	Portage	.0241
McHenry	.0010	Preble	.0049
McIntosh	.0012	Putnam	.0050
McKenzie	.0013	Richland	.0418
McLean	.0023	Ross	.0132
Mercer	.0015	Sandusky	.0119
Morton	.0055	Scioto	.0151
Mountrail	.0017	Seneca	.0175
Nelson	.0013	Shelby	.0081
Oliver	.0003	Stark	.1436
Pembina	.0029	Summit	.2404
Pierce	.0022	Trumbull	.0695
Ramsey	.0047	Tuscarawas	.0195
Ransom	.0014	Union	.0072
Renville	.0005	Van Wert	.0116
Richland	.0047	Vinton	.0012
Rolette	.0021	Warren	.0111
Sargent	.0013	Washington	.0139
Sheridan	.0005	Wayne	.0265
Sioux	.0002	Williams	.0095
Slope	—	Wood	.0239
Stark	.0081	Wyandot	.0039
Steele	.0006	OHIO–TOTAL	4.3030
Stutsman	.0086		
Towner	.0011		
Traill	.0020		
Walsh	.0028		
Ward	.0171		
Wells	.0018		
Williams	.0097		
NORTH DAKOTA–TOTAL	.2050		

OHIO	% of U.S.	SOUTH DAKOTA	% of U.S.
Adams	.0020	Aurora	.0007
Allen	.0400	Beadle	.0079
Ashland	.0102	Bennett	.0004
Ashtabula	.0227	Bon Homme	.0012
Athens	.0089	Brookings	.0045
Auglaize	.0094	Brown	.0130
Belmont	.0130	Brule	.0021
Brown	.0038	Buffalo	.0001
Butler	.0872	Butte	.0023
Carroll	.0024	Campbell	.0004
Champaign	.0059	Charles Mix	.0021
Clark	.0474	Clark	.0008
Clermont	.0161	Clay	.0021
Clinton	.0087	Codington	.0068
Columbiana	.0217	Corson	.0003
Coshocton	.0069	Custer	.0010
Crawford	.0135	Davison	.0080
Cuyahoga	.9169	Day	.0013
Darke	.0081	Deuel	.0009
Defiance	.0101	Dewey	.0008
Delaware	.0182	Douglas	.0009
Erie	.0198	Edmunds	.0009
Fairfield	.0189	Fall River	.0015
Fayette	.0058	Faulk	.0005
Franklin	.5210	Grant	.0022
Fulton	.0079	Gregory	.0013
Gallia	.0054	Haakon	.0009
Geauga	.0130	Hamlin	.0009
Greene	.0300	Hand	.0011
Guernsey	.0086	Hanson	.0003
Hamilton	.5812	Harding	.0002
Hancock	.0264	Hughes	.0050
Hardin	.0091	Hutchinson	.0023
Harrison	.0021	Hyde	.0006
Henry	.0048	Jackson	.0005
Highland	.0047	Jerauld	.0007
Hocking	.0038	Jones	.0004
Holmes	.0039	Kingsbury	.0017
Huron	.0131	Lake	.0026
Jackson	.0040	Lawrence	.0055
Jefferson	.0214	Lincoln	.0034
Knox	.0115	Lyman	.0005
Lake	.0675	McCook	.0014
Lawrence	.0068	McPherson	.0009
Licking	.0400	Marshall	.0010
Logan	.0074	Meade	.0026
Lorain	.0808	Mellette	.0002
Lucas	.2299	Miner	.0007
Madison	.0039	Minnehaha	.0543
Mahoning	.1178	Moody	.0013
Marion	.0206	Pennington	.0280
Medina	.0278	Perkins	.0012
Meigs	.0019	Potter	.0013
		Roberts	.0021
		Sanborn	.0005
		Shannon	.0009
		Spink	.0017
		Stanley	.0004
		Sully	.0003
		Todd	.0011

Figure A.2 Continued

		% of U.S.
Tripp	. . . .	0020
Turner	. . . .	0014
Union	. . . .	0023
Walworth	. . . .	0023
Washabaugh	. . . .	—
Yankton	. . . .	0060
Ziebach	. . . .	0001
SOUTH DAKOTA—TOTAL	. . .	2046

WISCONSIN		% of U.S.
Adams	. . . .	0006
Ashland	. . . .	0056
Barron	. . . .	0083
Bayfield	. . . .	0013
Brown	. . . .	0733
Buffalo	. . . .	0020
Burnett	. . . .	0014
Calumet	. . . .	0075
Chippewa	. . . .	0088
Clark	. . . .	0094
Columbia	. . . .	0094
Crawford	. . . .	0033
Dane	. . . .	1519
Dodge	. . . .	0147
Door	. . . .	0071
Douglas	. . . .	0096
Dunn	. . . .	0051
Eau Claire	. . . .	0290
Florence	. . . .	0004
Fond Du Lac	. . . .	0310
Forest	. . . .	0009
Grant	. . . .	0146
Green	. . . .	0074
Green Lake	. . . .	0041
Iowa	. . . .	0037
Iron	. . . .	0011
Jackson	. . . .	0036
Jefferson	. . . .	0214
Juneau	. . . .	0031
Kenosha	. . . .	0343

		% of U.S.
Kewaunee	. . . .	0036
La Crosse	. . . .	0387
Lafayette	. . . .	0016
Langlade	. . . .	0047
Lincoln	. . . .	0071
Manitowoc	. . . .	0248
Marathon	. . . .	0435
Marinette	. . . .	0111
Marquette	. . . .	0014
Menominee	. . . .	0003
Milwaukee	. . . .	5837
Monroe	. . . .	0075
Oconto	. . . .	0054
Oneida	. . . .	0105
Outagamie	. . . .	0554
Ozaukee	. . . .	0202
Pepin	. . . .	0015
Pierce	. . . .	0048
Polk	. . . .	0068
Portage	. . . .	0221
Price	. . . .	0033
Racine	. . . .	0665
Richland	. . . .	0030
Rock	. . . .	0440
Rusk	. . . .	0032
St. Croix	. . . .	0097
Sauk	. . . .	0124
Sawyer	. . . .	0025
Shawano	. . . .	0050
Sheboygan	. . . .	0419
Taylor	. . . .	0036
Trempealeau	. . . .	0043
Vernon	. . . .	0034
Vilas	. . . .	0026
Walworth	. . . .	0206
Washburn	. . . .	0019
Washington	. . . .	0235
Waukesha	. . . .	1079
Waupaca	. . . .	0090
Waushara	. . . .	0009
Winnebago	. . . .	0497
Wood	. . . .	0287
WISCONSIN—TOTAL	. . . . . .	1 7762

Figure A.2 Continued

Figure A.3

Note: It is easy to get carried away in drawing territory lines. You may look over the border to Kentucky and determine that Louisville is a lot closer to Cincinnati and even closer to Evansville than it is to Atlanta, Memphis, or wherever the Southern Region District Manager covering the territory calls his home office.

Remember that geography and the ability to make personal calls is only one aspect of servicing your customers. With the rising costs of sales calls, increased emphasis on telemarketing, and increased centralized computer usage, the number of accounts and their volume has become more important than their geographic closeness to each other. We're a long way from the drummer's three-month sales trips which depended on the rail lines.

MIDWEST TERRITORY (#3) PLANNING SHEET

Terr. #	
3A	Ohio
	Less Lucas County
	Total
3B	Michigan
	Plus Lucas County
	Total
3C	Illinois
	Cook County
	Winnebago County
	Boone County
	McHenry County
	Lake County
	Indiana
	Lake County
	Total
3D	Indiana/Illinois
	Less 4C Counties
	Total
3E	Wisconsin
	Minnesota
	North Dakota
	South Dakota
	Total
	Grand Total

Figure A.4

STEPS TO TAKE BEFORE SETTING TERRITORY QUOTAS

Let's first construct a worksheet that we'll use for a lot of our planning and reporting work. We're assuming that you don't yet have a computer setup, but the same format will work even better if you do, and still better if you are on line or interactive with your headquarters computer (Figure A.4).

Based on our index figures, from Figure A.2, let's fill in the percentages of the country as a whole that each territory represents and as a percentage of our total territory in a way that will be clear to our district managers. Figure A.5 shows what this looks like.

MIDWEST TERRITORY (#3) PLANNING SHEET

Terr. #		Potential (% Country)	Potential (% Terr.)
3A	Ohio	4.3030	
	Less Lucas County	.2299	
	Total	4.0731	20.54
3B	Michigan	3.4223	
	Plus Lucas County	.2299	
	Total	3.6522	18.42
3C	Illinois		
	Cook County	3.6637	
	Winnebago County	.1268	
	Boone County	.0109	
	McHenry County	.0430	
	Lake County	.1639	
	Indiana		
	Lake County	.1899	
	Total	4.1982	21.17
3D	Indiana/Illinois*	7.9405	
	Less 4C Counties	4.1982	
	Total	3.7423	18.87
3E	Wisconsin	1.7762	
	Minnesota	1.9795	
	North Dakota	.2050	
	South Dakota	.2046	
	Total	4.1653	21.00
	Grand Total	19.8311	100.00

```
*  1.9176
  +6.0229
   ───────
   7.9405
```

Figure A.5

Now, let's assume that your regional quota is $5,000,000. The first of the quota assignment steps (which will be summarized below) is to determine what portion each territory should bear—all other things being equal. You simply apply the percentage each territory represents of your total and get one input for your quota assignment determination. Figure A.6 shows the results.

Note that we've rounded off the figures so that they can be divisible by 12. You may have a seasonal business that would dictate assigning different quotas for each month or quarter, but the monthly arrangement is a good start. Also, while we want to be as fair as possible, a little fudge cushion is OK.

MIDWEST TERRITORY (#3) PLANNING SHEET

Terr. #		Potential (% Terr.)	Quota Based on Potential
3A	Ohio Less Lucas County Total	20.54	$1,080,000
3B	Michigan Plus Lucas County Total	18.42	960,000
3C	Illinois Cook County Winnebago County Boone County McHenry County Lake County Indiana Lake County Total	21.17	1,080,000
3D	Indiana/Illinois Less 4C Counties Total	18.87	960,000
3E	Wisconsin Minnesota North Dakota South Dakota Total	21.00	1,080,000
	Grand Total	100.00	$5,160,000

Figure A.6

The next step is to look at what actual sales were last year and break them down by the territories as you have defined them. You probably can't count on the home office giving you figures in the nice neat territorial categories you have defined. You may have a total for the territory, totals by state, or totals by major cities. Somewhere there are individual customer totals. You will probably have to do a lot of massaging to make the figures fit your categories, but this will give you a good feel for your region and who is making things happen. Take the time to do it and come up with a worksheet like the one in Figure A.7.

MIDWEST TERRITORY (#3) PLANNING SHEET

Terr. #		Potential (% Terr.)	Quota Based on Potential	Actual Sales Last Year	Actual Sales Last Year % Total
3A	Ohio Less Lucas County Total	20.54	$1,080,000	$ 760,520	17.22
3B	Michigan Plus Lucas County Total	18.42	960,000	816,647	18.49
3C	Illinois Cook County Winnebago County Boone County McHenry County Lake County				
	Indiana Lake County Total	21.17	1,080,000	1,060,916	24.02
3D	Indiana/Illinois Less 4C Counties Total	18.87	960,000	106,881	16.02
3E	Wisconsin Minnesota North Dakota South Dakota Total	21.00	1,080,000	1,071,036	24.25
	Grand Total	100.00	$5,160,000	$4,416,000	100.00

Figure A.7

Besides allocating last year's sales by your territory alignment, you have determined the percentage of your total region that each territory represented. Obviously, 3A, and 3D seem to be coming up short while territories 3C and 3E are wringing more out of the areas that the "potential"figures would seem to indicate. Let's not jump to conclusions yet, but put some specific numbers to the judgments we just came to. Let's work out a percentage of potential reached by dividing the percentage of actual total by the percentage of potential.

This would give you:

3E	115% of potential
3C	113% of potential
3B	100% of potential
3D	85% of potential
3A	84% of potential

This could be an indication of which territories are doing well and which need help. But, let's still not jump to conclusions yet. It is enough for now that we have a basis for setting quotas and this leads us to the following conclusion: When setting quotas, start with the percentage of the total region (country) the territory should represent and average this against the percentage of the total that the territory actually represented last year. This provides a "raw" quota figure that can be adjusted for special situations.

SETTING TERRITORY QUOTAS

Let's take the quota based on potential from column 2 of Figure A.6 and our "fudged" quota of $5,160,000, times the percentage of the total that each territory represented last year, average the two columns, and come up with our "raw" quota.

In Figure A.8, you will notice that we've rounded off in a way to make sure that we have allocated more than our regional quota of $5,000,000. As mentioned above, a small cushion like 6 percent or 7 percent doesn't keep us from insisting that "quota" is an absolute minimum demanded and expected, not a goal. Your district managers' *goals* should start at 120 percent of quota as should yours.

Now that we have our "raw" quota, let's look at some possible adjustments. Territories 3C and 3E are doing very well. Some investigation discloses two things. There is, indeed, a distributor in Chicago who sells throughout the Midwest, and the Chicago territory gets all the credit.

Also, there is a national mail-order house in Minneapolis that sells throughout the country with a significant amount of sales in your territory outside Minnesota and Wisconsin. Based on the amount of sales from both these customers last year and your assessment of what they will do in the present year, you adjust the "raw" quota figure and come up with the numbers shown in Figure A.9.

We have adjusted the 3C and 3E territories to recognize the extra business these territories get credit for because of the unusual situations that exist. Because they are unusual, your regional managers should be expected to get more from their territories than the raw potential figures alone would indicate. This is not unfair, since the home office sold these accounts and you and the home office are going to have to provide a lot of service.

The final quota figure that we will assign is 6.8 percent above the figure we have been given from the home office. This should raise a question or two since we have been advocating a "partnership" and a "same team effort" with our people. This is not out of line with our philosophy since it does have a solid foundation in reality.

There may be some truly unforeseen things that will come up during the year that are perfectly understandable reasons for not making quota. (If you believe that the "home office" will remember these things when review time comes along, I

Terr. #		Potential	Raw Quota	
			Last Year	Average
3A	Ohio Less Lucas County Total	$1,080,000	$ 900,000	$ 990,000
3B	Michigan Plus Lucas County Total	960,000	960,000	960,000
3C	Illinois Cook County Winnebago County Boone County McHenry County Lake County Indiana Lake County Total	1,080,000	1,240,000	1,160,000
3D	Indiana/Illinois Less 4C Counties Total	960,000	840,000	900,000
3E	Wisconsin Minnesota North Dakota South Dakota Total	1,080,000	1,240,000	1,160,000
	Grand Total	$5,160,000	$5,180,000	$5,170,000

Figure A.8

Terr. #		Potential	Raw Quota		Adjust	Final Quota	Last Year Actual	% Increase
			Last Year	Average				
3A	Ohio							
	Less Lucas County							
	Total	$1,080,000	$ 900,000	$ 990,000	$ (30,000)	$ 960,000	$ 760,520	26.2
3B	Michigan							
	Plus Lucas County							
	Total	960,000	960,000	960,000	(60,000)	900,000	81,6647	10.2
3C	Illinois							
	Cook County							
	Winnebago County							
	Boone County							
	McHenry County							
	Lake County							
	Indiana							
	Lake County							
	Total	1,080,000	1,240,000	1,160,000	200,000	1,360,000	1,060,916	28.2
3D	Indiana/Illinois							
	Less 4C Counties							
	Total	960,000	840,000	900,000	(60,000)	840,000	706,881	18.8
3E	Wisconsin							
	Minnesota							
	North Dakota							
	South Dakota							
	Total	1,080,000	1,240,000	1,160,000	120,000	1,280,000	1,071,036	19.5
	Grand Total	$5,160,000	$5,180,000	$5,170,000	$ 170,000	$5,340,000	$4,116,000	20.1

Figure A.9

have some land about 60 miles west of Fort Lauderdale I'd like to talk to you about.) Play it safe and fudge a little. After all, your effective management is going to make it possible for your people to do more than they ever thought they could. Right?

As a final test, the last two columns of Figure A.9 list last year's actual sales (from Figure A.7) and show the percentage increase. Since our investigation so far has indicated that territory 3C is resting on its perhaps undeserved laurels because of the large distributor selling outside the territory, and territory 3A has not adequately implemented the programs provided by the home office, we are satisfied that these admittedly healthy increases are not unfair.

REGIONAL QUOTA-SETTING CHECKLIST

Let's review what we have done to arrive at our quotas so we can convince our district managers that they are indeed fair, and that a great deal of thought was put into the exercise:

1. We looked for and found an appropriate index to determine equitable territory sizes and defined territories with a mind to equalization and logistical considerations.
2. We developed a planning sheet that will remind us of the territory makeup and be useful for all planning and tracking.
3. Using the index, we determined the potential each territory should represent as a percentage of the country and as a percentage of our (Midwest) territory.
4. We then applied our quota (with some rounding off) to this potential figure to get one input for our "raw" quota assignment figures.
5. Next, we determined what percentage of our total sales for the previous year each defined territory represented.
6. We developed a "raw quota" figure for each district manager territory by averaging the actual percentage with the potential percentage.
7. We made adjustments to the raw figure to allow for special situations within the territories, to come up with a final quota figure by district manager territory.
8. We tested our figures by looking at the final quota figures as a percentage increase over last year's actual figures and were satisfied that the quotas to be assigned are as equitable as they are likely to be in this world.
9. We gave ourselves the rest of the weekend off for doing such a good and thorough job.

SELECTING A LOCATION FOR HEADQUARTERS

Do you remember (a long time and a few pages ago) that your third assignment after defining territories and setting quotas was to select a headquarters office location? By now you've done so much work on the potential in your territory that you have probably zeroed in on the Chicago area.

This isn't exactly an inspired choice, but it *is* the weighted (by business potential) geographic center of your territory. It's also the site of a major airport that will get you where you want to go in your territory. But where is this area? Let's look at the selection criteria you should be considering:

1. Ready access to an airport that services your major cities—Columbus, Cleveland, Indianapolis, Minneapolis, Detroit, Sioux Falls, etc.
2. Nearness to major expressways so you don't have to travel for an hour before you get moving.
3. Reasonable closeness to desirable residential communities and community activities.

Before looking at the recommendation below, get out the maps you have been poring over to define territories and see what location you come up with. If you're not the Midwest Regional Manager, the criteria still apply even if the location does not.

Anyway, unless you're a sailing nut, a logical choice for you is Schaumburg. It's less than ten miles from O'Hare, very near the Dwight D. Eisenhower and Kennedy Expressways into Chicago, the office rental rates are a lot less expensive than in the downtown area and you can, except for sailing, find all the housing and leisure time activities you would want close by, and at lower cost, than the communities on the lake between Chicago and Evanston.

As Chicago is a natural for the Midwest, Los Angeles is appropriate for the West, Dallas for the Central Region, Atlanta for the South, and New York or Philadelphia for the East. You can, however, find "Schaumburgs" in each area.

Appendix B

Setting Equitable National Quotas

Basics are basics, so the principles and techniques for setting quotas for a national organization are the same as for a regional territory. National is probably easier since by dealing with larger numbers you have more room for error, with less attention needed to microeconomic situations like poor farming profits, the closing of steel mills, tourist business being off, etc., that would affect regional areas.

We chose a regional assignment first since it meant dealing with these detailed situations and concerns. Let's see how our "basics" apply equally well to a national situation:

HOW TO DEFINE NATIONAL TERRITORIES

The traditional East, South, Midwest, and West Territorial allocations with the growth of the "Sunbelt," have been realigned by many sales executives to include a Central Region which moves the Southeast east and the Midwest northeast. So, we're going to assume that there will be five regional managers with territories as equal as possible given the geographic and logistical considerations.

There is almost no logical way to avoid having the East as the largest territory by a considerable margin. There is no getting away from the short distances from Boston to New York to Philadelphia to Washington, D.C. as compared with traveling from Memphis to Miami or from Los Angeles to Billings.

Figure B.1

However, let's make an attempt to define nearly equal territories by taking out a map of the country and the same "NOPA County Buying Patterns for Office Products" that we used before. We will start by process of elimination as follows:

1. *Western Territory:* Decide that the West is just east of the Rockies and draw the line down the eastern borders of Montana, Wyoming, Colorado, and New Mexico.

2. *Midwestern Territory:* We already defined the Midwest earlier in this chapter, leaving out Iowa, but including the Dakotas, so this is already defined for us.

3. *Southeastern Territory:* In order to make room for the Central Region, we'll put the western border of the Southeast at Mississippi's and Tennessee's western borders. To try to even up the Eastern Seaboard and keep the Northeast as small as possible, we'll include West Virginia, Virginia, and Kentucky. This is a tough call since so much of Washington, D.C.'s business is done outside the capital in Virginia as well as in Maryland, but we have to draw the line somewhere. Let the Yankees be happy we didn't try to claim the nation's capital for the southern folk.

4. *Central Territory:* By process of elimination, we've defined the Central Region with Texas as the flagship state. Admittedly, Colorado and New Mexico are a toss-up for the Central or Western Regions, but *they think* they are *West.* El Paso could also be added to the Western Territory, but we've left it in Texas. Iowa is tough, but is demographically closer to Kansas and Missouri than Chicago.

5. *Eastern Territory:* This is what is left, New England, New York, and the Mid-Atlantic states, defined here as New Jersey, Pennsylvania, Delaware, Maryland, and the District of Columbia.

This then gives us our five regional territories (Figure B.1).

Now let's check this against our NOPA listing to see how our territories shape up for relative equality. We'll code the listing by our territory numbers and add up the states within the territories defined (Figure B.2).

This gives us the following potential figures by territory:

#1	Northeast	28.0536%
#2	Southeast	17.2819
#3	Midwest	19.8311
#4	Central	15.1228
#5	West	19.7106
	Total	100.0000%

Well, it looks as though we did fine in the West and Midwest and not too badly in the Southeast. Combining demographic and logistical considerations, however, we aren't likely to do much better. Let's live with this territory definition and move to the next step.

STATE	1983	TERRITORY
Alabama	1.2821	2
Alaska	.1928	5
Arizona	1.0602	5
Arkansas	.7126	4
California	11.5754	5
Colorado	1.5920	5
Connecticut	1.6531	1
Delaware	.3401	1
District of Columbia	.7417	1
Florida	4.4161	2
Georgia	2.1593	2
Hawaii	.4647	5
Idaho	.3368	5
Illinois	6.0229	5
Indiana	1.9176	5
Iowa	1.1702	4
Kansas	.9709	4
Kentucky	1.1764	2
Louisiana	1.6300	4
Maine	.3011	1
Maryland	1.9515	1
Massachusetts	3.1124	1
Michigan	3.4223	3
Minnesota	1.9795	3
Mississippi	.7208	2
Missouri	2.2539	4
Montana	.2670	5
Nebraska	.6778	4
Nevada	.3046	5
New Hampshire	.3890	1
New Jersey	3.2550	1
New Mexico	.4334	5
New York	10.5071	1
North Carolina	2.2818	2
North Dakota	.2050	3
Ohio	4.3030	3
Oklahoma	1.1395	4
Oregon	1.1024	5
Pennsylvania	5.1576	1
Rhode Island	.4372	1
South Carolina	1.0578	2
South Dakota	.2046	3
Tennessee	1.7644	2
Texas	6.5679	4
Utah	.5471	5
Vermont	.2078	1
Virginia	2.0169	2
Washington	1.6888	5
West Virginia	.4063	2
Wisconsin	1.7762	3
Wyoming	.1454	5
United States	100.0000	
Standard Metropolitan Statistical Areas	85.5183	

Figure B.2

PUTTING THE QUOTA WORKSHEETS AND CHECKLIST TO WORK

We will follow the same basic steps as in defining the Midwest Regional quota.

1. Start with the potential for each territory as defined by our NOPA index. (Again, most industries and industry associations have similar material.) See Figure B.3.

NATIONAL PLANNING SHEET

	Total	#1 NE	#2 SE (Territory)	#3 MW (Territory)	#4 C (Territory)	#5 W
Potential	100.0000	28.0536	17.2819	19.8311	15.1228	19.7106

Figure B.3

2. We'll assume that your quota as national sales manager is $25,000,000. This would provide a regional territory breakout and the first input for our quota determination (Figure B.4).

NATIONAL PLANNING SHEET

	Total	#1 NE	#2 SE (Territory)	#3 MW (Territory)	#4 C (Territory)	#5 W
Potential	100.0000	28.0536	17.2819	19.8311	15.1228	19.7106
Quota per Potential	25,000,000	7,100,000	4,200,000	5,000,000	3,800,000	4,900,000

Figure B.4

3. Now let's fill in last year's actual figures (the third line in Figure B.5) and determine the percentage each region represented of the total country (the fourth line on Figure B.5).
4. Next, average the following items:
   - — The determined regional potential as a percentage of the total of the country (the first line on Figure B.5).
   - — Last year's actual as a percentage of last year's total sales (the fourth line on Figure B.5).

   This gives us our "raw quota" figure for each region to be adjusted as outlined below. (Since we're in the home office now, our worksheet and other figures can be rounded off to hundreds.)

NATIONAL PLANNING SHEET

	Total	#1 NE	#2 SE	#3 MW	#4 C	#5 W
			Territory			
Potential	100.0000%	28.0536	17.2819	19.8311	15.1228	19.7106
Quota per Potential	$25,000,000	7,100,000	4,200,000	5,000,000	3,800,000	4,900,000
Actual Last Yr. ($000's)	$ 21,464	5,817	3,859	4,416	3,234	4,138
% of Total	1000.000%	27.1012	17.9789	20.5740	15.0671	19.2788
Average % (Lines 1 & 4)	100.00%	27.58	17.63	20.20	15.10	19.49
"Raw" Quota ($000's)	$ 25,200	7,000	4,500	5,000	3,800	4,900

Figure B.5

5. For the same reasons as outlined previously in setting district manager quotas, we've rounded up the regional figures. Now, we have to look at any unusual situations that might require adjustment to the raw quota figure.

In doing our "80-20" analysis of accounts from the listing of all accounts in descending order of volume, we made some interesting discoveries.

> For example, Lichtman Distributors in New York City, a national wholesaler, did over $1.5 million in sales, more than 25 percent of the total business in the Northeast. By checking further, you found that your president is a sailing buddy of Bert Lichtman and your president's wife is co-chairperson of the New York UJA with Sylvia Lichtman. Further, Dorothy Lichtman is dating your president's son. How much did your Northeastern Regional manager have to do with this account?
>
> This is not a rhetorical question; it should be investigated. In some instances, the Regional Manager could have initiated the contact, directed the development of the account, and is the main reason why the contacts are working to your company's benefit.
>
> Alas, this is not the case. In checking the customer file for Lichtman Distributors, you find a big bold note signed by David H. Stuart, your company president, "All contacts with this account, except for routine matters, will be made by D.H. Stuart."
>
> This is a pretty good indication that your Regional Manager plays a secondary role with the account and his territory gets the credit. However, you have to assume that some of the business Lichtman is doing is in the Northeastern Territory and that a portion of it would come from other accounts if there were not Lichtman Distributors.
>
> Let's assume 40 percent and add $600,000 to the Northeastern Territory for this windfall and get the Northeast Regional Manager to scramble for other accounts.

Note: These examples may seem somewhat fanciful and not wholly applicable to your situation. They are, however, intended to suggest the kind of thinking that is appropriate to do the job properly and thoroughly.

You will come up with your own examples using these suggestions as a springboard for your thinking.

In another example, your analysis has determined that there is a large regional wholesaler in the Southeast, headquartered in Atlanta and doing about $700,000 per year. While most of the business is within the Southeastern Territory, about 20 percent of the business of Krisher Office Products goes to the Central Region in the states of Arkansas, Louisiana, and Texas.

So let's add $150,000 to the Southeastern Territory and deduct $100,000 from Central. (The "house" always has to come out ahead.)

We find that Leewend Wholesale Stationery, Richardson, Texas accounted for $950,000 of the business done in the Central Region. They have a branch in Tempe, Arizona and another in Tustin, California that account for about one-third of their business.

All orders are entered from Richardson, so the Central Region gets all the credit. Now, they deserve a lot of the credit for setting up and maintaining the account, but some of the missionary and dealer work that the folks in the Western Region do winds up in the Central Region sales totals.

Let's, in our spirit of having the house come out ahead, add $200,000 to the Central Region quota and deduct $100,000 from the Western Region.

We now have our final quotas as shown in Figure B.6.

NATIONAL PLANNING SHEET

			Territory			
	Total	#1 NE	#2 SE	#3 MW	#4 C	#5 W
Potential	100.0000%	28.0536	17.2819	19.8311	15.1228	19.7106
Quota per Potential	$25,000,000	7,100,000	4,200,000	5,000,000	3,800,000	4,900,000
Actual Last Yr. ($000's)	$ 21,464	5,817	3,859	4,416	3,234	4,138
% of Total	1000.000%	27.1012	17.9789	20.5740	15.0671	19.2788
Average % (Lines 1 & 4)	100.00%	27.58	17.63	20.20	15.10	19.49
"Raw" Quota ($000's)	$ 25,200	7,000	4,500	5,000	3,800	4,900
Adjustments:						
Lichtman	.300	.600	(.100)	(.100)	(.50)	(.50)
Krisher	.50		.150		.100	
Leewend	.100				.200	(.100)
Adjusted Quotas ($000's)	$ 25,650	7,600	4,550	4,900	3,850	4,750

Figure B.6

6. Or do we really have our final quotas? You know your regional managers are going to provide a cushion in the quotas they assign to their district managers. Does a national field sales manager deserve less? As long as you can honestly say that the figures you have assigned to the regional managers and the field are within 10 percent of your minimum performance target, you need have no fear of being unfair.

Let's round the figures off to make them come out to even monthly amounts. We're going to assume no seasonality, forgetting about the July and December doldrums.

If "things are slow," your regional and district managers should have more time to do the creative selling as opposed to order-taking, which will eliminate the valleys. They should also be more successful in getting appointments and scheduling sales meetings or demonstrations since "no one calls on customers or prospects the first two weeks of July or the last two weeks of December."

You decide that your sales force is not going to participate in these doldrums and assign quotas one-twelfth each month and come up with programs to make it happen. Your paperwork will be easier and the factory and warehouse will love you as you make it happen.

This is not theoretical. It can happen. The author has personally put together July and December sales promotional programs that made the salespeople want to cancel their planned vacations so they could participate. In *all* cases the sales during these months amounted to more than 8.5 percent of annual sales.

Here's a real-life case history. The 1974/1975 recession was probably one of the most accurately forecasted and most anticipated in history. It was my job in 1973 to hold a sales meeting to announce an average 15 percent increase in quota for all district managers along with the programs that would get them there.

All of a sudden, every district and regional manager became an economist. They came armed with every fact and figure they could marshall to justify a *decrease* in quota. I listened to all of their persuasive arguments and then unveiled the banner: "*We choose not to participate in the coming recession!*"

The specifics of the promotional and other activities that justified this bold assertion are too lengthy to be covered here. The bottom line was that sales increased 28 percent over the previous year because we *chose* not to participate in a downturn others were calling inevitable.

You can make the same kind of choice in deciding to eliminate those doldrums from your sales charts. So, back to our "rounding up" exercise and the final quota assignments. We will also perform the same kind of test as we did for the Midwestern regional quotas assigned to Midwestern District Managers and determine the percentages over last year's actual sales. (Figure B.7).

In our final quota assignment, the Midwest and the West got a break and the Northeast took it on the chin in terms of increases over last year's actual sales. Let's take still another look at this to make sure it's fair (and to have the right answers for the Northeast Regional Manager's questions).

NATIONAL PLANNING SHEET

	Total	#1 NE	Territory #2 SE	#3 MW	#4 C	#5 W
Potential	100.0000%	28.0536	17.2819	19.8311	15.1228	19.7106
Quota per Potential	$25,000,000	7,100,000	4,200,000	5,000,000	3,800,000	4,900,000
Actual Last Yr. ($000's)	$ 21,464	5,817	3,859	4,416	3,234	4,138
% of Total	100.0000%	27.1012	17.9789	20.5740	15.0671	19.2788
Average % (Lines 1 & 4)	100.00%	27.58	17.63	20.20	15.10	19.49
"Raw" Quota ($000's)	$ 25,200	7,000	4,500	5,000	3,800	4,900
Adjustments:						
Lichtman	.300	.600	(.100)	(.100)	(.50)	(.50)
Krisher	.50		.150		(.100)	
Leewend	.100				(.200)	(.100)
Adjusted Quotas ($000's)	$ 25,650	7,600	4,550	4,900	3,850	4,750
Final Quotas ($000's)	$ 25,940	7,680	4,560	5,000	3,900	4,800
% Over Last Yr. Actual	20.8%	32.0	18.2	13.2	20.1	16.0

Figure B.7

The final quota for the Northeast is about 29 percent of your total. This is pretty close to the figure you should be getting from that territory based on the "potential" index of 28 percent. Based on what you found out about Lichtman Distributors, it looks as though your Northeastern District and Regional Managers have the time and territory potential to hit their quotas and stop resting on their cushions.

The Midwest has the smallest increase of all. Is this fair? Well, they are already doing 20.6 percent of the country while the potential would indicate only 19.8 percent and you don't want to penalize them for a good job. Also, you can't find any interterritory sales situation that would dictate a change. They (as indicated when we worked out their quotas) are in a transition mode so they probably deserve at least for now, a small break.

So, where are we? You have a pretty hefty 20.8 percent increase over last year's sales to make happen. You've done your homework and assigned this increase (plus a mere 3.8 percent cushion) to your regions as equitably as possible.

You've investigated, explored, and made adjustments for all of the "special situations" you could identify and are satisfied that you have covered them. Now you have the job of selling the quotas to your regional managers as discussed in Chapter 3, under the heading "Checklist for Communicating Quotas to Your People."

Appendix C

Making Prospecting Pay

In this practice example, we'll see how the accounting stratification steps work in FSM Computer Software Company and fit into their overall marketing plan in a very simplified and condensed way. Figure C.1 shows an example of a part of the marketing plan for this company.

FSM COMPUTER SOFTWARE CO.
1987 MARKETING PLAN

COMPANY IDENTITY:
FSM is a relatively small computer software company that is large enough to effectively support our present products and develop new ones, but small enough to provide personalized service and product customization where necessary.

MARKET AREA:
Since the software package, including documentation, can be sold through the mail and is easily shipped, and since our customers pay all expenses of on-site installation, our market area is the world.

WHAT WE HAVE TO OFFER:
A unique proprietary product used on the IBM PC HD with a PC DOS operating system that enables meeting planning consultants to effectively lay out, schedule, and provide cost estimates of events for their clients.

MARKET TARGETS:
Meeting planning consultants and, in some limited cases, travel agents to handle sales meetings, award trips, and training meetings for their clients. The ideal target would be a one-to-ten-person consulting firm or travel agent who does not yet have an installed system or whose system needs upgrading.

Figure C.1

FOLLOWING THROUGH TO TURN PROSPECTS INTO ACCOUNTS

Let's look at what FSM did to follow through on the information developed in the marketing plan:

1. Since their primary target was identified as meeting planning consultants, *these* were the people they had to find. There were a lot of travel agents in the yellow pages, but even the Philadelphia Yellow Pages goes from Meditation Instruction to Meeting Rooms, completely ignoring Meeting Planning Consultants.

   Under "Consultants," the directory goes from Plastics to Printing. There were City and Town Planners, but then the directory skipped to Planographers. (You probably have to be in the printing business to know what a planographer is.)

2. The Planning Committee was about to give up when one planner decided to call a friend of his—a management consultant who claimed to know everything about everything. They didn't expect much help, but what a beautiful way to put this consultant in his place.

3. The call. As expected, the management consultant didn't know where to find meeting planning consultants. Aha! But, he did know how to find them.

   He reasoned that since publishers publish books and magazines on everything from antique collecting to worm farming, there must be a magazine on meetings. He suggested going to the library and getting a copy of SRDS (Standard Rate and Data Service) and finding out who the publishers were.

4. To the library. Sure enough, there turned out to be more than one publisher dealing with meetings. And, at least one of them, *Meeting News*, actually published a directory of all kinds of suppliers of meeting services.

5. Call the publisher in New York. They were very helpful and offered to send along a copy of the January directory issue.

6. The directory did, indeed, include a section on almost 200 "Consultants, Planning," more than enough to get the preliminary marketing effort off the ground.

7. They "captured" this prospect list and batched the prospects in tens (they figured they could only follow up on ten at a time).

8. A mailing was sent out with an introductory letter, a broadside describing the software package and the company's capabilities and a reply card. The letter made the promise of a follow-up phone call.

9. Two inquiries came in before they even made the calls, so they followed up on the other eight and prepared their next batch of ten and so on.

10. FSM then expanded into the travel agent business with similar help from ASTA (American Society of Travel Agents—also helpful people), sold a bunch of packages, developed new products for the industry, and made a lot of money. All because they called a management consultant who *didn't even charge them!*

Remember, that even though the company and plan in this appendix are fictitious, the steps in this process have been used successfully in actual situations.

Appendix D

Figuring Available Selling Time

One of the most common misconceptions in selling or in sales management is the amount of actual selling time the salesperson has. This practice example provides a guideline for you to determine how much selling time your people actually have.

HOW MUCH SELLING TIME IS THERE?

Let's start with all the available time. There are 168 hours in a week. This is the "universe" we are dealing with. We'll deduct, on average, nine hours a day for sleeping, showering, and shaving. This leaves 103 hours to divide between work and personal activity. Assuming that your people are motivated enough to work a 60-hour week, let's see how this 60 hours might be spent by taking a typical (or atypical) day:

A TYPICAL SALESPERSON'S DAY

8:00	Drive to work to pick up some material and check the answering machine. Modify the "to do" list based on messages or orders.
9:00	Head for the first appointment with Mr. A.
9:30	Arrive and leave word with the receptionist. Wait for the least person to leave.

9:45	Ushered into the office. Exchange of pleasantries (perhaps a hunting or fishing story). Mr. A calls other staff members who he wants to hear the presentation your salesperson will make.
*10:45	Effective presentation, but people begin to get itchy after a half-hour.
11:00	Meeting adjourned with promise to discuss and review. Next appointment scheduled. On to the appointment with Mr. B, a luncheon appointment.
11:30	Arrive, park, walk to reception area and find Mr. B is finishing up a phone call—just a minute.
11:45	Leave immediately for lunch.
12:00	Arrive at restaurant. No wait. Order drinks, one white wine and one Perrier and look at menu.
*12:15	Approach the discussion and provide an overview of the pitch to be made.
12:30	Lunch arrives (an efficient restaurant). Mr. B changes subject to the impact of the price of the U.S. dollar on his business.
*1:00	Your presentation, as agreed, resumes over coffee.
1:30	A commitment is made by Mr. B to order. Leave.
1:45	Back at Mr. B's office, he gets out a purchase order, writes it up, and hands it over after a brief discussion on the importance of timely delivery to his production people.
2:00	Leave for Mr. C's office, cleverly scheduled for today since he is in the same industrial park.
*2:15	Arrive and go right in. Mr. C has an order waiting and a 2:30 appointment. Brief discussion of the new program. Literature left. Appointment made to go over in detail.
2:30	On to Mr. D. Travel, go through the receptionist, and right in.
3:00	Deal with questions about a fouled-up order. Mr. D gets his purchasing agent in after he gets off the phone. Particulars taken. Mr. D isn't going to listen until you resolve this, so at his request, you call the home office. Resolved—the customer used the wrong part number, the customer service people got it straightened out with the purchasing agent's assistant but didn't tell him, and the salesperson is a hero again.
*3:30	Present the new program with the purchasing agent there. Good reception but the PA wants to "check out a couple of things" before a recommendation.
4:00	On to Mr. E and no wait here either.
*4:15	Good reception but Mr. E has a plane to catch. He does, however, make a commitment to sent in a purchase order. Salesperson makes a folow-up note.

5:00   No point in attacking the expressway now. Go to a quiet coffee shop, call the home office (one hour behind the salesperson's time), place orders and get messages, dictate letters and review plans for tomorrow.

5:45   Head home.

6:30   Arrive and handle mail—light today.

7:00   Cocktail hour, family time, and dinner.

9:00   Catch up on some trade magazines till 10:00.

Now, what happened? This salesperson, admittedly an exemplary model, put in a 12-hour day. He (in this case, it was a he) was organized, knew what he wanted to accomplish, had set up appointments and had no last-minute cancellations. There were *none* of the ususal delays—traffic, detours, no parking spaces, customers who wanted to chat overly long, uncooperative receptionists, or any of the other things that are part of a normal day.

Yet, this person had only three hours of selling time. He put in a 12-hour day, but had only *three hours of effective time in front of the customer selling!* [This time is identified in the preceding schedule by the asterisks (*s).] Let's break down how ther 12 hours were spent. (Some arbitary divisions have been made between the categories, like traveling and waiting times):

Travel and Commuting Time	3.75 hours	32%
Waiting Time	1.25 hours	10%
Nonselling Customer Time	2.00 hours	17%
Paperwork of Administrative Details	1.00 hour	8%
Self-Development	1.00 hour	8%
Selling Time	3.00 hours	25%
Total	12.00 hours	100%

Two points from the above exercise should be very clear:

1. There really isn't that much actual, face-to-face selling time in a salesperson's day no matter how lucky the salesperson gets with regard to traffic, not waiting, or cancellations and no matter how well the day is planned.

2. It become extremely important, therefore to:

   a. Make sure that every hour, if not every minute, counts—making sure the time is used to see the right accounts (what to do while there is a different matter) and not waste it on the "C" accounts.

   b. Find ways to stretch out the conventional workday or workweek. (Some examples were discussed in Chapter 5.)

Appendix E

Running Your Sales P & L

In many companies there is a wall between the accounting and sales/marketing functions. Neither seems to understand or appreciate what the other is doing. As in most walls, the problem has more to do with a lack of communication rather than any intentional misunderstanding.

The way to solve a communication problem is to start with a common language or at least an understanding of the other person's language. The purpose of this practice exercise is to take the mystery out of accounting language. The assumption in this appendix is that you have no previous background in accounting.

UNDERSTANDING THE
PRO FORMA P&L STATEMENT

This is an appropriate starting point for our discussion since the Profit and Loss (P&L) Statement, with its "bottom line," is the final measure of whether a department, region, or company is successful. The most fantastic sales organization in the world is worth little if the efforts cannot product a profitable return on investment to the stockholders or other owners. The Profit and Loss Statement measures this return periodically. A Pro Forma P&L Statement estimates what the final official P&L statement will look like.

Understanding what makes profits happen and how a P&L Statement is constructed will enable you to get done for your region, group, or company what needs to get done. It's a tool that your controller may use to shoot your ideas down. It's a measurement standard that your top management will use to judge your performance and the efficacy of your ideas. It's also a tool you can use to your and your company's advantage. Let's look at the two basic formulas that comprise this scary document:

1. Sales - Cost of Good Sold = Gross Profit
2. Gross Profit - Expenses = Net Operating Profit

That's it. That is all there is to it. (We got into breakeven points and incremental costing in Chapter 6.) For now, let's just look at what makes up this P&L, according to the above formulas:

1. *Sales* is obviously the sum total of all the invoices billed to your customers, whether or not (in an "accrual" accounting system which most businesses use) you have been paid yet for the goods and/or services delivered. Any returns, discounts, or other allowances made are deducted from this figure to arrive at a "Net Sales" figure. This net figure is often referred to by accounting types as the "top line."

2. *Cost of goods sold* is just what it sounds like. In a manufacturing operation it's the sum of all the material, direct manufacturing labor, and "overhead" that goes into producing the product. "Overhead" includes a host of diverse things from depreciation (allocation of cost over a period of time) on the building and equipment to the cleaning rags used to wipe up the spilled oil which is also "overhead."

    In a retail or distributor business, the Cost of Goods Sold is the cost from a vendor, possibly with the addition of freight or other costs directly involved in the purchase. Because a discussion of manufacturing costs would involve at least another book, we will assume that you are either in the distribution business or that your area has been given a Cost of Goods Sold from Manufacturing that you have no responsibility for nor any control over except to the extent your sales volume can reduce costs.

3. *Gross profit*, then, is the difference between Sales and Cost of Goods Sold. Don't look for any concrete rules on percentages here. A trading business could conceivably operate very well on a gross profit margin of as little as 10 percent on sales while a medical equipment manufacturer with substantial capital equipment and research and development costs could be struggling to survive with an 80 percent gross margin level.

4. *Expenses*, for your budgets and P&L should be of two types—Administrative and Sales. The reason for the distinction is that administrative expenses will generally not vary directly with sales volume. If you rent an office or hire an administrative assistant, that expense stays constant whether you are at 60 percent of sales quota of 150 percent. At some point, of course, you may need a larger office or another administrative

assistant, but it's not a direct, variable relationship, so these expenses are looked upon as relatively "fixed."

Sales expenses, however, are expected to have a more direct relationship to sales volume. If you have straight commission salespeople or straight commission representatives who pay their own expenses, their commissions will be very direct or "variable." If you pay a salary plus an incentive based on sales volume, the salary will be a "fixed" component of your budget or P&L statement and the incentive "variable."

HOW TO CONSTRUCT THE BUDGET (P&L STATEMENT)

Since we said we were going to take the broadest possible case—a new start-up venture, the pro forma P&L statement will also be your budget for the coming fiscal period.

In Chapter 6, the "Checklist of Profit-Generating Budget Techniques" section, we showed how the numbers that we will use were arrived at, so we will create our P&L statement or budget according to what was explained in Chapter 6, on the "Pro Forma P&L Statement." Remember, that for our present purposes, the terms "Pro Forma P&L Statement" and "Budget" are interchangeable.

Figure E.1 shows a Pro Forma Profit and Loss Statement. (Don't let the term "loss' throw you—you will come up with only profits, but "Profit and Loss" is the commonly accepted term.) We'll discuss how we arrived at the figures below.

The assumption is that you are the computer software and services company selling to the meeting-planning consultants identified in Chapter 4 and you have to convince your headquarters that this is a proper venture for the company to embark upon. Unless you are in the banking or utility business, you can *count on* this being the proper format in which to do this.

To illustrate how budgets are set, let's look at how we came up with the figures in Figure E.1. We'll take it one category (line item) at a time to show just how a Pro Forma Profit and Loss Statement or Budget is constructed and, if we are successful, take the mystery out of it.

HOW TO ESTIMATE GROSS SALES

Admittedly, $10,000,000 sounds like too round a figure. However, when dealing with rough estimates, only small-minded accountants (the two terms don't necessarily go hand-in-hand) try to work things out to the penny or dollar. Here are the steps used following the guidelines outlined in the "Checklist of Profit-Generating Budget Techniques" section in Chapter 6 to arrive at this figure:

FSM COMPUTER SERVICES CO.
PRO FORMA PROFIT & LOSS STATEMENT
FISCAL YEAR ENDED 12/31/87

GROSS SALES		$10,000,000
Less Returns and Allowances		100,000
NET SALES		9,900,000
COST OF GOODS SOLD		6,000,000
GROSS PROFIT		3,900,000
ADMINISTRATIVE EXPENSES:		
Administrative Salaries	200,000	
Payroll Taxes	20,000	
Insurance and Benefits	40,000	
Office Rent and Utilities	160,000	
Stationery, Supplies, and Postage	50,000	
Telephone	40,000	
Office Machine Rental and Repairs	20,000	
Depreciation, Office Equipment	6,000	
Insurance	10,000	
Other Administrative Expenses	20,000	
TOTAL ADMINISTRATIVE EXPENSES		566,000
SALES EXPENSES:		
Management Salaries	100,000	
Sales Salaries	500,000	
Service Salaries	30,000	
Payroll Taxes	76,000	
Insurance and Benefits	152,000	
Travel Expenses	200,000	
Entertainment Expenses	70,000	
Samples and Demos	10,000	
Sales Administrative Expenses	40,000	
Incentive Compensation and Bonuses	240,000	
Advertising and Promotion	300,000	
Displays and Exhibits	80,000	
Other Sales Expenses	50,000	
TOTAL SALES EXPENSES		1,848,000
NET OPERATING PROFIT		$1,486,000

Figure E.1

1. Estimate the market for the product. We plan on getting the following installations of our software package, based on some additional market research done since our work in Chapter 4.

Meeting Planners (30% of list)	60
Other Meeting Planners	200
Travel Agents	1,500
Corporate Accounts	850
Other	90
Total	2,700

2. Estimate the average gross revenue from the sales. This is complicated since there will be a wide range of "add-on" services required by different customers. We estimated that it would break out about as shown in Figure E.2.

FSM COMPUTER SOFTWARE CO.
19XX MARKETING PLAN
ESTIMATED AVERAGE SELLING PRICE AND SALES VOLUME

INTRODUCTION:

In our planning, we have categorized accounts into three areas:

A accounts who will need a fair amount of customization and who will purchase additional hardware products like modems, cables, and peripherals from us and who will be prospects for our multi-user or site-licensing agreements at $500 per additional/package/user.

B accounts who may need a limited amount of these products or services.

C accounts who will buy the software package only.

SALES ESTIMATES:

	A Accounts	B Accounts	C Accounts
Software Packages	$ 1,250	$ 1,250	$ 1,250
Multi-User Licenses	1,500	—	—
Installation/Customization	5,000	3,000	—
Other Products	3,000	1,000	—
TOTAL	$ 10,750	$ 5,250	$ 1,250
Times Number of Customers	× 500	× 500	× 1700
ESTIMATED SALES	$537,500	$262,500	$212,500

NOTE: The total adds up to $10,125,000 which is rounded off to 10,000,000 in the interests of conservatism.

Figure E.2

As you can see, we didn't pull the figures out of the air. Based on our preliminary calls on prospects, we identified the likely needs in three different categories and developed an estimate of possible sales by category.

Notice that we used the information developed in previous chapters with some new quantification of our subjective guesses to develop these estimates. Different industries will, of course, require different approaches, different strategies, and different categorizations, but the basics are the same. We now have our Sales figure and are ready to move on.

ESTIMATING RETURNS AND ALLOWANCES

This is fairly simple. We estimate that 1 percent of our sales either won't stick or that we will have to make some kinds of adjustments, so we deduct $100,000 from our gross sales. This has nothing to do with not collecting the money due. This is a separate expense which might be called, appropriately enough, "Bad Debts."

Discussion of the reserve versus actual write-off methods belongs in an accounting textbook, so let's assume for our purposes that we've covered this possible expense in the "Other Administrative Expenses" category on our P&L Statement.

ARRIVING AT THE COST OF GOODS SOLD

To keep things simple, we're going to assume that we have a crackerjack controller who has accurately estimated all the manufacturing costs of producing our product.

For our information, however, he has provided the breakdown shown in Figure E.3 (which he doesn't expect us sales types to understand):

CALCULATING THE AMOUNT FOR ADMINISTRATIVE EXPENSES

Since we are involved in a start-up venture that we have developed from scratch, we have made some assumptions in putting our budget or plan together. Let's review just how we did this:

1. For "Administrative Salaries," we have decided that we will need a manager, a relatively senior person, and several other people at various skill levels. Here's how we worked out our budget:

Administrative Manager (1)	$ 40,000
Senior Administrative Specialist (1)	30,000
Senior Customer Service Specialists (4)	60,000
Other Personnel	70,000
Total	$200,000

FSM COMPUTER SERVICES CO.
COST OF GOODS SOLD
FISCAL YEAR ENDED 12/31/XX

MATERIAL COSTS:
(Based on the sale of 2,700 units for the fiscal year)

Diskettes	$ 3,800	
Documentation, Printed Material	140,500	
Packaging Material	78,700	
TOTAL MATERIAL COSTS		$ 223,000
LABOR COSTS, SOFTWARE PACKAGES:		
Reproduction	21,400	
Packaging	24,600	
TOTAL LABOR, PACKAGES		46,000
LABOR COSTS, INSTALLATION/CUSTOMIZATION:		
Installation	200,000	
Customization	600,000	
Support (Customer Queries)	100,000	
TOTAL LABOR, INST./CUST.		900,000
OVERHEAD COSTS:		
Indirect Manufacturing Costs	120,000	
Amortization of Research	4,500,000	
Other Costs	$ 211,000	
TOTAL OVERHEAD COSTS		4,831,000
TOTAL COST OF GOODS SOLD		$6,000,000

Figure E.3

2. "Payroll Taxes" and "Insurance and Benefits" were estimated respectively at 10 percent and 20 percent of salaries. It could be argued that these figures should be 7.6 percent and 21.8 percent, but we're not looking (for now) at the pennies.

3. We will need an office for our venture (or will have to pay our corporate headquarters for our space) so we have estimated that our space will cost $10,000 per month and that we will have to pay $40,000 in utility costs.

4. Since we want this effort to get off the ground quickly, we estimate that our stationery, supplies, and postage costs will be about $1,000 per week, so we budget this expense at $50,000 for the year.

5. Our telephone service costs were estimated by getting actual figures from the telephone company we will be dealing with. They told us $30,000 per year. But, since extra costs always come up, we've used the figure of $40,000 for our plan.

6. We will need a copy machine, a telephone answering system, and some other office machines. We know it's an imperfect world, so we have budgeted for repairs or maintenance contracts in addition to the rental costs and arrived at the figure of $20,000 for the year.

7. We decided to buy our minicomputer instead of renting it and we needed a modem, a monitor, a printer, and some other ergonomic office equipment. The total bill came to $30,000 and we are going to depreciate (allocate the cost) over a five-year period, so this cost comes to $6,000 per year.

8. The "Insurance" and "Other Administrative Expenses" costs were based on our past experience or what the controller told us we could figure for this category. This completes the "Administrative Expenses" portion of our Pro Forma Profit and Loss Statement.

DETERMINING SALES EXPENSES

1. We know that we are worth more than $100,000 per year, but our compensation will come from the incentive compensation plan, so we've budgeted the paltry amount of $100,000 for "Management Salaries."

2. To accomplish the sales goal of $10,000,000, we will need *at least* ten salespeople. Since we won't hire them all at the same time, we'll assume that we can get by for an average of $50,000 for the first year, so we have our "Sales Salaries" figure of $500,000.

3. We want our salespeople to spend their time selling, but recognize that there will be some bugs in our software program that will take a while to show up, so we want a service person to deal with any possible problems. We know from past experience that we can hire a competent person for between $25,000 and $30,000 per year, so we budget our "Service Salaries" at $30,000.

4. "Payroll Taxes" and "Insurance Benefits" are estimated respectively at 10 percent and 20 percent for our sales and service personnel in the same manner as for our administrative people.

5. To get this product off the ground, we'll probably have to do a fair amount of traveling. Since there are 12 people involved (even though the salespeople will be hired three or four at a time) we'll figure on an average of about $300 to $400 per week to compute our "Travel Expenses" figure of $200,000.

6. Since we want our sales and service people to be effective when they go out into the field, they will be working over lunches and dinners. This costs money since most purchasing agents don't pick up the check, so we'll figure on $70,000 for this activity to come up with our "Entertainment Expenses" figure.

7. We want to sell every product that comes from our manufacturing operation. Reality, however, dictates that there will be some occasions where we will leave a product with a customer at no charge. Reality also suggests that there may be some occasions when we won't get the product back. So, being realistic, we've budgeted $10,000 for this expense.

8. It's true that we have budgeted for an effective administrative support team that will handle most of the administrative chores (and expenses) but there will still be some instances when our salespeople have to incur administrative expenses—preparing a proposal in the field with the use of a hotel secretarial service, getting copies made, buying binders or proposal covers in the field, etc., so we have provided $40,000 for these kinds of expenses in the "Sales Administrative Expenses" category.

9. This ambitious budget of $10,000,000 isn't going to get accomplished by just wishing for it, so we've developed an incentive plan to reward the accomplishers (including the field sales manager). Besides their salaries, we're paying our salespeople 1 percent of sales up to quota and 2 percent of sales over quota.

    In addition, we will assume that the sales manager gets an override of .5 percent of sales up to quota and 1 percent of sales over quota. Because there will be some sales force performance disparities (some people at 70 percent of quota and others at 120 percent) we've budgeted $240,000 for "Incentive Compensation and Bonuses."

    If you do the arithmetic, you'll find that it works out like this:

$10,000,000 in sales × 1% =	$100,000
$10,000,000 in sales × .5% =	50,000
Total	$150,000

    This gives us an additional $90,000 to pay for the exceptional performances (that 2 percent for the plus-quota accomplishments) and to provide some extra "sprint," special or one-time bonuses to pick up the slack to make sure we don't have any slow periods. This gives us our figure of $240,000.

10. Instead of letting the "Advertising and Promotion" expenditures be controlled from a headquarters ivory tower, we've included them in the "Sales Expenses" budget. To be truly effective, effective field sales managers should control their companies' advertising and promotion budgets.

This means, of course,that you have to learn something about spending the money wisely—the subject of another whole new book. For now, let's assume that the $300,000 figure for "Advertising and Promotion" was arrived at wisely and a plan is in place to spend it in the most effective manner possible.

11. Demonstrating and showing your product in the field is an important part of a total sales effort. There will be countless opportunities to do this at trade shows, "tabletop" exhibits, and other interest-generating activities. Doing this well is covered in more detail in Chapter 12. For now, we'll assume that you have looked over the roster of display and exhibit vehicles, chosen the ones that are most likely to produce sales, and accurately estimated the costs of your participating in these soirees.

12. Finally, since all effective field sales managers always anticipate the unpredictable, we have an "Other Sales Expenses" category with an admittedly arbitrary figure of $50,000.

IN CLOSING. . .

Unless you are in the banking, insurance, utility, securities, or other field with its own accounting rules, the Profit and Loss Statement shown in Figure E.1 applies to over 95 percent of all budgeting situations you are likely to encounter. Take your own company's annual report or the report of a company you own stock in and you will see that, with the above exceptions, the format is similar.

Appendix F

Using the Time Management Worksheet

The tool explained in this practice example is a simple but effective way to analyze how you spend your time and develop ways of using this limited commodity more effectively.

HOW ARE YOU SPENDING YOUR TIME?

You can't go where you want to in any endeavor unless you first decide where you are. The first step is to keep track, for a week or two, of exactly how you are spending your time. A simple worksheet like that shown in Figure F.1 should suffice.

Keep the worksheet handy—right by your telephone and keep it constantly up to the hour. It you wait until the end of the day you may forget some of those time-wasters. The "code" section on the worksheet is a small timesaving device. After a day or two, you will be able to abbreviate your recording according to your activities. For example: ER for time spent reviewing expense reports, CR for time spent reviewing salesperson call reports, CC for customer calls, HO for discussion with home office, SM for staff meetings, etc.

Be specific about which customer or which project the discussions or meetings were about. This will be important in identifying those critical few items that accounted for most of your productive activity during the week and those many noncritical items that consumed your time less productively.

TIME MANAGEMENT WORKSHEET

Time	Code	Activity/Customer/Project
7:00- 7:30		
7:30- 8:00		
8:00- 8:30		
8:30- 9:00		
9:00- 9:30		
9:30-10:00		
10:00-10:30		
10:30-11:00		
11:00-11:30		
11:30-12:00		
12:00-12:30		
12:30- 1:00		
1:00- 1:30		
1:30- 2:00		
2:00- 2:30		
2:30- 3:00		
3:00- 3:30		
3:30- 4:00		
4:00- 4:30		
4:30- 5:00		
5:00- 5:30		
5:30- 6:00		
Other		

Figure F.1

Now let's fill out the sheets for a couple of typical (or atypical) days in order to go to the next step. Incidentally, don't take this lightly. I've given literally hundreds of worksheets like this to client executives and have heard all the reasons why it isn't really necessary "for me," all the excuses for procrastination, and all the justifications for an end-of-the-day summary instead of hour-to-hour listings.

The typical comment is "If you want me to save time, why are you asking me to spend time on another task?" Once the benefits became clear, however, the sheets become habit-forming. Several clients still use the system after several years as a checkup to see how their time is being spent and one still uses it every day to keep track of time. Another, an engineering consultant, uses it as a management tool and billing record. You may not bill time as consultants, CPAs, and attorneys do, but your time is costing your company real dollars and it's your job to maximize their and your return on this investment.

Figure F.2 and F.3 show what your sheet might look like for two days—one spent in the office and one as the first day of a two-day trip to work with your field manager.

TIME MANAGEMENT WORKSHEET

Tues. 1/14

	Time	Code	Activity/Customer/Project
B	7:00- 7:30	R&S	WSJ, Business Week over coffee
B	7:30- 8:00	T	To office—Listened to EFSM tape
B	8:00- 8:30	D/C	Dictated answers to last week's correspondence
A	8:30- 9:00		
	9:00- 9:30	M	Reviewed December flash report on sales. Computed %
	9:30-10:00		against quota and prepared sales bulletin.
	10:00-10:30		
A	10:30-11:00	D	Met with Lisa to review weeks assignments
	11:00-11:30		
C	11:30-12:00	PR	"Hand Holding" telecon w/Product Mgr., tapes
A	12:00-12:30	CR	Return customer calls—Tim's Stationery,
C			Harkins Wholesale
B	12:30- 1:00	RM	Racquetball & lunch w/Howard Davidson.
B	1:00- 1:30	RM	
B	1:30- 2:00	RM	Discussion of co-op ad program for distributors.
B	2:00- 2:30	M	Detail review of central region sales
A	2:30- 3:00	M	Disc. w/Central Regional Mgr. about
B	3:00- 3:30	M	performance report (dictated)—Confirm action
C	3:30- 4:00	SM	plan—Central meeting on A/I project
B	4:00- 4:30	SM/M	Ditto—Reviewed sales figures on the sly
B	4:30- 5:00	SM/M	Ditto—Pretended to be taking notes while writing
B	5:00- 5:30		sales bulletin on the co-op advg. program
C	5:30- 6:30	D/C	Reviewed day's correspondence & answered most.
C	Other		Sorted out AG's & PF/s memos.
C	8:00- 8:45	M	Reviewed AG & PF memos. Dictated reply to AG.
		D/C	Put PF in 2/1 up file.
			(Maybe she'll forget)

Figure F.2

    The use of time show isn't bad. Sometimes just having to account for time and being aware of the precious minutes ticking off causes managers to begin using it more wisely. This is a version of the application the "Hawthorne Syndrome." (In oversimplified terms, this principle holds that anything under study or review improves as a result of the study process.)

    You might question whether you really would have used the travel, airport waiting time, and airplane time as well as you did if you didn't know that you would have to "fess up" to where the hours went. If you really would have, you are eligible for sainthood and may skim quickly through the rest of the appendix to get on to something you need to know more about.

TIME MANAGEMENT WORKSHEET

Wed. 1/15

	Time	Code	Activity/Customer/Project
B	7:00- 7:30	R&S	WSJ, Sales Management over coffee
C	7:30- 8:00	T	To airport—Listened to news
D	8:00- 8:30	I	Plane late—Chatted with Red Carpet Room hostess
C	8:30- 9:00	M	Hostess busy—Reviewed notes for meeting
	9:00- 9:30 9:30-10:00 10:00-10:30	I	Plane finally leaves. Talked to co-passenger about his stained glass lamp hobby.
B	10:30-11:00 11:00-11:30	M	To first call. Laid out agenda w/Reg'l Mgr.
A	11:30-12:00 12:00-12:30	CC	Harkins Wholesale provided suggested catalog layout for fall catalog
A B	12:30- 1:00 1:00- 1:30	M	Discussed HW salesperson spiff and promotional programs over lunch
C	1:30- 2:00	CC	To Tim's Stationery. Discussed HW follow thru
C	2:00- 2:30 2:30- 3:00	I	Call on Tim's. He must have something on my RM. Little potential for my time.
	3:00- 3:30 3:30- 4:00	I	To B&B computer store. Passed by Harkins on the way. Talked about roads & traffic.
B C	4:00- 4:30 4:30- 5:00	CC	B&B call. The guy's a nut but has some ideas we can use. Must find a handle.
D	5:00- 5:30 5:30- 6:00	I	RM suggested a drink. Listened to Bill and Basil on their London trip.
A	Other		
	6:00- 7:00	I	To motel, shower, change, call home
B	7:00- 9:00	I, M	Dinner RM, review day, plan next & some B.S.
A	9:00- 9:30	D/C	Dictated follow-up letter to HW, TS & B&B.
A	9:30- 9:45	M	Called again to tell D. I missed her. (Smart move!)

Figure F.3

USING THE TIME MANAGEMENT WORKSHEET
TO SEE HOW WELL YOU SPEND YOUR TIME

Recording time is only the first step. Now let's analyze the worksheet to determine what we've learned and how we can apply it. Those letters—A, B, C, and D—to the left of your sheet are intended to be an extension of the Pareto time rule. It works something like this:

A projects take 10 percent of your time and account for 50 percent of your results or effectiveness.

B project take 30 percent of your time and account for 20 percent of your results or effectiveness.

C projects take 60 percent of your time and account for 30 percent of your results or effectiveness.

D projects are an almost complete waste of time and don't count for anything. You can charge this off to your leisure time and may feel badly that it was wasted instead of enjoyed.

Obviously, your goal should be to log in as much A time as possible. Let's discuss each entry on the Tuesday, 1/14, and Wednesday, 1/15, worksheets and the reasons they were classified the way they were:

Tue.

7:00 Good use of time, but won't produce immediate results, so it gets a B regardless of how desirable this kind of activity may be for your professional development.

7:30 Also good, but still a B for the same reason.

8:00 This is a composite. There was probably little in the correspondence that fell into the category of the "critical few" and a lot that belonged to the "noncritical" many.

8:30 Now we're getting to what your job is really about. While you could delegate some of the detail better, it's true that by doing the figures yourself, you get a feel for what is really going on. This kind of analysis and follow-up is the most important activity in which you can engage.

10:30 We gave this activity an A, assuming that it was not just conversation, but a real management discussion that involved delegating a lot of things that those less informed and aware field sales managers do themselves.

11:30 Some of this may be necessary, but it gets no points. Find a way to delegate this to your secretary, still remembering that we live in a political world and you can't afford to neglect your home office or lateral relationships.

12:00 You still have to be involved in important customer contacts no matter how much you delegate, so you get an A for Harkin's but a C for Tim's.

12:30 Nice move! You managed to squeeze in your racquet ball with a business discussion. It's future stuff, though, so it only rates a B.

2:00 This is the right kind of activity, but too general to rate a full A.

2:30 Now, here's the kind of thing that produces immediate results if it's done well. We're assuming that you handled this well, so it's worth an A.

3:00 You got an A on the discussion but the follow-through, however necessary, still rates a B.

3:30   You knew this would be a dumb meeting and you got out of it the last two times. This time they scheduled it to fit your schedule, so you had to be there. It's still dumb so it gets a C.

4:00   It's still a dumb meeting, but you found two things to do that would have to be done sometime, so you've turned a C (possibly D) into a B.

5:30   This isn't going to bring immediate results and is probably a lot of eyewash and nonsense, so this gets a C since it is the kind of activity that needs to be controlled and limited.

8:00   This is a good time to work on this kind of matter. Unfortunately, your judgment that it could be left until after dinner proved correct—it wasn't productive even though for political reasons you had to deal with it. The C is fair.

Wed.

7:00   Same comment as for Tuesday.

7:30   The news will keep you informed, but won't produce sales dollars in the direct way; so a C.

8:00   Your author wouldn't think of disapproving of this kind of activity, but it gets chalked up to leisure time and therefore gets a D for business effectiveness.

8:30   A nice try, but you should have done this before. The effort, however, gets a C instead of a D.

9:00   Since you are not in the stained glass business, this gets a leisure time D.

10:00   Planning is essential, but should be done in the car while you are going somewhere instead of in a coffee shop or motel room, so a B.

11:30   Good activity. This is a major account that deserves home (regional) office attention and it's quite fair and appropriate for you to be involved in the details. The last half-hour got a B since it is assumed you were telling war stories after one and one-half hours spent together.

1:30   Tim's get a C and your Regional Manager gets a lesson on how to use time effectively no matter what his relationship with Tim's receptionist is.

3:00   This time gets a C because it should have been reduced. Your RM should have scheduled things in a more geographically sensible way to avoid unnecessary travel time.

4:00   The first half-hour gets a generous B since the ideas might have some potential and the customer does a little business with us and you are humoring your RM. The last half-hour, however, was wasted on something that is not going to bring immediate business.

5:00 A waste of time and a deserved D. Your regional manager should have scheduled another customer or worthwhile prospect for 4:00 and left 5:00 for B & B.

6:00 All these activities are very important and deserve an A. While on the road, you're working two shifts. It makes sense to break, shower, and change to get mentally prepared for the second shift. Calling home is a must for a successful career/home life.

7:00 Besides some good management discussion, review of the day, and plans for tomorrow, we assume that you spent some time instructing your RM on the effective use of your and his time. Since this is also a time for socializing and telling war stories, this gets a composite B.

9:00 Smart idea. Dictating follow-up letters to the people you saw today was probably second on your "desirable" list to attending the Tupperware party being given at the motel pool. Your refusing to procrastinate on this important chore gets you an A on this activity and leads us to:

> As a general rule, when in doubt about whether to pursue a course of action, do it! When there is a question about the time, do it now!

9:30 Another smart idea. A phone call every day or two may be obligatory. An *extra* call when all you fun-loving types are supposed to be in the middle of the evening's revelry has to win you a lot of points, especially when you can answer the question "What are you doing?" with "Well, I just got through with some dictating and have some reports to go over before tomorrow." If you handle this properly and understatedly, you can actually make your spouse feel guilty about having just sat down to read a book after cleaning up the kitchen and putting the kids to bed.

We obviously took a hard-nosed approach to the classification of time as useful or not (A, B, C, D). It's true that you can't spend all of your time on what would be classified as A activities, even if you have complete control, but this kind of disciplined approach is necessary to change from spending 80 percent of your time on the "trivial many" to 80 percent on the "critical few."

Some new and, admittedly, arbitrary codes were introduced in the worksheet summaries. When you really get time-management sophisticated and are budgeting time according to categories, this kind of time division and coding may prove worthwhile. For now, let's explain the meanings of the codes used:

R&S Reading and study. A portion of every week has to be devoted to keeping up on what is going on. Read with a view of using the material and sending copies to your managers to make a particular point.

T   Travel time. The key is how you use this time for productive purposes.

I   Idle time. You are either having fun, which is fair, or you are wasting time and not enjoying it, which is not smart.

M   Management time. This is what you get paid for. The more time you spend in this category, the better the chances are of you reaching your goals.

CC   Customer calls. Good if they rate an A. Bad if they rate a C. Set standards for yourself and your managers about the kind of calls you want to be involved in and those you wish to avoid. Don't be afraid to say "no."

CR   Customer relations. This is an example of those little things that take a relatively small amount of time but can mean a great deal to the customers and your managers. Personal letters from the top honcho to a small account can have a lasting effect on the customer and your managers.

SM   Staff meetings. Often a waste of time, unless you called the meeting. Find a way to be productive when it gets boring as you did on Tuesday. For your meetings, we assume that you will follow the guidelines in Chapter 11 and are holding meaningful and worthwhile meetings.

D/C   Dictating and correspondence. A necessary job, but it doesn't have to be an onerous chore if you keep a dictating machine handy and don't get behind.

D   Delegation. Specially singled out since one of our effectiveness-increasing as well as time-management tools will be to look at the amount of work that can be done as well or better by someone else.

PR   We listed a category for discussion with the home office or your colleagues down the hall. This was meant for those useful discussions. This category is for those necessary (politically) discussions that don't add much to your job performance or effectiveness.

R   Recreation, as distinguished from idle time. This is a must if you're going to handle your responsibilities and stay on top of a mentally demanding job.

PINPOINTING TIME-WASTING ACTIVITIES

We accounted for a total of 27 hours in the two days we tracked. This is not an unusual number of hours in two days of a busy, ambitious sales manager's schedule. You remember that you have two full time jobs—home (or regional) office and field and that you have to get 75 percent of each done.

Let's summarize how those 27 hours were used:

A Activities	6.75 hours	25%
B Activities	9.50 hours	35%
C Activities	7.00 hours	26%
D Activities	3.75 hours	14%

You remember that the interpretation of the Pareto time rule said that you would normally spend 10 percent of your time on those activities that account for 50% of the results. In achieving the converse of the 80-20 rule, you would spend a great deal more time on the A activities to increase you effectiveness.

The 25 percent of your time spent on A activities is pretty good. Most managers spend only 10 percent to 15 percent. The rest of the percentage breakdown isn't bad either, compared to the ideal:

A Activities	50% of your time
B Activities	30% of your time
C Activities	20% of your time
D Activities	0% of your working time

So far, this worksheet exercise should have made you think more carefully about the time you spend. It should also have given you an indication of where you and your managers need improvement on the utilization of your time and the kinds of goals you have to shoot for. Let's try another way of looking at these 27 hours in more detail:

Code	Hours	% Total	Comments
M	9.25	34%	Very good. Again, it is just possible that knowing you were going to have to face yourself with a work-sheet summary persuaded you to concentrate on these activities. Keep this up.
I	7.0	25	Not good. Some idle or breathing time in a busy schedule is good, but most of the time designated as idle took place in the field and wasted two people's time. This would indicate a need to talk with your managers about the use of your and their time and the kind of calls you need and want to be involved in.
CC	2.5	9	In a day on the road, this should have been at least double. Obviously, more planning is needed to change idle time to customer call time. Also, how about dinner with one of your important customers when out of the office?

D/C	2.25	8	Depending on your management style and the demands of your home office or boss, this may be a bit low. Earlier we discussed ways to manage this aspect of your job.
SM	1.25	5	You did well to keep this low, especially if you're in home office. Be careful about those other activities during meetings. Some of your colleagues and superiors take their meetings very seriously.
R&S	1.0	4	You used your "wake up" time well. Since the days covered didn't include a weekend, this is probably enough.
T	1.0	4	This is usually a time-waster. You, however, found a way to use it well.
D	1.0	4	A very important hour. We'll look for ways to increase this so that you are planning and managing instead of doing.
R	.75	3	The combining with business was a good idea. Keep planning this kind of time to squeeze more hours out of those short days.
PR	.5	2	One of the realities of business life is that it is a political world and these kinds of contacts are necessary to do your job properly. Besides, you may pick up some useful information that you wouldn't get in any other way.
CR	.5	2	Probably not enough time since there is only one sales manager in your territory. You were, however, out calling on customers.

Even in a two-day period, this exercise enables you to pinpoint time-wasters and identify quality time. Try this for a few more days with the same kind of detailed analysis. Then go back to the worksheets and analyses periodically as a checkup, particularly if you begin to feel that there aren't enough hours in the day or that you aren't getting enough done.

Index